HORSES *Like* LIGHTNING

A STORY OF PASSAGE
THROUGH THE HIMALAYAS

Sienna Craig

WISDOM PUBLICATIONS • BOSTON

Wisdom Publications
199 Elm Street
Somerville MA 02144 USA
www.wisdompubs.org

Library of Congress Cataloging-in-Publication Data
Craig, Sienna R.
Horses like lightning : a story of passage through the Himalayas / Sienna Craig.
    p. cm.
ISBN 0-86171-517-9 (pbk. : alk. paper)
1. Mustang Region (Nepal)—Social life and customs. 2. Horses—Social aspects—Nepal—Mustang Region. 3. Craig, Sienna R. I. Title.
DS495.8.M87C73 2008
954.96—dc22
                                2008012113

12 11 10 09 08
5 4 3 2 1

Cover design by TLrggms. Interior design by Gopa&Ted2. Set in Berkeley Book 11/15.2. Cover photo by Thomas L. Kelly. Illustrations by Tenzin Norbu Lama. Mustang map by Digital Himalaya Project, www.digitalhimalaya.com.

Wisdom Publications' books are printed on acid-free paper and meet the guidelines for permanence and durability of the Production Guidelines for Book Longevity of the Council on Library Resources.

Printed in the United States of America.

This book was produced with environmental mindfulness. We have elected to print this title on 30% PCW recycled paper. As a result, we have saved the following resources: 27 trees, 19 million BTUs of energy, 2,369 lbs. of greenhouse gases, 9,832 gallons of water, and 1,263 lbs. of solid waste. For more information, please visit our website, www.wisdompubs.org. This paper is also FSC certified. For more information, please www.fscus.org.

Horses Like Lightning

FOR KEN

TABLE OF CONTENTS

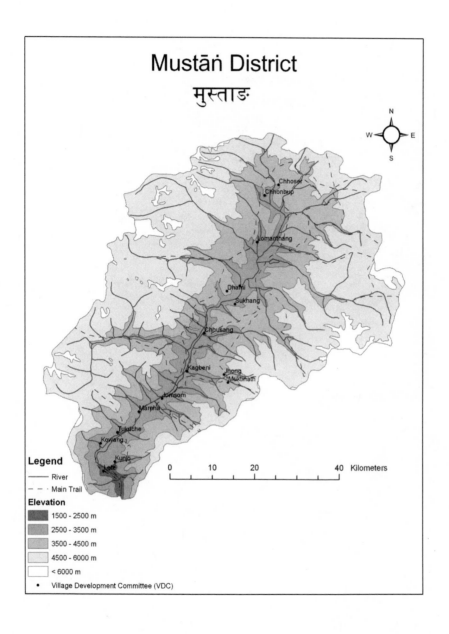

Mustāṅ District
मुस्ताङ

- Chhoser
- Chhonhup
- Lomanthang
- Dhami
- Sukhang
- Chhusang
- Kagbeni
- Jhong
- Muktinath
- Jomsom
- Marpha
- Tukuche
- Kowang
- Kunjo
- Lete

Legend

—— River

– – · Main Trail

Elevation

- 1500 - 2500 m
- 2500 - 3500 m
- 3500 - 4500 m
- 4500 - 6000 m
- < 6000 m

• Village Development Committee (VDC)

0   10   20   40   Kilometers

PROLOGUE

Beauty is the moment of transition, as if the form were
just ready to flow into other forms.
—RALPH WALDO EMERSON

MY FATHER IS TRAINED as an archaeologist. He has sculptor's hands and an astral stare that can see right through me. When I was small, he wore a beard and often smelled of earth. In those years, he worked with Chumash Indians who lived in and around Santa Barbara. We took long walks together, and he would point out arrowheads and shards of pottery in the dirt. Archaeology eyes, he called them. To me, his perceptiveness was a small miracle. He was a scavenger, a finder of lost things. His imagination could piece together village histories from soil, sky, and stones. There was hawk in him: piercing, graceful, and often alone.

My mother is a painter. To her, anything torn apart can be reassembled. There are no wrong lines. This sense of creativity enlivens her, that seized moment of seeing and then seeing again. Even now, more than three decades after I was born, I can imagine her as the young mother she once was, a long braid down her back, her knees rough with paint. Her studio is sacred space—a place where she can be alone, most fully herself. It is an intimate place she rarely opens up to others. But as her young child, and therefore as an extension of herself, I sometimes joined her. I drew and wrote stories, watching as she worked a piece, moving across her medium of collage, the white expanse of walls cluttered with her different reckonings of art. She kept a shrine in the corner—feathers and stones and other found offerings—above which was tacked a small piece of paper. "Go, little picture!" it read.

I suppose that California in the seventies was anything but *normal*, but when I was small, Kraft macaroni and cheese and Barbie dolls were my exotica. Instead of a swing set in my backyard, we had a sweat lodge. On weekends or after long days at a dig, the house would be given over to my father's colleagues. I watched as the crew of Chumash and longhaired white folk stripped down in the California sun and crawled into the lodge, with its willow branch spine and eucalyptus leaf skin. Part of me was embarrassed by the bareness of it all—the incongruity in what was otherwise a suburban tract house neighborhood, near the freeway—but I still love the smell of white sage and steam rising off rocks.

Sometimes the discrepancies between my upbringing and those of my schoolmates jarred, embarrassed, disappointed me. I can remember longing for my mother to pick me up from school wearing anything but her shimmering Dolphin running shorts and cutoff T-shirt, invariably splattered with paint. "My mom is an artist," I would say to my friends as they glanced at their mothers with their station wagons and matching pantsuits, and then stared at my mom. In my heart, I felt I knew what being an artist or an archaeologist meant. I could sense, if not articulate, something of the intersubjective tension that is at the creative heart of what has also become my discipline, my vocation: the practice of moving between worlds, charting differences, and understanding how meaning is made across human experience. But in my youth I also learned to live this dissonance, and to accept the fact that some things would not translate. In that sense, I have been preparing for Mustang for as long as I can remember.

My parents nourished my curiosity and, by virtue of their own choices, helped me to feel comfortable living between worlds. And, as much as painting and archaeology are intuitive, my parents gave me confidence in my own ability to decipher, to draw lines, to dig things up.

I remember being small, thigh-high against my father's wiry legs. He had taken me out to an archaeological site on the northern edge of Santa Barbara, near Point Conception, the most westerly jut of the California coastline and the point at which, according to Chumash cosmology, spirits leave this world. Although at the time I simply knew it as a place where dolphins streamed through the Pacific and osprey flew in circles overhead, I could still appreciate it as sacred ground.

When we arrived at the site, my father and I began to explore, looking for things. Eucalyptus trees rustled in the afternoon wind and the air grew still. An eagle feather lying on the ground caught my attention and I reached down to pick it up. The shaft of cartilage felt cool in my hand. I knew eagles were rare, and the brittle plume felt like a gift.

I shook the feather. As I shook it, the earth itself began to shake. In seconds, the asphalt buckled and kneeled. My father picked me up—feather and all. We tried to stand still while the ground beneath our feet swayed and rumbled. As a native Californian, I had experienced earthquakes before, but, for me, there have been none like this one since.

When the ground stopped shaking, my eyes darted between the wrinkled road and the feather I still held in my hand. "Papasan, did I do that?" I finally squeaked. "Maybe," he said, smiling. He had seen me shake the feather, and had witnessed the sense of power and magic that accompanied this gesture and its aftermath. Despite our own rationality, for that first kinetic moment, my shake was eagle and earth and energy through me, beyond me, toward something deeper—the ways humans and other animals share worlds, bleed into each other.

I am an only child. As parents went, and as far as I could tell when I was young, mine seemed well matched. But this match, made when they were young themselves, ended with difficulty by their early thirties, as I was turning ten. I was given my first horse around the time of their separation, and my adolescence passed mostly at the barn. I mucked out stalls, fed oat hay and alfalfa pellets to my four-legged charges, and swept the aisles. These tasks helped to earn my horse's keep. My fingernails were never clean, but my mare's coat glistened like a wet seal in the sun. I kept my brushes and hoof pick, fly spray and bandages in a tin trunk painted blue. It bent easily, and after a few weeks of my sitting on it as I pulled on my riding boots, the top caved in. But it was mine, and the mare was mine, and that was enough.

In the years when my parents' marriage incinerated, I found solace at the barn. The other girls who hung out at the stables were more sisters than any friendships since. We spoke first of horses and only later of boys. Gathered on the fence like crows when our trainer schooled a horse, we were initiates, learning through participation and observation to belong to this horse culture, to know its language. After our rides, we played in the hay barns until dusk. But my barn sisters had their own families to contend with, and there was little to say or talk through with them about my parent's dissolving marriage. I could talk to horses, though.

Summit, a chestnut-colored gelding with a dished face, was neither the strongest nor the most beautiful horse I ever rode, but he was the best listener. On days when I didn't want to be found, I sat in the corner of his stall, just talking quietly to him. Summit nibbled alfalfa, using his upper lip to separate it from the wood shavings that made his bed, as I confided in him about late-night arguments and my worries about our dissolving family. If I happened upon Summit early in the morning or late in the evening, when he was lying down in his stall, he would let me curl up next to him—something horses don't usually tolerate. That gesture felt more intimate than the arms of most lovers since. One winter, when Summit was nearly dead from pneumonia, he took to laying his entire neck and head in my lap—a heavy weight for a twelve-year-old girl to bear. But I was strong and I managed. I stroked him between the ears as he labored for breath.

By the time I was a teenager, I had ridden and cared for a succession of horses, each more challenging than the last, and had had success in competitions. The ribbons that lined my bedroom walls insulated me from the domestic chaos beyond them. While my parents were breaking up, I think I spoke to their answering machines more than I did to them. I would tell all to the tape: school grades, slumber party schemes, details of that afternoon's riding lesson, or even deeper murmurings. That way my parents would register something of my daily life, would know where I was, and would show up on time, I hoped, to take me home.

College wasn't really a place for riding. I dreamed about horses, though, and counted paces in horse strides. I even spent some time as a member of the Brown University Equestrian Team. But the Californian in me had a difficult time riding indoors, and the academic demands of college precluded long afternoons at the barn, when time seemed to stop.

During my tenure at Brown, the world's cultures and religions fascinated me and likewise directed my studies. I knew that I wanted to go abroad and was drawn to Asia. In 1993, during my junior year, I went to Nepal for the first time. The last month of that semester was to be devoted to conducting an independent project, and I entertained the idea of living with Tibetan nuns. That is, until I found out that there were horses and a rich "horse culture"—in a place called Mustang, no less.

PART I

We often walked away from the town in the late afternoon sunset.

There were no paved roads and no fences—no trees—it was like the ocean but it was wide, wide land. The evening star would be high in the sunset sky when it was still broad daylight. That evening star fascinated me. It was in some way very exciting to me.

I had nothing but to walk into nowhere and the wide sunset space with the star.

—Georgia O'Keeffe

 རྟ་མགྲོ་བསྐུན་འཇིན་ནོར་བུ།

Finding Mustang

M Y MIDDLE NAME, Radha, recalls the days when my parents ate too much bee pollen and brown rice, when they stuffed Robert Graves' poetry and the *Bhagavad Gita* in their pockets. Radha is the consort of Krishna, the playful yet fierce incarnation of Vishnu the Preserver within the Hindu pantheon. This young girl, a simple cowherd by birth, is often depicted in gardens, reclining on swings, listening to Krishna play his flute. At once demure and powerful, Radha keeps Krishna—that blue-skinned scamp, that trickster—coming back.

When I was a teenager, I despised the name Radha. My best friend at the time was Rebecca, a girl nearly three years my senior with freckles and blonde hair whose life, in contrast to mine, seemed exceedingly normal. I'm not sure when I made the decision to change my middle name—without informing my parents—but my diploma from high school reads Rebecca, not Radha. And by then I had read the *Bhagavad Gita* myself.

Yet by the time I first traveled to Nepal, Radha was back on my passport.

"Ah, Radha," a portly Nepali immigration official with a betelnut-stained smile remarked as I waited for him to stamp my student visa. "Good Hindu name," he offered. "Welcome in Nepal." And I was.

I emerged from the Tribhuvan International Airport and was overcome by contrast: aural, sensory, aesthetic, natural. Enormous cumulus clouds billowed above fluorescent paddies, bursting with moisture. Even the most dilapidated of brick buildings shone in the afternoon light. On first impression, this city seemed burnished and used, by turns. There was the smell of *chiya*, Nepali sweet tea, petrol fumes, and cow dung. As my fellow students and I were driven by bus through the capitol's crowded, narrow streets toward our program house, I was struck not so much by abject signs of poverty as much as I was moved by a sense of resourcefulness: children transforming discarded paper clips, rubber bands, and empty instant noodle bags into the stuff of play, while others combed rubbish piles for bits of recyclable material; entire families shuttling through traffic on one motorcycle; tailors sewing scrap pieces of fabric into coin purses or baby slippers. In contrast, the sense of waste, and of excess, that seemed to me so obvious about my own country was made more so after only hours in Nepal. Those first few weeks in the country, as I began studying Nepali language, learning more of the country's history, and experiencing its culture by participating in my home-stay family's daily rhythms, I felt at once overwhelmed and deeply happy.

Kathmandu at the end of the twentieth century was also a city of paradox and multiplicity, and made me acutely aware of the passage of time. Stone statues of gods, thousands of years old and more delicate than the flowers offered them, stood along thoroughfares and in back alleys, near motorcycle repair shops and stores that sold pirated videos from Beijing and New Delhi. Women on their way to work as beauticians at five-star hotels took the time to offer vermilion and incense to temple deities. On the streets, lorries halted for befuddled cows. White-gloved policemen conducted traffic: three-wheeled electric cars called "tempos," stuffed full of school children and commuters; porters weighted down by wide-screen televisions or refrigerators; diplomats and Nepali politicians in imported SUVs with tinted windows. The country captured me immediately.

By early October, Kathmandu still rode on the edges of a verdant monsoon, yet the days dawned crisp, and pockets of morning fog wisped and gathered like a long, smooth veil. On this morning, as I peddled my bicycle to the program house, I felt grateful that the night's downpour had cleansed the polluted city air. I could see the Himalayas rising up from the northern horizon. I pulled in to the program house, parked my bicycle, and joined some of my fellow college students on the roof. Some were smoking Yak cigarettes, others were sipping *chiya* before the day officially began. Downstairs in the kitchen, Lawa, the Tibetan cook, was chopping onions for the midday meal, reciting Buddhist prayers as he worked. He had been a monk before he left Tibet and still carried with him something of a monastic presence.

The unstructured lull of morning was broken by the sound of a bell ringing downstairs, signaling that it was time for lecture. Charles Ramble, a British anthropologist, had come to give a talk about Mustang, one of Nepal's seventy-five districts nestled deep in the Himalayas, and the site of his research for more than a decade. In anticipation of his lecture, my fellow students and I had read some of Charles's work. As with other visits to our program house by Nepali and foreign experts, it was not lost on this rather motley crew of American college students that this was a precious way to learn. My fellow students and I filed into the common room, sat down on cushions or the low platforms that lined the space, and listened.

"I'd like you to think for a moment," Charles began, "about the difference between cultural and political borders, about how language and religion relate to the landscape." Charles sat cross-legged on the floor in front of us. His hands looked more like those of a muleskinner than a scholar. He wore years in the corners of his eyes and had a beguiling smile.

"Mustang is a good example. It lies between Dhaulagiri, the sixth tallest mountain in the world, and the Annapurna massif. In the southern reaches of this district, the Kali Gandaki River forms earth's deepest gorge." Charles showed a slide, taken from out the window of an airplane, to illustrate. A serpentine of frothy gray-green water coursed through crags and solid rock, conifers clinging at all angles from the gorge's edge. Even from this arial view, I could sense the power of this river—a visceral understanding of this landscape's extreme nature, of its beauty and danger.

As Charles spoke, I learned that Mustang was located in Nepal's Karnali Zone, and that Jomsom, Mustang's district headquarters, was about a five-day walk away from Pokhara, a mid-hills town below the Annapurnas. Though there were flights between Pokhara and Jomsom, most people from Mustang walked this passage. What did it mean, I wondered, to measure distance not in miles, but in days, in footsteps?

That morning, I learned that the Kali Gandaki valley was not only the deepest gorge on earth, but also that it had been a thoroughfare of trans-Himalayan trade for centuries. Pictures of mule trains and yak caravans bespoke an ancient exchange—highland salt for lowland grains—as much as they also captured a sense of Mustang's place as a trekking destination *par excellence*. Some of the animals in Charles's slides were loaded down with crates of Coca Cola bottles, Rara instant noodles, Cadbury chocolate bars, and muesli.

Charles flipped through more slides. Images of a stark landscape came into focus. Soil and sky seemed to part irrevocably here. Cliffs and ruins resembled eroding sandcastles—not an inaccurate description considering that hundreds of millions of years ago, all of the Himalayan range was ocean floor, above which ran the salty currents of the Tythes Sea. As we watched, two of my Nepali language teachers, high-caste Hindus from Kathmandu, whispered to each other.

"Oh my! Can you believe people live there?"

"I've been to Mustang once, to go on pilgrimage to the temples at Muktinath. The wind blew so hard that I couldn't see. Everything was dirty!"

Slides of coniferous forests and apple orchards in southern Mustang soothed their tone. Beneath the whir of the slide projector, they conferred about the price of Mustang apples in Kathmandu markets. But even southern Mustang, with its forests and glacial streams, was rough country. Windswept and arid, most of Mustang's villages lie between eight and twelve thousand feet.

I was entranced by this landscape. Homes, monasteries, and trailside cairns were striped with earthen pigments of gray, white, and red. These marks symbolized Rigsum Gompo, a trinity of Buddhist deities—Avalokitesvara, Manjushri, and Vajrapani—that protected this sacred geography. Doors and windows seemed built on a Hobbit-sized scale, and some were marked with suns and moons. Charles explained that these doors were small to ensure that people bent over as they entered—to prevent *ro lang*, or zombies, from entering homes. Stones the size and shape of ostrich eggs were brought up from riverbeds and formed the foundations of dwellings. Groves of poplars and willows rustled along riverbanks in an otherwise treeless place. Wood is wealth here, I learned.

Most people in Mustang are agro-pastoralists and traders. They raise crops, herd animals, exchange goods, and now cater to tourists. Village temples and monasteries punctuate this landscape, a place of oxidized earth, chalky hillsides of borax and salt, and eroding cliffs speckled with caves. Fields of barley, buckwheat, and rapeseed create a tapestry of green, pink, and gold.

Small Himalayan horses dotted the hillsides and villages in Charles's photographs, as did herds of sheep and goats. Mules carried enormous loads, their heads crowned with tassels made from yak tails dyed red, and their necks encircled in bells. Yak herds wandered the high pastures. At seventeen thousand feet, these were bucolic realms speckled with wildflowers and medicinal plants during the brief summer, and snowbound most of the year. Lower down, *dzo*, yak-cow crossbreeds, intermingled with smaller bovines, horses, and miniature donkeys.

"I should clarify what is meant by the name 'Mustang,'" Charles said. "Since I'm speaking to a group of Americans, I should tell you that the scruffy ponies you see in my slides bear no relation either to the feral horses of your country or this region's name. Mustang is the Nepali misnomer for the Tibetan *monthang*, meaning 'plain of aspiration.'"

Charles went on to tell us that although many people use the terms "upper Mustang" and "Lo" interchangeably, they were actually different. What Nepalis call upper Mustang includes the seven counties of the kingdom of Lo as well as an area called the Shöd Yul. These regions, distinguished by language as well as by local lineages and rituals, had been closed to foreigners until the previous year, mostly because of its proximity to Tibet, and had only the previous year become open on a restricted basis. Lower Mustang was part of the Annapurna trekking circuit, and saw thousands of travelers each year.

"This entire region was once made up of many different principalities, loosely bound to the ancient western Tibetan kingdom of Zhang Zhung. Today only one of these principalities, the kingdom of Lo, remains active. The king of Lo lives in the walled city of Monthang, just a few hours' ride south of the Nepal/Tibet border." As Charles spoke of the regions encompassed by Mustang District, I learned that many different cultural groups live along this passageway between Nepal and Tibet. My notebook was a scribble of unfamiliar names and places: *Bhote, Baragaon, Shöd Yul, Bön.* I noted that clusters of settlements were sprinkled throughout the region, housing ethnically Tibetan and Thakali people. While the Thakali were one of Nepal's smallest ethnic groups, their reputation as middlemen on the ancient trans-Himalayan salt-grain trading route was legendary. I followed along as Charles described this region, which, like so much of Nepal, was a crossroads of culture, religion, and landscape.

Charles also spoke of the religious diversity of the area, how Hindus, Tibetan Buddhists, and Bön practitioners—followers of Tibet's pre-Buddhist traditions—all lived among each other. Charles wove together stories about the transmission of Buddhist teachings from India to Tibet beginning in the seventh century with Mustang's history, and the rise to power in the "more recent past"—the 1380s—of Lo's first king, Amepal.

This description of Mustang made me wonder what sort of a place would make the fourteenth century seem recent. Though the shards of California's past were familiar to me, my ability to identify a midden pile or an arrowhead could not erase the concurrent reality of strip malls and condos, conquistador heritage as a tourist attraction. When it came to imagining a place that had passed through history and yet remained somehow more consistent, if not unchanged, I had little to refer to. Rome and Florence and Oxford were ancient cities I had experienced, and yet they, like Kathmandu, were also unmistakably modern.

As I first encountered Mustang, I struggled to keep myself from conceiving of this region as an area existing outside of time, romanticizing the landscape and culture. I would soon learn that this was precisely the image Nepali tourism ventures and foreign travelers, alike, were invested in promoting—despite local realities, local histories. To many, Mustang had become known as a "lost" and "hidden" Tibetan kingdom that was now accessible. But, Shangri-la fantasies aside, what I really came to learn from Charles's lecture was that I had no reference point from which to understand subsistence—living by the land. This both fascinated and disturbed me.

"Regardless of where you are in Mustang, villages can startle you," Charles continued. The next slide revealed just such an image: a cluster of houses built above a river valley, and an oasis of green barley fields. Sheer rock faces loomed on either side.

"This is the village of Kagbeni, or Kag in the local Tibetan dialect. The name means 'stop' and this village has been a checkpoint and trading post for hundreds of years. It now divides the restricted and non-restricted regions of Mustang. One can't travel beyond Kagbeni without a special permit." Charles clicked forward the slides to reveal smooth, barren looking hills framed by sky: natural and manmade structures of equal providence, both eroding.

As Charles spoke, I wondered what he saw when he looked at these photographs. Did he feel comfortable here? Was this home to him?

By later in the fifteenth century, the kingdom of Lo was secure enough in wealth and power that its kings invited artisans from great distances—Kathmandu, Lhasa, India, and even Persia—to paint murals and make statues. Although many were in disrepair, the monasteries in Lo were among the grandest buildings intact in the Tibetan-speaking world.

In 1769, King Pritvi Narayan Shah and his army from Gorkha swept through the Himalayas and conquered the Kathmandu Valley, eventually creating the nation of Nepal. At that time Lo and other principalities in what is today Mustang District were still closely connected to the kingdoms of western Tibet; yet during the Nepal-Tibet wars in the eighteenth and nineteenth centuries, the kings of Lo sided with Nepal. Despite these alliances, Lo's ties, in terms of culture, language, and tradition, are to Tibet. Lo eventually became politically part of Nepal, and the king, or *raja*, of Lo retained a good deal of local autonomy. ⌐

Mustang's history rolled off Charles's fluent tongue. I began to understand how someone could become addicted to this process of becoming an "insider" in a foreign place. It struck me that knowing local languages, as Charles did, was part of this puzzle—but only part. For what belied language in this sense of fluency was the way a place's wind or sky becomes a part of your own skin; the way the tinny lilt of a horse's bell can call you home.

As the lecture proceeded, I realized that people couldn't live here if it weren't for their animals. I'd seen ponies, brightly decorated in Tibetan saddle blankets. It began to dawn on me that this was a land that *needed* horses. In a flash, I understood why I'd come to Nepal: halfway around the world and here I was, still horse crazy. In that sense, I was also doing what many an anthropologist and traveler before me has done. I was searching out the familiar in an unfamiliar landscape, drawing on a vocabulary of equivalents as a way of learning, of asking questions.

After the lecture, I approached Charles. "Do horses play a cultural role in Mustang?" I asked.

"Do you read French?" he responded. An unlit cigarette dangled from his lips.

"Excuse me?" I said, taken aback.

"Sorry. Yes. Horses are very important. People pay a lot of money for them, especially these days. They used to have little bearing on much beyond transport. The nobles rode, but not many other people could afford horses. Why do you ask?"

"I grew up riding. I was thinking of going to a nunnery in the Khumbu for my independent project, but if there are horses in Mustang, well…" I paused. "But where does the French come in?"

"Oh, yes. There's a French Tibetologist named Blondeau. She's translated a Tibetan book about horse care. I skimmed it years ago. Frankly, it is not my cup of tea. But I suppose an equestrienne would get excited about things like the significance of a horse's coat color or the ways to cure a horse who's been attacked by a wolf."

"That sounds fascinating," I said. "I would love to see the book…but I don't read French." I glimpsed a brief wave of disappointment pass across Charles's face.

"Spanish," I fumbled. "Grew up in California."

"I see. Well, perhaps one of your fellow students could help you with translation. I have a copy of Blondeau's book somewhere."

"That would be great. But what about Mustang? How do people care for horses? Do women ride? Do they figure into local religion somehow? Are there horse gods? Would people consider me really odd if I went to Mustang to do a project on horses?"

"People are quite particular about their horses," Charles hinted. "At certain times of the year horses are taken to a sacred lake to drink and be bathed. Other times they let blood from horses, sometimes from their nostrils, other times from their tongues. I've never really asked much about this. But there are definitely things to explore."

"You mentioned Tibetan horse texts," I probed.

"Indeed. The texts translated into French are facsimiles of manuscripts found in the T'ung Huang caves—a place in China that was once part of greater Tibet. But there are others, and some are local in origin. The king of Mustang owns some beautiful ones. But he's quite particular about who can browse his library."

On mention of the king of Mustang, I was overcome. It was as if a small piece of information about a man I'd never met in a place I'd never been held something not only of my future but also of my past. Charles coughed, rubbed out a cigarette and reached for another. A fruit salesman called out prices for bananas from behind the gates of our schoolhouse compound, and a bicycle bell sounded in the street below us. The feeling passed.

"Horses are becoming more and more important, economically speaking, especially now that upper Mustang has been opened up to tourism," Charles continued. "Both the people who live in southern Mustang as well as people from Lo are vying for the horse rental market. There is serious competition these days."

"So, if I went to Mustang, where should I start?"

"Go to Jomsom, the district headquarters. You could start by finding a local doctor named Tshampa Ngawang. *Tshampa*, by the way, means someone who has completed a three-year Buddhist retreat. You won't hear it used often. Anyway, this Tshampa has worked with many students. He has some horse texts, one of which I think he borrowed from the king of Lo. He and his wife, Karma, run a lodge near the airport, the Dancing Yak. He many not be in Mustang when you arrive, but it's worth a try." Charles paused, took a long drag, and motioned for me to hand him my notebook.

"Nirmal Gauchan is a local politician and a lodge owner. He's also a good friend." Charles scribbled his name into my journal. "He'll help set you up with a translator, if you want one. Go to the Hotel Alka Marco Polo, across from the airport. I don't know how much he knows about horses, but he is a good person to speak with, regardless. A big man about town."

I felt my first wave of fieldwork fear. What was I doing? Going to a strange place alone to ask strangers about horses? If I hadn't been so intrigued by the notion of horse texts—ancient words that could perhaps reveal something deeper about this curious bond between human and animal, between girl and horse—maybe I would have abandoned the idea altogether. But that initial burst of excitement, coupled with the beauty of Mustang as revealed by Charles's photos and the fact that I was not actually out there on my own yet, facing more pressing challenges of language and loneliness, kept me going.

"The other person you should try to find is Nyima Dandrul. He should be in a village called Chongkhor in the Muktinath Valley. He's looking after my horse these days."

"You have a horse?" I said with kindred excitement.

"Of course," Charles smiled warmly. "It is the only way to travel in Mustang."

Come as a Guest, Go as a Friend

B Y LATE OCTOBER, a damp winter fog began to blanket Kathmandu each morning and evening. Fruit sellers and tailors and bicycle repair men wrapped thin wool scarves around their heads and shoulders. Street cows huddled together near garbage piles for warmth, settling into the winter. I stuffed my backpack with warm clothes, chocolate, a few books, a tape recorder, and a stack of notebooks, said goodbye to my host family, and headed off to Mustang.

Initially, I did not travel alone. Several of my fellow students were also planning on conducting their independent research in northwestern Nepal, including other villages in southern Mustang. There was Klaus, a wiry young man from New Hampshire, who planned on learning about rural Nepali education along the Annapurna trekking circuit. CL planned to research *cham*, Tibetan ritual dance, and would spend her month of independent study living in a Thakali village south of Jomsom. Bronley was blonde and earthy, from New Mexico, and interested in Bön, the pre-Buddhist shamanistic religion of the Tibetan region of Dolpo made famous by Peter Matthiessen in his book *The Snow Leopard*.

Klaus, CL, Bronley, and I traveled together by bus to Pokhara. On the day of our departure from Kathmandu, we met early in the morning just outside the gates of the main bus park. We squeezed in, three to each hard platform seat, on the rusting blue buses that ferried most Nepalis across their country. Klaus climbed up alongside two young men—a pair who looked no more than sixteen, and who turned out to be the driver and the ticket taker—and helped to load bags on top of the bus. Bronley, CL, and I claimed seats next to several families.

"Miss, you are going to Pokhara, yes?" a young schoolgirl in a gray pleated uniform said to me, breaking her shyness.

"*Hajur. Ma Pokhara jaanchu,*" I replied. "*Tapaai kahaa jaanahunchha?*" "Yes. I will go to Pokhara. Where are you going?" I asked in Nepali. The girl giggled, as did the entire row behind her, and I realized my mistake. I had referred to her using the respectful form of the verb "to go", rather than the form reserved for those younger than myself. Despite all the hours of language instruction, my intuitive response was to speak using the most respectful form of address, regardless of to whom I was speaking. The delineation of social status by different pronouns and verb endings made cultural sense, but was still, somehow, a deeply foreign concept to me.

In teaching, or perhaps just as a gesture of generosity, a matronly woman wearing a bright pink *saree* reached out and tapped CL on the shoulder.

"*Khao, khao,*" she said, treating me, linguistically speaking, as the younger person that I was, holding out a still warm stack of flatbread stuffed with coriander and potatoes. "Eat, eat."

For the next seven hours, the bus belched and sputtered its way along the Trisuli River. Bronley and I stared out the window, watching as women and children washed clothes, cut fodder, and crushed large rocks into gravel with rough-hewn hammers, towels folded on top of their heads to shield the subtropical sun.

That night, we all camped out in one room at the Emerald Guest House, just down the road from the Pokhara Airport. Each of us seemed nervous, here at the edge of our first independent foray into parts of Nepal. As we prepared our backpacks and then settled into our sleeping bags for what would be our last night together for a whole month, we each expressed concern and trepidation for the coming period. CL was nervous about language acquisition, while Bronley was afraid her vegetarian diet would not be practical in Dolpo. I was nervous about meeting Tshampa Ngawang. I had sent him a letter from Kathmandu, but had received no response. I feared that he had never received it, or was a generally unwelcoming individual, or even worse yet, away on vacation.

Klaus shut off the light and slipped into his down sleeping bag. Our four cocoons lay still and quiet in the room, but our nervous energy was palpable as we tried to drift off into sleep.

A loud knock on the door startled us awake. My watch read 5:15AM, and it was still dark outside.

"Wake up! Tea ready. Airport open. Must hurry. First flight on time. Weather good," said the Thakali woman who ran the guesthouse. My classmates and I dressed, stuffed our sleeping bags into our backpacks, laced up our hiking boots, and headed out for this next adventure.

An hour later, Klaus, CL, and I waved goodbye to Bronley and boarded Everest Air Flight 101 to Jomsom. High winds and bad weather had grounded all flights into the area for days, and we were nervous about what we were flying into. The engine spun to a frothy, high-decibel whir. As we taxied to the end of the graveled tarmac, the stewardess handed out hard candies and cotton balls for our ears. With a rush and a push, we were at once airborne, skirting the verdant hills, as Machupuchare, the "Fishtail" Himal, flickered gray gold in the early morning light.

I had never before witnessed so dramatic a shift in landscape. As we traced the Kali Gandaki by air, I watched green fade to gold then to bare fawn-colored earth of the trans-Himalayan rain shadow, rimmed, as it was at the early edge of winter, by clear skies and snow. Trees became a rarity as we began our descent. What foliage there was came in the form of conifers clinging to south-facing slopes up side valleys, and stands of willows and poplars that lined the riverbank in places. Clusters of flat-roofed whitewashed homes and fields already stripped of harvest gave way to a dusty clearing, mostly straight, that was the Jomsom Airport runway. We braced ourselves for the landing, and rejoiced when the plane wheeled up next to a pile of Gore-Tex and burlap: the cargo waiting to be loaded on the return flight to Pokhara. A group of cheering, slightly desperate looking tourists rushed to get on the plane past us.

In the hullabaloo of arrival it took me a moment to notice the air—or, rather, the lack of it—but the moment I reached down to pick up my backpack I was overcome, not only by the dearth of oxygen, but also by the stark, intense beauty of the place we had landed in. Nilgiri Himal towered over this outpost of a town, regal and nearly perfect in its crystalline symmetry. Klaus and CL decided to join me as I headed off in search of the Dancing Yak Lodge. We would have breakfast together, we decided, and then they would head off, CL down to the village of Syang, Klaus across the river to the settlement known as Thimi. We walked out through the airport, with its canary yellow concrete walls, past rows of local women selling apples from woven *doko* baskets, apples whose crispness and sweet flesh was nearly palpable, there in the cool morning air.

"You buy. Good price. Sweet delicious," they said. I vowed to return soon.

"Where is the Dancing Yak Lodge?" I asked.

One of the ladies gestured over her left shoulder, pointing the way with pursed lips. "*Ootha*," she said. "Over there."

At first, I worried that it would be difficult to find the Dancing Yak. But the wood and concrete building on the edge of the airport side of town would have been impossible to miss. A large sign, painted in primary colors, showed a picture of a yak doing a jig, a goofy bovine grin across its face. The name *Dancing Yak* refers to Buddhist ritual dances in which one dancer is costumed as the head of a yak and another as the tail. The image of the dancing yak became a frequent doodle in the margins of my letters home.

I had envisioned Tshampa Ngawang, the local Tibetan doctor, or *amchi*, that I was about to meet, as round-faced and plump, perhaps bald. Undoubtedly, I had grafted too many images of Tibetan monks onto my expectations for Mustang. When I entered the lodge, I was surprised to find Tshampa Ngawang to be a thin man in his late forties with high cheekbones and long hair that was braided and coiled around his head. He had a slightly crooked, toothy grin and beautiful hands. He wore a sunflower turtleneck under a saffron vest—a quintessentially Tibetan color palate that marked his status as a *nakpa*, a householder priest.

"Namaste," I introduced myself. I had grown relatively surefooted in my use of Nepali while in Kathmandu, but I stuttered now, in the face of this potential teacher. "I am interested in horses and have heard that you know how to take care of them, train them...That you have books about them. I sent you a letter, but maybe you didn't receive it."

"No, no letter. But yes, I have worked with students before." Tshampa said. His voice was at once smooth and buoyant, exuding confidence.

"May I study with you? I hope to stay in Mustang for one month."

"Of course. *Most welcome*," he said, using some of the few English words he knew.

"These are my friends," I said, introducing CL and Klaus. "They are also students who want to study in Mustang—but not about horses." A laugh betrayed my nervousness.

"Everyone is *most welcome*," Tshampa repeated.

Over the next day, as Klaus, CL, and I adjusted to the altitude, Tshampa engaged each of us in turn, asking about our families, what we thought of Nepal, and what we wanted to study. He helped place CL in a family in the village of Syang, and told her that he would write a letter to the abbot of the monastery of Marpha—a place known for annual cycles of *cham* dances—on her behalf. For Klaus, Tshampa called on a "cousin-brother" to take him over to Thimi, a settlement across the river from Jomsom, and introduce him to the school masters, including a resident Peace Corps volunteer.

Once CL and Klaus had both headed off the following day, I found Tshampa in the kitchen.

"Has anyone studied about horses with you before?" I asked.

"One woman came from Germany to study my horse books. She still comes to see me sometimes." Tshampa paused. He looked me over before continuing, as if to see if I really liked horses, if I might belong here. I sensed he was also considering what I would do for him, in exchange for his tutorials.

"But she did not like to ride. She was too tall, and was scared of falling. You ride." The latter was spoken as statement, not question.

"Yes. I ride. I can train horses, too." My smile nearly ate my words. It couldn't be this easy, could it?

"You can stay upstairs, in room 104." He handed me a key. Behind him, painted in blue letters on the second floor railing, were written the words: *Come As A Guest, Go As A Friend.*

I spent that first day wandering the length of Jomsom, making note of the numbers and types of horses—ponies by my American standards—

tethered outside guesthouses. I watched how men guided their mounts, and observed just how different the physical gestures that prompted a horse to move were here, as compared to how I would signal for a trot or coax a horse to canter back home. In the late afternoon, I climbed up to the bluff behind the Dancing Yak, and sat down amid the dust and goat dung, the shrubs and wildflowers, to write in my journal. The entry was simple: *I have only just arrived, but I will need to come back here. I already know this.*

During the month I spent at the Dancing Yak, Tshampa and I rode all over southern Mustang together. Before that trip, my body could not remember a time when I felt awkward on a horse. But those days in Mustang, when I learned to lean back against the wind and balance myself as my mount sped forward at an extended trot that locals call a *droo*, I felt as if I were learning how to walk. Everything was different: the size of the horses, my center of gravity in these hard Mongolian-style saddles, the length and position of my stirrups, how I held the reigns. And neither my Nepali language lessons nor my equestrian training prepared me to speak the local dialect of "horse" Tibetan. It had not occurred to me that I would need to learn anew the commands that would send a horse forward, or the words and tone of voice that would settle a horse if it shied.

As the weeks passed, I learned how to saddle Tshampa's ponies with carpets and the local wooden frame saddles. I helped him load animals with bushels of grass and woven baskets piled high with manure. We shod his horses together, and I watched as he worked leather strips and metal buckles, bought in a Kathmandu bazaar, into a new girth or bridle. I was coming to understand what it was like to actually rely on a horse, not for blue ribbons, but for transportation, farming, and commerce.

In the evenings, Tshampa and I studied his small collection of Tibetan horse texts. Some bore the chopmarks of New Delhi printing houses: reprints of old medical treatises translated from Sanskrit into Tibetan. I wrote down the names of books that seemed both crucial to my understanding and beyond what I could learn on this first trip to Mustang. Later, Tshampa brought out small stacks of loose-leafed, local folios that smelled of earth and revealed precious line drawings: horses being saddled, mares giving birth, horses to illustrate Buddhist metaphors of transcendence and skillful means, horses of different colors and shapes. Tshampa would read a folio aloud in Tibetan and then synopsize these passages into a simplified Nepali vocabulary that I could understand. I knew that much was being lost in the translation, but I was transfixed, nonetheless, as Tshampa spoke of origin myths and methods of healing horses and other animals.

The Tibetan people are often said to be the offspring of a monkey incarnation of Avalokitesvara, the Bodhisattva of Compassion, and a mountain ogress. One night, as we studied together, Tshampa spoke about how Horse's mother was Eagle, and Horse's father was Monkey.

"Finally, nearly one year after Monkey had first met Eagle, the eggs that Eagle had been guarding broke open in one big crash, just like an avalanche," said Tshampa. "Five tall, four-legged animals emerged from the eggs. The creatures began stumbling around on their new legs, whinnying. At first they could not walk well at all. They stumbled back and forth, wandering in and out of the waters of Tso Mapam," continued Tshampa, who had explained that this magical event took place beside the shore of one of Tibet's most sacred lakes, at the foot of Mt. Kailash, the giant snow-capped mountain in western Tibet that itself was the proverbial "navel of the universe."

"But as these new creatures took long sips of the cool, blue-green waters of Tso Mapam, they revived," recalled my teacher. "And so, from that moment, the horse was born. Clever like the monkey, strong and swift like the eagle, the horse grew and flourished. Soon they were flying across earth and up mountains as quickly as Eagle pervades the sky."

During the evenings, when Tshampa would read to me from the horse texts, I learned that other *nakpa*, Buddhist and Bön householder priests like himself, performed rituals to protect horses and other livestock from wild animals, disease, and harmful spirits.

"Many people here know how to set a bone or break a colt," said Tshampa one evening, as we talked about the birth of a horse and the first three years of a foal's life. "But not many people know about horse medicine. Horses and humans are similar. So are their medicines. People usually know when a horse will be born because their gestation period is known to be twelve months."

"Not eleven?" I asked, thinking back to all of the horse books I'd read growing up.

"Remember, our months are different than yours. We follow the moon. Sometimes there are more days in a month, sometimes less. Sometimes we need to repeat days or lose days because they are very lucky, or very inauspicious," Tshampa continued.

"As the time draws near for the mare to give birth, the owner should make a nice spot for the mare to live. A smart person will not ride a pregnant mare once the mare's nipples stiffen and spread apart and her woman's parts become wide and begin to sweat. When this happens, birth is soon to follow. After the new horse is born, you should feed the mare some oil and *tsampa*, roasted barley flour. Mix it into soup. This will replenish the energy and vitamins she lost while giving birth. If the placenta comes out quickly, fine, but if it is late in coming, give the mare hot food. You can also rub oil on the mare's back and place wool over this area to help. After the birth, keep the foal and the mother inside for a few days and let them rest. If many people come to look at the mare and foal—and especially if they comment on what a good foal it is—the foal might die." I later learned that the same held true for human births: that newborns were most vulnerable to the whims of jealous neighbors and nefarious spirits, and that either too much preparation for a birth, or too much anticipation about the nature of a child, could result in that child falling ill, or dying.

The first year of a horse's life is called the *milk-drinking year*, a time of nursing and of growth, when the colt wears a special protection cord and amulet around its neck. The second year is called the *hair-cutting year*, when a colt is weaned and its tail is shorn and shaped.

"Sometimes, if a horse is strong and ready, the owner will look in the calendar for an auspicious day and make a small offering and then ride the horse for the first time when the horse is only two. But most people only start to ride a horse in its third year. This is called the *saddling year*," Tshampa explained.

One evening, as Tshampa and I were leaning over the Tibetan texts together, he suddenly looked up at me, his finger resting on a specific passage and smiled. "Know what you do if a woman can't give birth and the baby is ready to come out?"

"No idea," I replied.

"Put her on a horse and make her ride backward!"

"How do you know?" I asked. I was amused by the story, but like some of the remedies Tshampa had read to me earlier that night—crushed beetles to cure a horse's cold, bloodletting from a horse's tongue to cure colic—I was skeptical.

"I watched my father prescribe this once for a woman. She was in pain from all the weight in her stomach. She couldn't sleep, and refused to eat. All she wanted to do was give birth, but the son inside her was stubborn. He sat high in her belly, like sons always do, and wouldn't move. So my father got her on an old gelding, facing the horse's tail, and had her husband walk her around the village for an hour or so. Within a day she had given birth to a healthy boy."

"Then it must be true, Tshampa-la!" We both laughed, but in some sense I found myself wondering if my knowledge of Western veterinary care was actually limiting my experience in Mustang, making it more difficult for me to dislodge my sense of truth from that which I was now learning.

Some days reinforced this sense of cultural dissonance, and the need to reach beyond what I was comfortable knowing, how I understood the difference between empirical realities and so-called "belief." Other days, this dissonance dissolved into the simple yet fantastic nature of all that Tshampa knew.

"In Tibetan culture," Tshampa explained as he read, "Three swirls of hair, *tsug*, on the horse's head bring the owner luck and wealth. This very auspicious sign is like a *norbu*, a precious jewel. But a cowlick on a horse's back, under the saddle, brings nothing but trouble. The owner of such a horse will surely face an early death, under bad circumstances."

"And what if you find a great horse with such a marking?" I asked. "Would you not buy it?"

"Probably not. Too risky! But if the price was good, I'd buy it, and use it to carry loads. Early death cannot come to a bag of potatoes or barley." Tshampa laughed. "Besides," he said, turning more serious, "I will live until I'm at least one hundred."

"Says who?"

"Tibetan astrology. It is very reliable," said Tshampa. "Besides that, there is the healthy mountain air, and my Buddhist practice and belief in the *dharma*. With that, especially, I can die whenever, and go without fear." As Tshampa spoke, I began to realize what it meant to be a part of an *amchi* lineage of healer-physicians.

As the weeks in Mustang passed, I learned a bit about Tibetan medicine, and, through this process, more deeply understood that illness and health are never just facts of biology, that medicine is, at its core, a cultural system. Tshampa explained some of the principles of *Sowa Rigpa*, which in Tibetan means "science of healing." In this system, every substance on Earth has the potential to be used as medicine. A healthy environment is a cosmo-physical space in which the elements of earth, water, fire, air, and consciousness exist in balance with the three "deficiencies" or humors: wind, bile, and phlegm. This environment is not only an external tableau, in which plants grow and are harvested and used for healing, but it is also an internal geography—a map of the body. To an *amchi*, sickness among sentient beings—"People, but also horses," Tshampa was quick to point out—is thought to be the earthly manifestation of deeper imbalances that are moral, spiritual, and karmic. It is essential to pay attention to these deeper causes, for the path to wellness begins here, in the journey away from the three poisons of ignorance, anger, and desire.

As simply as he could, Tshampa explained to me that *Sowa Rigpa* seeks to unify the body's struggle with illness with the spirit's quest for liberation. As such, a Tibetan definition of health encompasses much more than physical well-being; it is a quest for wholeness in mind and body, a challenge to our workaday Western notion that our bodies are capable of being healed without engaging our minds in this process. Pointing out the very desires and aversions that define our contracted lives as "unhealthy," Tibetan medicine builds from there. Medicine is found not only in pills and powders derived from ingredients carefully gathered and prepared according to the precepts of Tibetan medical texts, but is also in the food we eat, the behaviors we adopt, and the practices of mindfulness and attention in which we engage, guided by right motivation. Long-term health is nothing if not spiritual transformation.

As Tshampa instructed, the duties and practices of an *amchi* arise from the *bodhisattva* mind—a place of good intentions and clarity of judgment, at once grounded in the sentient world and also transcendent of it. Ideally, a physician's services are offered without thought of material gain, because *Sowa Rigpa* is a manifestation of the Buddha's teachings. *Amchi* should make medicines to the best of their abilities, using the materials available to them. *Sowa Rigpa* expertise, then, is a way of being in the world that not only confers a type of authority on its practitioners but that also grounds an individual within a community and within a particular landscape.

As I heard more about Tshampa's life history, and the ways he learned medicine from his father, I also began to see how *Sowa Rigpa* finds its most profound expression in the marriage of oral and textual knowledge—transmitted through study, practical apprenticeship, and a deep connection to a root teacher. Expertise in this medical practice manifests as the ability to subdue imbalances, harmful spirits, and mental obstacles, and to use wisely the "divine nectar" derived from plants, minerals, gems, and animal products, which have been empowered by the Medicine Buddha, the Healer King of Physicians.

From Tshampa, I also learned that what is today called *Sowa Rigpa* has existed in some form throughout Tibet and the Himalayas for thousands of years. A corpus of classical medical texts, the *Gyushi* or *Four Medical Tantras*, emerged after the spread of Buddhism to Tibet in the seventh century, and was refined in the eleventh century by lineages of medical practitioners. During the seventeenth century, under the leadership of the Great Fifth Dalai Lama, new commentaries and a series of illustrated medical scroll paintings were produced, and Tibet's first college of medicine and astrology, called Chagpori, was founded. Tibetan medicine has historical and philosophical links to Ayurveda, as well as to Chinese medicine, and yet it is a fully developed system in its own right.

During the reign of the Thirteenth Dalai Lama (1895–1933) Tibetan medicine thrived and a new medical college in Lhasa, called the *Mentsikhang,* or "house of medicine and astrology," was established. Even though Tibetan medicine suffered during the Chinese annexation of Tibet in the 1950s and the subsequent chaos of the Cultural Revolution, I learned that this system continues to be taught, and that today there are prestigious colleges and institutes of Tibetan medicine both in India and in Tibetan areas of China. Tshampa also explained that in places like Mustang, most medical knowledge is transmitted according to lineage, passed from father to son, as well as from one monastic to another.

"I learned by studying with my father and other masters, reading and memorizing books, and receiving initiations into teachings through oral instruction," Tshampa told me.

Most of the intricacies of Tibetan medicine bore little superficial resemblance to how people in Mustang cared for their horses. Yet these systems were connected, not only in how horses were treated but also in how people in Mustang reconciled their own complex ideas about how and why illness and suffering occurs—in horses or in humans—with less locally grounded practices of healing, such as that meted out by Nepali veterinary technicians or the doctors at the Jomsom District Hospital.

As the first snows fell in Jomsom, Tshampa and I talked late into the night over cups of sweet milk tea. Karma, Tshampa's wife, snoozed in the nearby bedroom, their youngest child curled around her sleeping form. When the electricity failed, which often happened, we read by candlelight. While my eyes drooped under the weight of too much information and sleepiness, Tshampa never seemed tired.

On the fifteenth day of the month, Tshampa and I traveled back to his home village of Drumpa for a *tsog* offering, in which lamas honored the local village deities, and solicited their protection. Given the high regard with which Tshampa spoke about his home village, and the sense of responsibility he seemed to impart when he explained the importance of paying respects to the spirits that guarded Drumpa, I was expecting to find a lively, well-kempt house in a vibrant village. Instead I was confronted with the poverty and destitution of an all but abandoned place. As he showed me around his family home, Tshampa mumbled prayers while walking through rooms blackened by layers of woodsmoke, overrun with dust and mouse droppings, and filled with the last year's apple crop. Tshampa assured me that when he lived in Drumpa, the house was clean and organized. But he no longer lived here. Rather, he returned as a matter of obligation, of duty. After all, his mother still lived here.

As I watched Tshampa perform the *tsog* ritual, I thought about the home I'd left behind in California. What did it mean that I was choosing to build a connection to a place that was, literally and figuratively, so far away from my roots?

In many ways, these weeks with Tshampa had initiated me into the practice of anthropology, and to what it meant to come to know a new place that was also on the cusp of many transitions: social, economic, political. From the few local people my age I got to know during that first trip to Mustang, the generation gap was palpable, not unlike the river gorge that divided this landscape. Likewise with a sense of what the recent opening of upper Mustang would mean for those who lived throughout the district. For my part, I began to understand how horses fit into Mustang—as commodities, symbols of social status, and a medium of exchange. These rugged mountain steeds had carried their culture through centuries. They had enabled trade, enlivened community festivals, and were so often spoken of as a metaphor for strength, power, and insight. I realized I wanted nothing more than to delve deeper into these questions about what horses meant to this place.

On the day I left Mustang, Tshampa said good-bye with these words: "Keep these things in your head and heart. You have a good mind for it. Good luck and go slowly." He placed a *katag* around my neck, a ceremonial scarf that marks partings and felicitous occasions, the blessing of cool, white silk. He also put a small painting of a horse in my hand, one that I had commissioned from him earlier in the month.

Next, Karma wandered out. Although I had spent more time with Tshampa than with her, Karma had still welcomed me into her home as more than a guest. Where Tshampa and I spent hours on the topic of horses, Karma taught me about the necessities of life in Mustang: from dirty jokes to how to make a meal over a wood fire. Unlike her husband, Karma looked permanently disheveled: the ample bosom that had nursed six children always poured out of her dirty frock. That day, she threw her hair into a loose bun, wiped her hands of flour, and embraced me before I set off.

CL and I met up in Syang and spent the next four days walking our way out of Mustang. Often, I found myself crying. The tears came partly because I did not know if or when I would return to Mustang, and partly because this initial experience had stirred in me emotions, expectations, and questions about the world that I had never asked myself before. The tears also came, I think, because I realized that even returning to Kathmandu would be something of a shock. I began to wonder how I would translate this experience into something both of and beyond myself. I thought back to college life in Providence, and my roommates who were off in Paris and Seville, and wondered how I would be able to communicate with them, or with my family. What would I know how to share, and what stories would feel too distant, or simply too embedded in a different language and culture, to tell?

I carried my painting of Tshampa's horse on the top of my backpack, cushioned by my sleeping bag. A poem Tshampa had written for me rested safely between pages of my journal. The poem was written in Tibetan, but before I had left Jomsom, Tshampa had explained it to me in Nepali. It was crudely translated, but no less powerful for its lack of grace. In that sense, the poem was an apt entrée into the meticulous, imperfect, and yet magical act of translation. The fact that it was written at all, and written for me, was enough.

A good horse is a very lucky horse.
Within the world of animals, horses are the best.
They run in competition with birds in the sky.
Horses and humans share a similar mind,

this is why horses and humans are the best of friends.
Even when work must be done far away, the horse is expedient,
up, down, or over flat terrain, the horse travels well and swiftly.
Therefore, Horse's name is also "windhorse."
In times of peace, horses are happy with us.
In times of war, horses help us defeat our enemies.
The horse's Father, Eagle, is an excellent being.
Mother Monkey is also very clever.
From this pair comes the Excellent Horse.
Horses have helped man for centuries
with their quick feet and quick minds.
Share good faith with your horse and ride your horse well.
Horses, like lightning, move quickly in all directions.

I wouldn't return to Mustang until autumn 1995, nearly two years after I'd first come to Mustang. Upon finishing college, I had been granted a Fulbright fellowship. My proposal had talked about translating some of Mustang's horse texts, learning more about the role horses played in Mustang's economy and its rituals, and trying to understand the connections between Tibet's past and Mustang's present through the vehicle of the horse. Tibetan creation myths speak of a land that would have included Mustang as "the center of the sky, the middle of the earth...an enclosure of glaciers, the head of all rivers, a place where custom is perfected, where horses grow swift." Horses were everywhere I looked, and I wanted to learn more about them,

After my initial month in Mustang, I had come to feel a certain dissonance between how Tshampa and other local healers and horsemen regarded these horse texts. To some, the myths, stories, and practical instruction contained in these books were accessible and important. To others who knew Mustang's horses intimately, this bookish knowledge was irrelevant or, for those who could not read, simply inaccessible. I wanted to learn more about this divide. More generally, I was fascinated by the relationship between humans and other animals, and I longed to grasp these interdependencies, outside of the familiar realms of the stables where I had spent so much of my childhood. I was also touched by

Mustang because being there made me realize just how little I knew about this animate earth. I trusted the Tibetan sensibility that sees life in rivers and sky and mountains, making a sacred and living landscape out of the everyday environment. I intuited that horses were a metaphor and a means of seeing how Mustang and its people were changing— and of bearing witness to a culture that was in the midst of profound transitions.

Beyond this, I knew that Mustang had touched me for reasons I could not explain intellectually, and that to not return would have meant the death of something that had just begun to live in me.

THE DANCING YAK

A<small>T FIRST GLANCE</small>, the Dancing Yak Lodge seemed unchanged. The door squeaked behind me—the same long, low drawl of welcome to which I had become accustomed two years ago. The pine floors in the dining room had weathered well. Dusty plastic geraniums still stood at attention in simple vases atop the lodge's dining tables. Rickety tin buckets, which cradled embers and kept visitors warm in the winter weather, peaked out from under the skirts of woolen blankets that served as tablecloths.

My traveling companion this time was a friend from Brown named Sara, who was now a student on the same study abroad program I'd participated in two years before. We had become very close during the interim years at Brown. While we were still in Kathmandu, I told Sara about Tshampa and suggested she meet him before beginning her independent study project on women's religious practice in lower Mustang. In the letters we'd exchanged over the past two years, I'd learned that Tshampa was helping to build a new nunnery in the Muktinath Valley, on the model of the large monastic institutions of historic Tibet, and those that had sprouted up in India and Nepal since the 1960s. The money for the building was flowing forth from the private coffers of a reincarnate lama who lived most of the time in Singapore, but whose previous incarnation had been a driving force behind Buddhism in Mustang in the 1950s and 60s. Sara's own work dealt with *chomo*, female religious adepts who did not necessarily live exclusively celibate, cloistered lives—indeed many of them had been traders and some had even borne children—but who devoted significant parts of their lives to religious study. She had been intrigued by the plans for this new nunnery, for it represented a stark contrast to the ways that Mustang's *chomo* tended to live and practice the *dharma*.

After three days of canceled flights, Sara and I finally boarded a plane to Jomsom. As we collected our bags and exited the tarmac, I could see Tshampa and Karma waiting for us outside the airport gates. Tshampa's hair was tucked under a woolen cap, and his signature gold polo shirt and red vest looked stiff, as if they had been recently washed and dried in the sun. Karma stood next to him, holding a *kathag* in her work-worn hands.

"Welcome back," said Tshampa, his hands folded in a *namaste* gesture. "We've been expecting you."

Sara and Tshampa made a quick connection with each other, discussing the new nunnery and the issues surrounding its completion. Tshampa was talking rapidly and ceaselessly, describing everything from religious texts the nuns would use to study, to the construction of door frames. But I was surprised when Tshampa mentioned in passing that one of his daughters was prepared to enter the nunnery as well.

"Who? Yangmo?" I asked. Tshampa nodded. Yangmo was Tshampa and Karma's third child. Shy and contemplative, she tried not to look at her father as he spoke of her future, but instead busied herself by playing with her younger sister as we talked. Middle born, she was well suited for the nunnery, according to Tibetan tradition. Still, I couldn't help but wonder what she was thinking as her father planned her future.

"Yangmo will do well at the nunnery," Tshampa continued. "And the religious life is a path of much merit." He looked at Sara and smiled sheepishly, "Ah, maybe you should become a nun, too, since you're interested in studying them. The building will be done in a year. Come back then and I'll shave your head!" We all laughed—everyone, that is, except Yangmo. She looked frightened.

That night Sara and I shared my old room and whispered into the early morning, kept awake by Mustang's oxygen-starved atmosphere and the nervousness of the work ahead of us. Sara left the next morning, letters of introduction written for her by Tshampa for her new host family in the village of Lubra and the *chomo* at Garwa Gompa, a small local nunnery in the Muktinath Valley. We embraced and said goodbye, for the time being.

After Sara departed, Tshampa decided to reorient me to the Dancing Yak. "We are making many improvements," he said. "Let me show you."

"This," he said, leading me into what had been a storeroom, "is now going to be the *lhakhang*, the shrine room. I've made all the carvings myself." The room smelled of newly cured wood and juniper incense. Tshampa had been hard at work, sculpting lotus blossoms, endless knots, conch shells, and parasols, a pair of fish, a victory banner, a treasure vase, and a *dharma* wheel: images that make up the eight auspicious symbols of Tibetan Buddhism. Two snow lions were emerging from a pair of pine blocks. It was clear that Tshampa's shrine room was meant as a space not only for contemplation and meditation, but also for cultural communication. This was a family room, and one that Tshampa would open up to local dignitaries, friends, and patients who came seeking his medicine, but one that was, as he described it, *not* a place for tourists.

Tshampa then led me out of the room and up the stairs to the second floor, past the row of guestrooms, to a portion of the flat adobe roof, facing Nilgiri, with plenty of southern exposure.

"This room will be our solarium," Tshampa continued. "Just like some of the other hotels in Jomsom, now it is our turn to build one here."

Tshampa prattled on about his plans for a room of glass walls in which tourists could watch the sun set while sipping a cup of local apricot brandy. While he spoke, I began to understand that in designing this "new and improved" Dancing Yak lodge, Tshampa and his family, like other Mustangis, were creating an increased divide between private, family life and the chief business of tourism. As Mustang became increasingly open to foreign travelers, Tshampa and many others like him were capitalizing on the trade, and using this increased wealth to expand the comforts of their own domesticity, as well as the amenities they offered to tourists. Yet these areas of expansion and improvement rarely overlapped. Indeed, they often represented very different value systems.

A deep ambition infused how Tshampa discussed these new developments.

"I thought you weren't really interested in running a hotel," I said, as Tshampa discussed the preparation of foreign foods and the painting of flower boxes. On my previous visit, Tshampa had taken pains to convince me that he felt his duty was to teach, to heal the sick, and to practice his religion. The hotel, he had stressed, was more of a bother than a blessing, imposed on him by his younger brother, an antiques dealer who darted between Kathmandu, Hong Kong, and Taiwan.

"Exactly right. I am not so concerned with business," Tshampa responded, unconvincingly. "But Karma can manage the hotel. And we do need to pay for school fees!" Tshampa's eldest son and youngest two daughters attended the relatively inexpensive local schools, but he had two children in a prestigious Kathmandu boarding school—paid for in part by a former Peace Corps volunteer who had befriended Tshampa and his family.

"And Karma, how will she manage on her own?" I asked.

"I've sent for a young girl from Dolpo. She arrived just a week ago and will help with the cleaning and cooking. Dolpo is not as developed as Mustang. It's a great opportunity for her to stay here and learn some English," continued Tshampa. Dolpo, the region just west of Mustang where my friend Bronley had traveled two years ago, was an area of even rougher topography and generally poorer folk. Tshampa's new employee was from a village located in a remote valley in upper Dolpo, near the Tibetan border. There, residents depended for survival on herding and the trade of Tibetan salt for lowland grains much more than tourism.

It did not surprise me that Tshampa had hired this out-of-towner to be the hotel maid. Undoubtedly, Tshampa would get his money's worth out of this young woman. And she would give Karma, whose eldest daughter was away at school, a younger female helper in the household. But I was surprised to hear Tshampa willingly discuss the social divide so easily. Nepal's strict high-caste Hindu state hierarchy afforded people from both Mustang and Dolpo the same derogatory *bhotiya* designation as meat-eating, Buddhist, alcohol-drinking people. The fact that Tshampa referred to Dolpo as an underdeveloped area showed that he was creating yet another layer of power relations—not between "the

West and the rest," or between Kathmandu and the rest of the country, but rather internally, based on social and geographic hierarchy.

The young woman from Dolpo appeared on the balcony, carrying two cups of tea, which she offered up demurely. She looked about my age, and our round faces in some ways mirrored each other. Dressed in a *chuba*, the traditional Tibetan dress, and wrapped in her rainbow-striped woolen apron, she was quite short, her black tresses pulled back in a neat bun. Her hands, of course, looked ancient. I took the tea and asked her name.

"Dolma," she replied in a voice barely audible.

"You are from Dolpo?" I asked. Dolma nodded in reply.

"Do you like Jomsom? Is Mustang very different from Dolpo?" I asked, using the few Tibetan words I then knew.

Dolma glanced shyly at Tshampa before responding. "Very different. Here, there is wood to cook on. Here, people are rich." Our eyes met, she glanced at her employer, and was gone.

When I first met Tshampa, he impressed on me his plan to set off for a cave and spend several years in retreat, upon his fifty-fifth birthday, which was then only five years away. Now, it seemed his priorities were shifting. As we talked over Karma's *dhal bhaat* and curried potatoes that afternoon, Tshampa shared with me not only his more local plans, but also his desire to travel to the United States.

"Retreats are important," said Tshampa, when I reminded him of his plans. "But going to America would also be very good. It would benefit many people if I could help spread Tibetan medicine and Buddhism in your country. I think first America, then retreat."

Through our conversation, I realized that many aspects of life in Jomsom had changed in just a few short years. I wondered how I, too, had become someone different, and whether my changes were as obvious as those I was beginning to observe around me.

That second day back in Mustang, Tshampa and I talked through the day and into evening. Tshampa was attempting to teach Tibetan and the rudiments of *amchi* practice to his son Jamyang, but at thirteen, Jamyang was acting like a typical teenager, bent on leaving the small town behind.

"Since you were here last, I also have a new clinic. It is at the Eco-Museum," Tshampa continued, enthusiastically. "Tibetan medicine is becoming famous throughout the world. Wait until tomorrow, when you see my visitor book," he continued.

The Jomsom Eco-Museum loomed above the southern outskirts of Jomsom airport. Made of wood and concrete, the building stood two stories tall on a bluff. The museum's construction had been funded by a Japanese foundation, with national support from the King Mahendra Trust for Nature Conservation (KMTNC), a semi-autonomous arm of what was then Nepal's "new" democracy, still nominally included within the king of Nepal's sphere of influence.

During my first trip to Mustang, the museum had been little more than timber frames and concrete slabs. Tshampa and the Japanese project coordinators had spent hours drawing up plans for the medicinal clinic and herbarium, shrine room, and library. The museum itself had felt like a skeleton. Tshampa had begun to carve an altar in the otherwise empty library *cum* shrine room. The main exhibit hall was empty, save a pile of rather battered and very Caucasian-looking mannequins that would someday be dressed in Mustang finery, "to show the Tibetan and Thakali culture." Now, two years later, the building had been completed.

By eight that evening my eyes burned with exhaustion. Tshampa and I had spent the day together, talking and touring all of Jomsom, taking in every new building and feature. I now longed for bed, the quiet candle on the nightstand that I had come to love during my last stay. "I'm tired, Tshampa-la. Maybe I should head off to my old room."

"No," answered Tshampa, surprising me. "You are family now. I made a special single room for you. Come." He walked toward the top of the stairs and worked the sliding lock on a new plywood door that, two years ago, led to their stock of grain.

"See, we have made a nice place." As Tshampa swung open the door, I tried not to gasp. The first flimsy portal gave way to an ante-chamber, no bigger than a closet, from which two more doors, equally thin, had been built to the right and left. Tshampa opened the door to the left, revealing a small cot. Across from it, a window looked out on the Dancing Yak's water tanks and stocks of firewood. Sawdust carpeted the floor. White-wash flaked and peeled. The windowpane still bore the grease pencil mark of its price, and the hinges strained and squeaked in protest as I tried to open them.

"Very cozy," I finally sputtered. "But not much place to put my books or clothes."

"There is space on the windowsill, and your bag will fit nicely here, under the bed," Tshampa raised the bed skirt to reveal a few lumpy burlap sacks that smelled of potatoes. "Right now Karma and I are sleeping just across, here," he said, opening the other door, as if that were consolation. It seemed as if he wanted to convince me that there were no barriers between us.

"Once the shrine room gets finished, Karma and I will move into the room in the corner, downstairs." Perhaps noticing the look of dismay on my face, he added, "We're quite comfortable here, though. We don't need much, really. Marriage keeps me warm!" he smiled. I felt queasy.

"You can stay here as long as you want. This way, you don't have to spend so much money, now that you are a student and staying a while." Tshampa went on. "We only need to charge a little for this room."

"Okay, Tshampa." I was too newly arrived, too eager to place myself in the good graces of this teacher, to answer otherwise. I thought back to Tshampa's family house in Drumpa and to the fact that privacy did not exist in the same way here as it did back home. Here, conception, birth, and death happened between four shared walls, warmed by the hearth, divided by long shadows, small windows, and the evening's descent into darkness.

Tshampa and Karma's nighttime chatter turned to deep breathing, and then silence.

The Family God Horse

TSHAMPA ALWAYS stirred before Karma awoke. From my cubbyhole bedroom on the opposite side of the plywood partition, I could hear him slip his arms through his shirt and into his vest, buckle his trousers, and begin his morning prayers: Tibetan syllables, deeply voiced and strung together in a melody that infused the house with calm. It was an aural equivalent of the smell of juniper incense that accompanied these morning prayers. Soon enough, Karma stirred, making her way down to the kitchen where she blew the hearth's embers awake. As with our cozy domesticity, Tshampa and I, too, soon fell into a working rhythm with each other. Each morning we left the Dancing Yak early, nothing in our stomachs save a cup of sweet tea, and walked up a small hill to the Eco-Museum.

The museum was a strange mixture of local pride and various attempts to market "traditional Mustang culture" to tourists trekking through the area. The main exhibition room was lined with a collection of photographs accompanied by blocks of text describing Mustang's physical and cultural landscape, written by foreign scholars. Although the museum had been open less than a year, most of the pictures were already dusty and faded—a testament to the severity of Mustang's elements. Glass display cases in the center of the room housed ammonite fossils. Known as *saligram* in Sanskrit, these smooth black stones, when split, reveal the perfect simulacrum of an ancient sea creature. Hindus believe the fossils are considered offerings from the god Vishnu, and they pour down the Kali Gandaki with summer swell, only to be gathered up and sold in the Jomsom bazaar to tourists. The collection in the museum looked chipped and handled—the dregs of a harvest that couldn't be sold. Other display cases held shards of pottery and other terra cotta artifacts excavated by teams of German and Nepali archaeologists who had been working in Mustang for years, dissecting its caves and cataloging the contents of its earthen mounds.

But the mannequins stole the show. A pile of naked—and very Caucasian—arms and legs and heads I'd seen two years before had been righted, positioned, and dressed. Now they stood along the back wall of the main exhibit hall: a battalion of cultural soldiers, dressed in their turquoise and coral necklaces, their hand-dyed, woven aprons, with turbans of white cotton, as worn by Thakali men on special occasions.

Despite the cultural artifacts, resident doctor, library, and video lab, the museum passed each day without many visitors. Locals were reluctant to trudge up the hill just to see books they could not read, or see pictures of the place they inhabited. The video room was popular with the younger residents, but mainly so that they could watch popular Bollywood movies. Visits by tourists were comparatively greater, but still small—a fact that seemed a product of the museum's location. Towering as it did over the trekking trail, one upward glance at its steep staircase made you lose all interest in climbing to the top. The small olive-green signboard posted at the base of the stairs, which most visitors failed to notice, conjured up the image of an army barracks rather than a museum.

Tshampa's medical clinic, however, was neatly organized and functional. The freshly painted walls were lined with shelved bottles of herbal powders and pills, marked with precise, calligraphic Tibetan. A statue of Sangye Menla, the Medicine Buddha, decorated the far wall, his hair painted signature bright blue, and his begging bowl brimming with plastic fruit. The adjacent medicinal plant storage room also had a curated feel to it, but the bittersweet herbs achieved the effect of casting Tshampa as a skilled healer. The room smelled of ginseng, juniper, and cinnamon, with canvas bags of herbs lining the room from floor to ceiling in some places. Dried leaves and gnarled roots had been gathered by hand, and sweet flowers and astringent bark were organized in neat piles.

But I was confused by the fact that Tshampa's impressive clinic was housed in a museum. I was fairly certain that most locals would only seek out Tshampa's medical care at his home, or ask that he make a house call. While the museum's mission was to highlight and "preserve" this and other aspects of Mustang culture, it also seemed to be precipitating its transformation. I could not help but wonder who the Eco-museum clinic would really serve.

For all its incongruities, the museum was a quiet place, "good for study," as Tshampa liked to say. During my first weeks back in Mustang, Tshampa and I passed many hours at the museum, talking about all manner of things equestrian. My field notebook became filled with coat colors, drawings, anecdotes, and Tibetan idioms, all surrounding horses and the spirited culture that lived around them.

I learned that white horses were used especially for weddings, as they reflected the whiteness of conch shells, a metaphor for the clarity of the Buddha's teachings. Chestnut-colored horses were considered lucky, but if a chestnut mare had white socks, she also meant trouble. Only lucky people should consider riding such a horse. A golden palomino was preferred by lamas, but if the horse had white eyes, it was known to "act drunk" in the sun, and fall short in snow. A horse with a slightly red coat would be the choice of kings, whereas horses with "blue" coats—the type of horse I knew back in California as a "gray"—would be ridden by everyday, "middle class" people.

Diagnoses were also made for equine diseases based, in part, on the appearance of the horse, as well as specific symptoms. A type of colic was recognized by a swollen and infected tongue, failure to eat, and pawing at the ground. The usual causes of such an illness were unclean food or water, most likely stemming from human urine contaminating the horse's stall or feeding area. The recommended treatment involved puncturing a vein on the underside of the animal's tongue, bleeding it, and finally rubbing salt onto the wound. As with colic back home in the U.S., Tshampa recognized that failure to catch and treat the disease could lead to a fatal twisting of the intestines.

I also learned that caring for horses was not just about maintaining their physical well-being. Tshampa spoke to me about Tandrin, a horse-headed god who helps to protect horses from nefarious spirits, disease, even attacks from wild animals. He showed me the small rainbow-colored amulets made of yarn and stuffed with mantras to this deity that people hung around their horses' necks in Mustang.

Tshampa and I talked about how our cultures differed when it came to feeding animals, also. In Mustang, locals partitioned rangelands for grazing and shared the duty of caring for their resources. Tshampa spoke of how these systems of land management had operated in his youth, and how things were changing now.

"When I was young, everyone knew where the good grass was and where we were allowed to go with our animals. We took turns having the good pastures, rolling dice to see where we would go each season," Tshampa explained one day. "Some areas were better for horses, other areas were good for the sheep and goats. Sometimes people would fight over borders, or say 'you owe me five *manna* of barley because your horse went in my field,'" he continued. "But today there are different problems. Young people go off to school and they don't know about these rules. There is less water now in some places. And the climate is changing, which means there is more rain and less snow."

As Tshampa explained the various problems affecting Mustang, it became obvious that these issues were as much developmental and political as they were brought on by the environmental and economic effects of modernization in Nepal. During the time I lived in Mustang, joint "conservation and development initiatives," such as those implemented by the Annapurna Conservation Area Project, had begun to proliferate. And yet, while these projects worked brilliantly in some areas to harness a diversity of local knowledge and transform them into more formalized community-led systems of natural resource management, in other regions such efforts were thwarted by politics and misunderstandings. Tshampa's comments about the changing nature of Mustang's environment were prescient.

During these conversations in the museum courtyard, I began to understand not only what it means to be from a place, but also what it means to be forced—or compelled—to leave. Throughout the year, I watched as countless people from Baragaon and Lo headed to Benares and Assam in the winter to sell sweaters, returning with cash in their pockets and rice on the backs of their mules, but thinner and more tired than they had been at the start of the trading season.

Through our conversations about grazing patterns and pasture boundaries, and in Tshampa's reminiscences about his annual trips to the high mountains to gather medicinal plants, I began to understand how Tshampa's *amchi* practice related not only to the care he could offer horses and other animals, but also to many other aspects of life in Mustang.

Tshampa had spent his entire life learning to listen. He had learned to listen to his father, who served as his primary teacher, and to his patients when they complained of ailments. And he had learned to listen to the natural world around him, discovering how to heal others based on elements he found in his environment—roots, leaves, bark, minerals. It was his success as an *amchi* that made him interested in spreading Tibetan medicine throughout the world, acquainting people far and wide with its practice. But discussing the problems Mustang was already suffering from the effects of globalization and modernization, I wondered what such a new popularity in Tibetan medicine would mean for the people of Mustang. I was beginning to sense something of the subtle dance between tradition and modernity, movements at once global and local in their implications, in which Mustangis were engaged.

"Tell me more about your childhood, Tshampa-la," I asked one morning, as we sat in the Eco-Museum courtyard. "About how you lived before you came to Jomsom."

"The best way to tell you such stories," Tshampa answered, "is to talk about the family god horse."

During our initial month together, and also from the bits of Tibetology reading I'd been able to do in the intervening years, I'd learned that people recognized certain animals as guardians of their ancestral lineage—an incarnation of a deity tied to their specific clan or village. I had also learned that animals—a horse, a yak, sheep, or goat—were sometimes "freed" as a way of appeasing local deities and atoning for a variety of sins, including killing animals for food. I wondered if this "family god" horse was related to these customs, and what, exactly it had to do with other things I was learning about Mustang's horse culture.

"Please!" I answered.

"I remember the first time I saw the colt that would be our family god horse," Tshampa began. "I must have been about twelve. I had been out collecting yak dung and brambles with some of the other children when I heard a faint, high-pitched sound coming up the canyon from our home. At first, I thought the sound was the wind. But the sound grew louder as I walked closer to the village, and as I listened, I realized that it was my father returning."

Amchi Pembar, Tshampa's father, had been away gathering medicinal plants for the past month. "When I heard the bells jingling from his horse's neck, I knew that with his return would come a busy month of medicine making. But I did not know that I would be meeting our family god horse, too. I can still picture it, my father on his *nangpa*, a golden-colored horse, coming through the archway at the entrance to the village, with a *kyangpa*, a fire-colored colt, following behind. He was one year old, maybe less. My father said, 'This is a *lhata*, a god horse. It will help guard our family. I will never sell the animal, and we must take good care of it.'

"During the sixth Tibetan month, everyone in the village harvested barley," Tshampa continued. "It was hard work, cutting stalks of grain and pounding them, but we had picnics and sang songs as we worked. The men and women would line up, face each other, and sing as they threshed, taking turns. They sang songs about all sorts of things, including horses," Tshampa smiled. He then began to sing:

> *Horse's face is like a long copper pot*
> *The pots from Tibet are just as good.*
> *The swirl on Horse's forehead is a half moon,*
> *Just like the half moon in Tibet's night sky.*
> *Horse's eyes are the blackest of stones,*
> *Just like the pits of ripened fruit.*
> *Horse's voice echoes the sound of conch shells,*
> *Just like the horns blown by the lamas.*
> *Horse's mouth is the sun and moon united,*
> *Just as sun and moon share the space of Tibet's sky.*
> *Horse's teeth are as white as a cow,*

Just like the cows that roam the low pastures.
Horse's tongue is like a religious text
Horse can hear the gods with his ears.
Listen. The gods of our place are calling.
Horse's mane is like strong green grass,
Just like the grasses of Tibet's plains.
Horse's neck curves like a golden pipe,
Just like the gold that runs through Tibet's mountains.
Horse's back stretches out like a rich summer meadow.
Horse's front legs are double arrows,
Just like the weapons made in Tibet.
Horse's back feet are two taut bows,
Just like the bows made to fit Tibetan arrows.
Horse's stomach is like a lake
Stretching across the Tibetan landscape.
Horse's breasts are a lama's double cymbals.
Horse's tail is as strong as hand-spun rope,
The twine used for harvesting and trade in Tibet.

"I used to listen to these songs as I worked with my family," Tshampa explained as he sat down, a bit winded from the effort of song. "But the year that my father brought home that horse, all I could do was watch him. After the harvest, we would allow horses into our fields, to eat the stubble. While we were working, I could see my father's horse and the family god horse grazing together under a juniper tree, near the edge of our family fields. All I wanted to do was ride the horse. But it would still take some time. The horse was still in his milk-drinking year."

Tshampa's gaze left me and went up toward the thick clouds in the sky. "I remember looking at the horse as we worked in the fields, thinking how strong he would become, how powerful. Since I could not yet ride him, I started drawing it," said Tshampa. When we had visited Tshampa's family home in Drumpa, he had pointed out a painting of this family god that he had done in their private shrine room, where Tshampa had spent his years of retreat. I remembered the horse was a deep red, and that the creature it carried looked wrathful, almost demonic, to show that the horse was an important protector of the *dharma*. Through Tshampa's descriptions that morning, I could see how he might have imagined the animal all those many years ago, and been inspired to paint it: from the peaceful colt grazing beside a field to a horse emblazoned, prancing, circled in fire.

"My father encouraged me to paint horses," Tshampa continued, breaking my reverie, "but really he wanted to teach me how to care for them. This was his duty. Amchi Pembar used to tell me, 'Son, horses and humans are not that much different, when it comes to medicines.' We made medicines that were used for both."

During the first few days of medicine production, Tshampa followed his father, taking out measurements of roots, fresh plants, powders, and minerals according to Pembar's instructions, and placing them in the grinding stone. Some of the ingredients had been freshly harvested, while others needed to be cured and dried for a number of months before they were ready to be made into medicines. Tshampa spent days pounding twigs, leaves, and flowers into fine powders.

"Each stage of this grinding process removes latent poisons from the ingredients and helps fuse one medicine with another," Tshampa explained. "After our family god horse arrived, I learned how to use herbs, ground flowers, and even pine cones to treat horses, donkeys, and mules."

"So when did you start breaking the *kyangpa*, the family god horse?" I asked.

"During the horse's hair-cutting year, I would feed the horse a mash made from barley, water, and sometimes the soaked grains left over from making *chang*. I used the mash to try and catch our horse. But the horse was smart and he liked to run away. Sometimes I slept with him in the animal shelter, so we could know each other and he would not be afraid. After many months, I could put a halter and lead rope on him, and he would listen to my voice." These descriptions sparked similar memories in me, of the young horses I'd helped to break and train back home in California, and I knew well the waves of anxiety and calm that marked this movement toward communion of two creatures, one human, one horse. The deep, earthy snorts from a horse's nostrils, scared but curious. The arch of a neck poised to run, or to submit.

"By the next summer, the *kyangpa* would lead," continued Tshampa. "I mixed brown sugar, honey, and a bit of milk into the mash of barley and wheat that I fed him each day, hoping that he would begin to trust me. By winter of the hair-cutting year, I started putting metal into his mouth, but only slowly. My father did not want me to rush. The following spring, I started saddling the *kyangpa*, but he did not feel my leg swing over his back until the spring of his third year.

"Before we rode the family god horse for the first time," Tshampa went on, "my father had to consult the calendar to find an auspicious day. Once we found one, during the first half of spring, I was allowed to swing up onto the horse. He kicked and squirmed so much that I nearly fell off. But we kept working, and my father taught me how to guide the animal using my body weight, legs and hands. Soon, the horse was moving well.

"Sometimes he broke away, ignoring the metal across his gums. He would just run and run. This is how we knew he was a powerful horse, good enough for our family god, and so much fun for me!" As he recalled this story, Tshampa's usual enthusiasm for life multiplied into a giddy, childlike exuberance. I could see him as a youngster, flying over river stones, poised atop this living red flame, warding off the demons of his imagination, flying with the wind. We met each other here, caught up in the warm memory of horses we had known.

Keeping Up Appearances

WHEN I WASN'T up at the museum with Tshampa, I occupied myself with haphazard language acquisition, aided in part by Nepali and Tibetan books I'd bought in Kathmandu. But mostly I learned by listening and repetition. I spent hours in the kitchen, my ears trained to Karma's demands of Dolma, Tshampa's teachings, business deals, and jokes, and the cacophony of visitors' voices over tea and local liquor. Evening "entertainment" often consisted of peeling potatoes, reading novels that bore no relation to Asia or anthropology or horses, and making the occasional meal for tourists. Dolma could make less sense of the Western menu than could Karma, and I ended up improvising pizzas and enchiladas out of slightly moldy cabbages and carrots, cans of tomato sauce, yak cheese, and *chapati*, the South Asian version of the tortillas I had grown up eating in Southern California. More than one tourist was shocked when I, a blonde-haired, blue-eyed girl emerged from the kitchen.

When I first visited Mustang, I did not think to wear local dress. The garments seemed too old for me, stiff, formal, and uncomfortable. I opted instead for sturdy hiking gear and frumpy flannel dresses that I had made by Kathmandu tailors. Upon return to Mustang, I still felt that the *kiti* and *kaou*, a rainbow-striped woolen apron and matching cummerbund customarily worn by married women, seemed inappropriate for me to wear. But I had bought a plain *chuba* in Kathmandu and somewhat reluctantly got into the habit of wearing it. The snug bodice flattered a woman's frame and the folds of fabric that wrapped around the back of this garment swished when I walked and made me feel elegant, for all the dust in this place.

One morning, I sat in the kitchen of the Dancing Yak with Karma. Tshampa had been called to Marpha to do some work in the new monastery, and our horse-related work had been put on hold for a day or two.

"I've got some work to do in one of our fields today, down near the village of Syang, on the near side of the river," Karma said as she forced a comb through Yangmo's hair and pulled it into uneven pigtails.

"Okay," I replied. "What sort of work?"

"Picking potatoes and removing rocks. I'll bring a picnic for later. Will you come and help?"

I nodded, my hands floured with the morning's chapati dough.

"Girl!" Karma grunted, now addressing Dolma, "After you finish that work, make some buckwheat cakes and tea. Put it in the basket with some apples from the storeroom." Dolma nodded from her perch atop the large slab of concrete that served as a kitchen sink, doing the previous night's dishes. Water gushed into a twenty-gallon drum at her side through an old hose, Jomsom's version of indoor plumbing. In the corner, Shanti, Karma's youngest child, was sucking on a piece of dried mango that my friend Ken had sent me from Kathmandu. Ken and I had met through Sara at a Halloween party the night before I left for Mustang, and had struck up a friendship. His regular care packages and letters were kind gestures that made me feel not entirely disconnected from life in the city.

"What can I do to help?" I asked Karma. "I can make the bread. Dolma has enough work to do."

"Whatever you like. But I'll have to get you a *kiti* and *kaou*. Otherwise your back will hurt and you might have problems with the damp earth. You're not bleeding, are you?"

As in many other cultures, the blood of menstruation, as well as that from childbirth, was viewed here as a source of pollution. Women were discouraged from doing certain kinds of labor during their menses. Work in fields was careful business, and required honoring and not upsetting the *lu*, serpent spirits that were at once guardians of the *dharma* and, if offended, capable of causing illness or environmental disturbances.

"No," I answered.

"Good." Karma left the kitchen and returned a few minutes later with a worn, faded apron and cummerbund. "Come here," she beckoned. "Now, you fold the apron into a triangle, like this. Then tuck the right side snug around your waist. Left goes over the top. Is it snug enough?"

"Yes. Feels warm," I said.

"This is good for women's bodies. Keeps them healthy through all the work we have to do. Having babies, making food, washing clothes..." Karma's voice trailed off as she wrapped the long cummerbund around my waist then tucked the end tassels under the rather formidable layer of wool that had accumulated around my middle. The contraption, though snug, felt comfortable. Not unlike an embrace.

Soon, we set out toward Syang. Karma and Dolma each carried a basket load of mulch and dung, on top of which rested several hoes. I was not sorry to have been given the task of carrying lunch. I was thankful for the slow pace, as I'd never before carried a basket on my back, Nepali-style, secured by a rope that rested across my forehead and spread the weight down my spine.

Karma, Dolma, and I worked for several hours, hands in the dirt, digging out tubers and preparing the ground for another year of growth. Remarkably, the woolens around my waist prevented me from rounding my spine, protecting my back and knees.

We ate our simple lunch in relative silence, under the noonday sun. Karma, her belly now full and her eyes grown heavy by the food, leaned back against the stone wall of her family's field, and began to ask me questions.

"What does your family do, now that you are so far away and helping in our fields?"

"We don't have fields," I explained. "And if I were in America, I wouldn't be living with my parents. I haven't lived at home since I was seventeen."

"A-bi!" Karma gasped. "Not since you were seventeen? What do your parents do without your help? You must have a very large family. The only way I can manage with Zompa and Tsewang off at boarding school is to have Yangmo and Dolma to help. Shanti will help too, when she's older."

"No, I don't have brothers or sisters. But my parents manage." Although I felt close to Karma, I couldn't see her understanding my family life. I didn't know how to explain that my parents were divorced, my dad was repartnered with a man who I called my "godfather," and my mother's new husband had an adopted son from a previous marriage who, a decade my senior, seemed more like an older friend than a sibling.

"Besides," I continued, "they are glad that I have gotten a good education."

"Lots of good your education is doing now that you're picking stones out of our field!" Karma laughed heartily. I couldn't help but join her.

"True, but I am learning here."

"What will you do when you leave?"

"I'm not sure. Write things. Teach. *Jagir khane*, maybe" I said. Literally, this Nepali phrase meant to eat by someone else's labor, and referred to a time in Nepal's history when high-caste middlemen did explicitly that. Now, the phrase had come to mean earning a salary from government or other office work—plowing with a pen. Even though the emphasis in meaning has changed, the alienated quality of this work still stands in opposition to *kaam*, the work of subsistence, of hands and land.

"Maybe I'll get married, have a baby," I continued.

"You're too young now," Karma said. "Wait a few years—unless you find someone here!"

That evening, after we'd returned home, Karma pulled out a new apron and cummerbund from a locked trunk she kept in the storeroom.

"I made them myself," she said. Karma's upright loom in the back courtyard held a cummerbund of similar design, not yet finished.

"I give you *good price* for them. These colors suit you." The apron was striped in blues, reds, and yellows, bordered in black. The cummerbund bore a pattern of crosses on a background of vertical, multi-colored stripes. It looked beautiful.

"How much?" I asked, without much sense of what this suite of woolens should cost.

"For you, *very cheap. I made.*" In Karma's sudden shift from Nepali to English, I resurfaced as an outsider, even after the closeness of a day together, working as family. The more time I spent at the Dancing Yak, the more I came to understand that the trust and rapport fieldwork can foster

is not something to take for granted, and that building up "family ties"—
be they bound by blood or fictive—is an iterative process, one in which
small moments of transformation can only account for part of what it
means to forge a lasting bond.

"How much?" I felt awkward asking, but asked anyway. Here, the line
between being a surrogate daughter and a paying guest became clearer,
perhaps more honest.

"Rs. 5000 for both. *Good price*." This sum seemed expensive, but I had
little to compare it with. Had I been in a bazaar shop, I would have set
to bargaining. But here, what was I to do? Naively, I thought our proximity to each other—the fact that I took care of Karma's children, that I
cooked alongside her—would be enough to bridge the gap between
commerce and friendship, and to make her see me as something other
than a *kuiere*, a foreigner. Also, as a measure of my own insecurity, I
longed to appear as "authentic" as possible—a foreigner, yes, but at least
one with a sense of local style. I agreed to her price without bargaining.
Later, I learned that had I haggled, Karma would have respected me for
it, and the interaction might have brought us closer.

At the time, I was most concerned with trying to get used to the
rhythm of my new Mustang life, getting over homesickness and becoming re-acquainted with this place I had chosen, but hardly knew. I was
just beginning to comprehend that people here would always see me as
they wanted to see me, not necessarily how I would like to be seen. In
that sense, Karma and I were trading illusions, keeping up appearances.
At the time, it was too difficult for me to admit that the reality of life at
the Dancing Yak was different than I had remembered it, after having
traveled so far, and worked so hard to return.

But when Tshampa returned from his work in Marpha, he smiled as
he saw me stooped on the floor, dressed in these cultural fittings, my
hands clutching a pestle and pounding dried red chilies, Tibetan salt, garlic, and water into paste.

"Good," he smiled. "You're becoming a local. All you need to do now
is learn our language," he said. It was true.

Nepali came relatively easily to me. Its singsong rhythm and straight-
forward grammar, combined with my desire to communicate, led to a

quick sense of basic linguistic ease. After a month or two in Mustang, I could not understand jokes. But a short time later, I was making them. Most people in Mustang, save a few old men and women, spoke Nepali even though it was not their native tongue, and I could get along well in casual conversation and interviews.

The local dialect of Tibetan was another matter entirely. In his preface to one of the many Tibetan-English dictionaries he has authored, the eminent anthropologist Melvyn Goldstein quoted a Tibetan proverb: *yig che go be log*, "Half of the words are read by implication." The warning was apt. Initially, I found Tibetan an impossibly poetic language: tonal, hierarchical, and deeply metaphoric. Before I returned to Mustang in 1995, I'd spent some time taking Tibetan lessons with a monk from Sikkim who was studying for his Ph.D. at Harvard. The lessons had helped, and I'd learned enough to read and write and speak simple sentences, but when I returned to Mustang and began to listen to the local dialects, I was completely lost. The verb endings were different, as were many nouns, and even when I could ask for something in basic Central Tibetan, I would be answered in dialect—an ancient form of Tibetan related, scholars believe, to dialects from Kham in the east and the old languages of the Zhang Zhung kingdom, in the west.

Tshampa and I were at our best when we could talk alone for hours about our common love, horses, or when I listened to him speak about Tibetan medicine. But these conversations were limiting as well. While we spoke Nepali together, many of the words and terms crucial to my research were spoken in Tibetan, which Tshampa would approximate in Nepali and then write down in Tibetan, for me to translate later. And while our work was productive, the hours we spent poring over texts at the Eco-Museum or chatting around the fire at the Dancing Yak did nothing to bring me competency in local Tibetan. I knew that if I wanted to speak the language of horses, naming their gaits, coat colors, ailments, and their rituals, I would have to move beyond a dependence on Tshampa's guidance and experience. While his knowledge was without question, his voice was representative of only one perspective.

The methods of ethnography required that I step out of this key relationship as well as maintain it, in order that it might grow. And, as I began to realize, my proverbial "key informant" had a somewhat controversial reputation in the area. Some of his contemporaries thought he was much too taken with his foreign "friends." Others considered him too proud. Everyone I came to know in Mustang spoke of him as a gifted doctor, but his reputation as a healer was not enough to keep the other perceptions at bay. And so, the choice to work with Tshampa also meant that I was feeding, if naively at first, other people's perceptions about who I was and why I was in Mustang. My decision to live at the Dancing Yak impacted how others in Mustang saw me.

I knew, though, that I had to also consider how my presence in Tshampa's home was bearing on his life as well. At first, it was much easier—or perhaps more comfortable—for me to imagine the ways Tshampa and Karma's lives and personalities were shaping my experience in Mustang than it was to fathom how I was affecting them. Tshampa's ease about working with me sometimes masked the extent to which my place among his family changed the household dynamics. Although I was not the only researcher to pass through or take tutorials from Tshampa, I was beginning to feel the pressure both in the kitchen with Karma and out around Jomsom.

As I would later learn, people outside the Dancing Yak took pleasure in gossiping about what Tshampa was getting from his Western students, by way of payment for his expertise, and of course it is difficult to say what role Tshampa and Karma played in feeding these rumors. Beyond this, the fact that I was a young woman impacted how people outside the Dancing Yak saw me, "read" my relationship with Tshampa, speculated about my intent, abilities, and qualifications—even inquired into my marital status. My gender, more than my citizenship, bore on Tshampa and Karma. Indeed, it would weigh on my interactions with other local veterinarians and *amchi*, all of whom, in Mustang, were older men.

Living with Tshampa and family meant something different, still. Payments for room and board, or money Karma snookered out of me for aprons and turquoise, seemed insignificant when I thought deeply about my role in their lives. In fact, these transfers of goods and services often masked other aspects of this cultural exchange, and rendered priceless the lessons I was to learn about our expectations of each other, the vacillations of illusion and clarity that passed between us.

PART II

Be nobody's darling

Be an outcast

Take the contradictions

Of your life

And wrap them around

You like a shawl,

To parry stones

To keep you warm

—Alice Walker

Mustang Elements

As the seasons shifted from autumn to winter, I took to chasing light. Early in the mornings, just past dawn, I often climbed up on the bluff above the Dancing Yak, or up to the hotel's flat roof, sheltered as it was by stacks of firewood, and observed the scene below. These were precious moments, between sleep and waking, when the cold air nurtured me and my journal was my home.

Half-past dawn in Jomsom, I began one morning. Hands numb from writing. Women are hawking last spring's apples in front of the airport as a helicopter sets down, muffling them. Tinkling horse bells and bleating sheep surrounding the lodge are similarly muted. Men and their mounts crowd round the airport gates, gossiping. The Tibetan word for "Jomsom" is dzong samba, "new fort," and this morning the name seems particularly appropriate given the movement through this town, the center of what might otherwise be thought of as an out-of-the-way place.

A saffron-swathed lama rides by with the speed and grace of a red-tailed hawk, his cloaks swallowing up wind in stride. His sagpa—a deep auburn-colored horse with white socks—prances while overhead an Everest Air helicopter whirs. The lama wears sunglasses and holds his chin high. A flash of Mt. Dhaulagiri is reflected in his bespectacled eyes, then he is gone.

Now, the planes have landed and the winds have picked up. I watch as men ride by. Some of them look awkward in the saddle, but most are so pristinely poised—their center of gravity leaning ever so slightly back, their feet unmoving in silver stirrups, just above the girth, their right hands dangling a hand-braided leather whip, just enough to tease their mounts forward—that I imagine they could carry a cup of tea across this rough terrain. They lend the landscape a different kind of grace than its own harsh beauty inspires.

With its wind and dust and cowboys, Jomsom recalled the image of a Wild West outpost. Wind marked time, granted a rhythm to the movement of human days. Outside, the wind seemed to carry with it new arrivals into town as well as news from Pokhara and Kathmandu. Inside, time was constantly spent gossiping and drinking, waiting for the wind to quell. I could not imagine this place without considering wind, without accounting for dust. Wind has sculpted this landscape, carving flutes into cliffs, eating away at the edges of riverbanks and fields. Dust was a metaphor for the commotion, and then the settling, that defined daily rhythms in this market town. I came to know the time of day in Mustang not only by the position of the sun on the horizon, but also by tracking gusts and howls, noting the ebb and flow of human traffic down Jomsom's main street, such as it was.

And, as in the American West of centuries past, the horse was both a status symbol and a necessity here. It was easy to spot a certain pride and swagger in Mustang's horsemen as they came and went past the Dancing Yak. Most loved their horses, and there was a certain pageantry to how people rode into or out of town. This palomino, tethered near the Snowlands Hotel, or that dark, robust bay saddled with fine Tibetan carpets, were considered the finest transportation around, the Cadillac of the Himalayas.

From a functional perspective, horses were less economical than sheep, goat, yak, and yak-cow crossbreeds—animals critical to pastoral lifeways of the Tibetan Plateau and the Himalayas. These animals could be transformed into cash or kind when sold or bartered at market. They provided milk and wool, tilled earth, and pulled plows. When their muscles grew sinuous, their bodies otherwise spent, they "accidentally" fell off cliffs and found their way into stews, or transformed into strips of jerky, smoke dried on rafters.

Horses, particularly fine riding mounts, were valued differently. Of course, horses provided people with a means of transporting themselves and their goods across these steppes, up craggy cliffsides, across rivers. Horses were more costly to maintain than animals, and were much more expensive to buy, but one must never underestimate the power of social capital. While they confered prestige, moreover horses epitomized freedom, strength, swiftness, and beauty to the people here.

Mustang is frontier territory. The Tibetan Plateau looms in the north, large as the sky, to which this landscape is beholden. To the south lie villages and valleys, fields of rice and millet, giving shelter to a different lifestyle than is practiced here, among the *tsampa* eaters. For all the ways Jomsom is Nepali—a Royal Nepal Army garrison at one end, a passage to the middle hills at the other—it is also on the margins of this Hindu kingdom.

As I worked to broaden my own sense of purpose in Mustang—to shift from being Tshampa's student to being, rather, a young ethnographer—I began to speak more with hoteliers and development workers, local politicians, other *amchi*, even the women selling apples outside the airport. While these began as conversations about horses, they led to many other discussions—about the nature of foreign aid in Nepal, the benefits and drawbacks of tourism, the purpose of education and the value of different languages, and even Western influences and generation gaps.

As I had initially intuited and continued to learn, horses played into both a sense of regional identity and economics. What I had not anticipated, however, was the ways in which the horse culture had actually changed in recent history. The more I asked about the history of horses in Mustang, the more I learned that, until quite recently, horses were a noble pastime, almost without exception. Fine riding horses belonged to the king of Lo, and the inheritors of aristocratic lineages in and around the Muktinath Valley, but to few other "common" people. They might have owned horses, but these, then, were usually beasts of burden more than the fancy icons of wealth and social standing, as they had now become.

The late twentieth century had brought a striking shift in the relationship between social status and occupation for Mustang's inhabitants. Access to cash could now be obtained not only through family inheritance and standing, but also through tourism, wage labor, or trade. This

opened economy enabled Mustangis to cut across social boundaries in
new ways, thereby making more "egalitarian" the possibility that someone could buy a relative "luxury" item like a fine riding horse. Particularly through the advent of the trekking industry, it had become easier
for people of lower social standing to have access to new wealth than it
was in other moments in Mustang's history. People who, even a generation before, might not have owned a riding horse, now sought to acquire
several in the hopes of renting them out to tourists.

In at first assuming a certain porousness between the Mustang of
today and the Tibet of yesterday, I also failed, initially, to account for the
ways that the presence of the Tibetan Resistance soldiers in Mustang
from 1960 to 1974 had directly impacted what people knew about
horses, how they valued them, and why they sought to acquire them.
The Tibetan Resistance soldiers—locally called "Khampa" after the
region in eastern Tibet where the armed guerrilla movement was born—
brought with them not only the violence and ravages of war, but also
many forms of cultural knowledge. Among the texts, stories, and other
artifacts to filter into Mustang through the soldiers' presence (and later
through the settling of Tibetan refugees at Tserok, a camp in southern
Mustang, near the village of Marpha) were bits and pieces of "horse culture," as well as much of what I learned about ethnoveterinary medicine.

I was coming to see how Mustang has grown into its infatuation with
horses. They were now as much a part of the economy and social life as
they were in many places to the north, in Tibet and Mongolia. But the
fact that horses in Mustang did not always mean what they did now
intrigued me. Much of the popular literature about Mustang referred to
the region as a "lost" or "hidden" Tibetan kingdom—a place that had
escaped the political turmoil of Tibet, and where traditional Tibetan culture could be witnessed intact. These images promoted Mustang as a
"timeless" place, and horses played a part in the creation of this image.
People now paid a premium to approach the ancient walled city of Lo
Monthang on horseback.

Yet what did it mean that much of Mustang's cultural authenticity, at
least as it was marketed, found its origins, in part, outside Mustang, carried in on the backs of Tibetan soldiers and refugees, carried in through

books such as the horse texts Tshampa possessed? Or simply conjured up in people's imaginings of how Mustang's present could speak to a Tibetan past? One value of tradition rests precisely in its ability to evoke the past in a way that is meaningful, even iconic, in the present, even if this act renders more permanent a set of ideas or practices than they ever were before being labeled a "tradition." But the invention of tradition is no less meaningful because it is just that, an invention. We are made by history as much as we are its makers.

One day during my first winter in Mustang, I sat in the dining room of the Hotel Marco Polo, sipping tea and talking horses with Nirmal Gauchan, the proprietor. Nirmal was one of the people to whom Charles had initially directed me, but who I did little more than meet on my first trip to Jomsom. In addition to being a hotelier, he was also a local politician who eventually became the District Development Committee Chairman for all of Mustang. Nirmal came from a prominent Thakali family. His father had been equally important in his day, serving as a *subba*, a form of civil servant and customs officer that was historically held by Thakali men from one of several clans.

Like many of his fellow Thakali, Nirmal and his wife Laxmi traveled across an uneven, and very interesting, ethnic and religious terrain. Laxmi wore a *tikka* between her brows and, more often than not, dressed in a *saree*. They both spoke commanding Nepali and some English, in addition to their Thakali mother tongue and the local dialects of Tibetan. They were able to more fluently and gracefully maneuver between worlds of the Hindu south and Buddhist north than were many of their compatriots from upper Mustang.

In part, this was a product of history. Indeed, the Thakali, like the Newars of the Kathmandu Valley, had made names and fortunes for themselves by being consummate middlemen and savvy traders, particularly between Nepal and Tibet. In the words of Don Messerschmidt, an anthropologist who had spent many years doing ethnography among the Thakali, they were people of "great economic and political acumen" who had a flair for entrepreneurship. These days, some experts on Thakali history and ethnology were remarking on what they saw as deep, even irrevocable, changes in religious orientation, social forms, and material culture—in essence, a sea change away from their northern, Buddhist and Bön roots toward the ways and means of Nepal's Hindu majority. Others argued that these changes belied a deeper continuity, indeed a flexibility, in how Thakali maneuvered through a web of cultural, religious, and political meanings and practices.

"We didn't have many nice riding horses here in Mustang when I was a child," said Nirmal. "And the ones there were all belonged to *thulo manchhe*—"big" people like the king of Lo. Because my father was a *subba*, he did have some nice horses over the years. One of the Khampa even gave him a horse from Tibet as a gift," Nirmal continued.

"In appreciation of his services as a customs official," I chided.

"Precisely," laughed Nirmal. We were still getting to know each other, but I quickly learned to value, and keep step with, Nirmal's sense of irony and humor, and to enjoy the sheepish yet also visionary qualities in him that were part and parcel of being a politician.

"But now that people are doing well from tourism and business, going off to Kathmandu, India, and other countries to make money, there has become this craziness about horses," Nirmal continued. "Who has the nicest saddle blankets? Who spent the most money on his horse? Today everyone is trying to buy more horses."

Nirmal was able to provide me with a cultural and environmental perspective on Mustang, one that was carefully attuned to local and regional politics. Through his work, he was busy monitoring the effects of open tourism and trade. In keeping with the idea that upper Mustang was a "fragile" ecosystem in need of conservation and protection, organized tours of trekkers to upper Mustang were mandated to be as "self-sustainable" as possible. While this policy made good sense in theory—after all, the skirts of Mt. Everest were now littered with foreign garbage—it ended up translating into a further marginalization of the people from Lo, or Loba, from opportunities to be in control of, or economically benefit from, the foreigners who passed through their villages and valleys.

Take nothing but pictures. Leave nothing but footprints. The classic conservation motto, borne out of the Sierra Club and Western environmentalism, had been adopted by ACAP, the Annapurna Conservation Area Project.

Though I could appreciate this sentiment, in reality this policy meant that people from Lo were not allowed to open teashops or otherwise serve tourists directly, unlike their southern neighbors who were free to run shops, lodges, and restaurants, provided they complied with ACAP regulations on resource use. It translated into a widening gap between the people of northern and southern Mustang.

"What do you think of this idea to make a horse lottery?" I asked Nirmal that morning, as we sat talking. In recent interviews with program directors and project managers at the ACAP office, I had learned that there were plans afoot to try and create a rotational pool of horses to be used by trekking groups that would travel to upper Mustang from Jomsom, in order that Loba would have a more equal chance of earning money from the horse and mule trade. Supplies for trekking parties were carried north by animals owned by various private families, but a few Thakali families had enjoyed a monopoly on the pack trade for decades and they did not wish to relinquish business easily. ACAP envisioned a system by which Loba, as well as people from lower Mustang would rent out their riding horses and pack animals on a rotational basis. They would set the daily price-per-animal, accounting for the rising costs of hay and access to grazing land en-route up and down the length of Mustang District.

"I know that the Loba need to make money from tourism, and horses are one of the ways to do this," answered Nirmal, being politic, "But I don't think it will work."

"Why? Because Thakali like you have cornered the market on tourism?"

"In part, yes," answered Nirmal, lightheartedly. "We won't give up on a business opportunity without a struggle. What do they say in America? *Let the best man win*," he laughed.

"But, seriously," Nirmal continued, "It won't work because there is too much mistrust of ACAP, and between people from different parts of Mustang. We will fight among each other, and people will cheat," he went on. "But most importantly it is not the job of ACAP to be running this sort of local enterprise. This should be the job of local government—of district and village development committees." Nirmal was known to be a staunch proponent of truly grassroots development, and, though he had worked with many different NGOs and governmental agencies, he often resented plans for change that seemed to be in the hands of outsiders, as opposed to projects that were derived from local ideas, expertise, and needs. This example of the horse lottery was no exception.

As Nirmal and I spoke that morning, I began to understand why local resentment of ACAP and the politics of opening upper Mustang to tourism seemed to run so deep across the district's ethnic and economic terrain. Nirmal explained that, even while businesspeople like him were benefiting from renting out horses and mules to trekking groups bound for Lo, the real problem lay in the fact that funds from the expensive trekking permits being charged to foreigners who visited Lo were collecting in Kathmandu pockets, far away from the realities of life in upper Mustang, or the larger concerns of district-level rural development budgets. This fact represented a breach in contract and in trust between the people of Lo and the government of Nepal.

"The Loba had been promised 60 percent of the profits, to be used for local conservation and sustainable development initiatives," explained Nirmal. "But they have yet to see hardly a rupee. And given the rules ACAP has made for *how* foreigners must travel to Lo Monthang, this means that the Loba are getting very little benefit. I understand why they are angry and mistrustful."

Beyond this, Nirmal explained, there was the perhaps unintended consequence of inflation that had come in the wake of Nepal's democratic revolution in 1990 and the expansion of private tourism and business enterprises. Everyone in the district, even the Thakali businessmen who benefit the most from tourism throughout Mustang District, spoke of the inflation in rice, corn, and the price of hay in recent years.

Still, Loba rode into town on the finest-looking animals—horses whose flowing tails and thick chests recalled the stories I had heard about the Siling horses. Siling is the Tibetan name for Xining, a city in present-day Qinghai Province, China—an area of vast grasslands and rolling hills that encompasses much of the historical Tibetan region called Amdo. Siling has been known for its horses for centuries, and indeed was part of the ancient tea-horse trade route. During the height of the trans-Himalayan trade through Mustang, before the Chinese occupation of Tibet, local nobles and Thakalis grown rich off their monopoly of the salt-grain trade sought out these horses. The animal's elegance embodied their owner's high social standing. Long in leg, these horses bore more resemblance to the fine Central Asian mounts by which the Mongols built their empire than they did to the scrawny local breeds, more pony and billy goat than horse.

One morning, I walked the length of Jomsom, past the pale yellow airport terminal with its peeling paint, the curio shops and the Nepali Police checkpost, toward the wooden bridge that divides the airport side of this way station town from the cluster of older residences on the other side of the Kali Gandaki River. The planes had come and gone, but the sun had not fully risen above the mountains and the valley leading to Lo glowed purple. A herd of mules, their flanks filled to capacity with kilos of fodder, clanked along ahead of me. I slowed my pace, allowing them to cross the bridge first. As I waited on the near side of the bridge, I glanced down at myself. Dressed in a *chuba* and awkwardly sturdy hiking boots, I remembered that I had dreamt in Nepali the night before for the first time.

A man mounted on a fire-colored gelding waited on the other side of the bridge. After the mule train ambled away, I motioned for him to proceed.

"You have a nice horse," I called out. "Where did you get him?"

"Tibet," the man answered with an air of indifference. As the horse and rider drew closer, I noticed the horse had a number of well-placed cowlicks on his neck and head.

"Very auspicious *tsug*," I said, pointing to the horse's head. "You are a lucky man to have such a horse."

The man slowed. "Yes," he responded. "Very good *tsug*. And his gaits are excellent." As if to demonstrate, he and his horse took off, the horse's hooves beating in lyrical four/four time. The man turned around and flashed me a smile.

Sacrifice at the Jimi Hendrix Restaurant

EARLY ONE WINTER morning, I woke to the whir of the airport tower announcing the arrival of the first flight from Pokhara. I layered up in long underwear, *chuba*, and woolen shawl before heading downstairs for morning tea. Karma was still half asleep as she made her way through the kitchen. Tshampa lingered in the semi-private space of their sleeping quarters, saying his morning *mantra*. Dolma blew at the kitchen embers and I watched her, warmly, in the interstices between sleep and waking.

These early winter days had grown increasingly cold. My breath remained visible until midday, when the sun rose above the Himals, only to usher in long shadows and a biting southern wind by mid-afternoon. On the days that we continued to work together, when I was not out interviewing other locals, Tshampa and I had taken to settling down in the Dancing Yak kitchen until after the mid-morning meal to avoid the stone cold courtyard of the Eco-Museum. The barley and buckwheat crops had been harvested, giving way to dusty, barren months of winter—months defined by the contrast between earth and sky, soil and light. Horses grazed in the empty fields, rummaging for roots and other agricultural remains. Domestic sheep and goats clung to lower hillsides, leaving the higher pastures to the wild blue sheep, their tawny coats a perfect camouflage against the cliffs.

Winter quieted Mustang in many ways. Tourists came and went, but something about the drop in temperature subdued them. They hunkered down against the wind, zipped up their anoraks, and moved steadily on. By late November, many local Mustangis set off for a winter of trade in India, while others headed toward Kathmandu and the comfort of a winter spent among city-dwelling family: electric space heaters, gas stoves, and pilgrimage. I thought about this quietude now, with only Dolma for company, as we slurped our scalding tea, thankful for the warmth.

The stable door creaked open, then shut with a clap and Tshampa's younger sister emerged in the doorway of the kitchen.

"Your friend, he's come," she said, angling toward me. She joined us by the fire, and Dolma handed her a cup of tea.

"What friend?" I asked.

"You know, the one who used to live in Lubra. He came on the first flight, and went to the Hotel Marco Polo. There is some other young person with him, too. Maybe he's from your country."

"Is it Charles Ramble?" I asked.

"Yes, maybe. I don't know his real name. People from Lubra call him Yungdung Tsewang. He's been coming to Mustang for a long time."

It must be Charles, I thought. I had not seen him since we'd first met in 1993, but I had phoned him upon arriving in Kathmandu. As far as I knew, he was the only anthropologist who had spent years in the village of Lubra. I'd hoped to see him—to ask for some fieldwork advice and to reorient to Mustang after my two years away—but we were only able to speak briefly by telephone before I left for the mountains. That was several months ago now, and I had forgotten that he said he might come up to Mustang for a brief stint of fieldwork in the early winter.

I had not fully realized how much I missed being understood—the cultural ease that comes from sharing language, if not citizenship. These respites from the work of living and learning in Mustang were moments in which I was able to reflect and bridge the gap between the raw experience of fieldwork—scribbles in my notebooks, hours of interviews, new relationships based on neither shared language nor shared culture—and my American reality. At the time, it was still a disquieting fact that this process of forging connections and learning what it means to translate between worlds, for myself and for others, was precisely why I had come to Mustang. At a certain level, horses supplied the medium for this exchange, but they could not fully constitute its form. To talk about animals was also to talk with animals, and as such, to talk past the humans that harbored them.

I finished my tea and headed off to the Hotel Marco Polo.

Charles sat at the main dining room, chatting with Laxmi, Nirmal's spunky, bright-eyed wife. Beside him sat a young man, about my age and very blonde. "Fancy meeting you here," I said, breaking the breakfast chatter.

"Ah, welcome—though I suppose you should be welcoming me," said Charles. "This is Justin," he continued, gesturing toward the young blonde. "He's also an American."

As it turned out, Justin had come to Nepal under the same auspices of my first visit, as a study-abroad student. He waved, faintly, and said, "I'm, like, interested in shamanism and Bön, y' know all that pre-Buddhist animism and stuff?" The thin oxygen of Mustang's high-mountain air seemed to be getting to Justin, for he spoke softly. Although Justin's aspirations and ambitions struck me as naïve, this act of judgment, this fluttering of ego, was also a reminder to be humble, particularly in the face of someone like Charles who knew so much more than me about the area, and about anthropology.

"Please, join us," said Charles. Although I had only spoken with him briefly several times before, Charles seemed more alive here in Mustang, and less distracted than he had during our interactions in Kathmandu. I sat down and Laxmi brought me a cup, from which she then poured out a serving of syrupy, dense coffee from a stovetop espresso maker.

"Charles's special coffee," she whispered. Indeed, I had not tasted real caffeine since my arrival, but had instead resigned myself to the metallic buzz of Nescafé.

"Thank you," I said, "What a treat!"

Charles took my gratitude in stride, and then offered an explanation for his current trip. "I've come up for a week or so to answer a few lingering questions for an article, and to watch a ritual. Should be quite a spectacle. A protection ritual, of sorts."

"Yeah, by, like, this Bön shaman guy," Justin broke in.

"A ritual specialist called an *aaya*," Charles corrected. "In the years I've been coming to Mustang, I've never seen this protection ritual performed. So, instead of waiting for the off chance that I would be here when one happened, I decided to sponsor it. The family—I've known them for years—agreed. It could be a long day, but I think you'll find it interesting. Nyima's just gone off to make the final arrangements." Nyima Dandrul was Charles's local assistant and, by all accounts, his best friend.

Nyima returned and, in a jocular tone, intimated to Charles that preparations were underway. We headed off in the direction of old Jomsom toward the Jimi Hendrix Restaurant.

I'm still not sure how morning passed into afternoon, then evening. Rather, I note the experience as a series of snapshots that, ironically, reminded me of just how much life there is in Mustang, how much movement and complexity. Although our destination was the Jimi Hendrix Restaurant, a small, whitewashed building at the far end of the main wooden bridge that divided old Jomsom from new, we would only end up there after paying proper respects to a number of other families.

As the anthropologist and his motley crew moved from one house to another, we charted time not by the movement of the sun but rather in what we imbibed, the hospitality we were offered. Really, the offerings were for Charles. We drank sweet tea, butter tea, and strong local *arak* tinged the color of a gecko, as the day waxed and then waned. Fried yak meat and steaming bowls of instant noodles fortified us, kept us drinking. I hardly saw the sun that day, save trips to the backside of houses to relieve myself. And when I did, the harsh outdoor reality blinded me. Mountain sun seemed too strong a counterpart for Mustang's dark interiors, the air too biting and too clear in comparison with the smoky haze of wood cooking fires.

I spent much of the day not understanding many of the conversations Charles had with his local interlocutors, as they were fast-paced and filled with jokes, nearly all of which were told in the local Tibetan dialect that I was still struggling to understand. Did Charles really follow all of the jokes we were told? Did he know every word? What did it mean to be truly fluent in a language, a culture?

Here, amid tattered Hindi film posters tacked to dirt walls and dingy glasses of local liquor, the outline of anthropological truisms began to

take form: there is no such thing as a free gift. Acts of giving and of rec-
iprocity are, by their very nature, designed to further enmesh the giver
and the receiver in a web of meaning and relations that come with specific obligations and responsibilities. By sponsoring this ritual of protection, as well as a ritual of blood, Charles was making his way into the
history and fortune of a family—a foreign strand woven into the fabric
of this place.

By nightfall, we'd settled in to the Jimi Hendrix Restaurant and Lodge.
The *aaya* had been called. A small man with a wiry face nearly overtaken
by wrinkles, he said little after he arrived, but gladly took the glass of
arak offered him by the proprietress. He hacked and spat on the dirt
floor, preparing his voice for the long night of chanting and recitations
ahead. Then, he set to work, gathering the ritual implements he would
need to complete the ceremony. Unlike the image one might have of a
shaman—all feather headdress and drums—this simple man asked for
some bowls of grain and barley flour, sprigs of juniper, rapeseed oil, a
frying pan, and a knife. It was a ritual composed of everyday things.

In the center of the room, near to the door, sat a chair on which was
stacked a pile of male clothes neatly folded. "My husband," the woman
of the house said to me, indicating that the pile was meant to represent
her spouse. "He's away, doing business in Hong Kong. But he has to be
here, too. Otherwise, all this won't do him any good. The gods won't pay
attention," she said, gesturing toward the *aaya*.

Our conversation was interrupted by the piercing bleat of a goat.
Nyima Dandrul appeared at the doorway, wrestling with the animal. He
had a wiley grin, and for a "good Buddhist," he also seemed to take a certain pleasure in knowing the goat's dismal fate.

"Where do you want it?" Nyima asked the *aaya*, who then gestured
toward the roof. Nyima slung the animal over his shoulders and hoisted
himself and it up the second story ladder. In a few minutes, the goat
began skittering across the roof, knocking loose bits of dirt and dust from
the ceiling of the sitting room.

In many respects, Mustang is a Buddhist land where people are guided
by an ethics of compassion and *ahimsa*, non-harming. It is a place where
people strive to heed the Buddha's admonishment against killing other

sentient beings, and the negative *karma* such acts can produce. But like other Himalayan landscapes, Mustang is a harsh place, where people raise more animals than grain, and where meat is both enjoyed and needed for sustenance. I had been a vegetarian for the six years before my return to Mustang, but I only lasted about two weeks before I broke this self-made taboo. Even though most meals at the Dancing Yak consisted of Nepal's ostensibly vegetarian staple of *dhal bhaat,* chunks of mutton, slivers of yak meat, or bony chicken bits were often sautéed into sides of spinach, cauliflower, or potatoes. I knew that meat added expense and, in that sense, respect, to a meal, and it was simply too difficult to decline that which was offered me. Of course, that did not stop me from sneaking out to trekking lodges for the occasional plate of spaghetti or a cheese sandwich. Nor did it mean that I could tolerate all local delicacies. Nettles soaked in sour buttermilk and red chilies, served with a five-pound glob of buckwheat paste, pushed my gastronomical limits.

Later that night at the Jimi Hendrix Restaurant a goat would be martyred for the well-being of the household. Of course, it would also be eaten. As we prepared for the sacrifice, I struggled with the fact that it seemed to go against everything I'd read about Mustang's Buddhist heritage. Charles laughed as he explained.

"Many people like to think of themselves as proper Buddhists—no killing, only offering pseudo-sacrifices of *torma,* barley-flour cakes. But as we're about to see, this is really not the case. Buddhism is only one force at play here. The pantheon of local deities and the sense of sacred landscape that predates orthodox Buddhism is just as important. They're tangled up in each other. Syangpa Rinpoche, that old Tibetan lama who tried to convert locals to 'proper' Buddhism in the 1960s, would be turning in his grave if he saw what we'll see tonight—or rather, what the men will see tonight. Sienna, I'm afraid you will not be able to watch the main part of the ritual, the sacrifice. No women allowed."

I swallowed this mandate. There seemed little else I could do.

By seven that evening, the smoke from burning fronds of juniper infused the Jimi Hendrix Restaurant. Our figures and those of the *aaya* could be made out only partially, in the half-light of dim bulbs powered by a small hydroelectric plant down the Kali Gandaki River. The *aaya* worked in the corner. Fresh juniper springs lay flayed across the frying pan, which had been set on a small metal pot aglow with embers. The *aaya* sat cross-legged, conjuring a household god in syllables that I could not understand. Movements that were as aural as they were physical ebbed and flowed within the swaying *aaya*. He had a rhythm both within and beyond himself, for part of a shaman's gift is his ability to transcend to the realms of mountain gods, or bring them down to the mundane, earthly realm. This mediation between worlds was his genius and his burden. By the end of the ritual, the *aaya* would be spent, physically, emotionally, and even, it seemed, spiritually.

During these rounds of ritual, the woman of the house appeared intermittently from the kitchen, carrying a clutch of live embers in her bare hands, which she then tossed onto the smoldering pile of ashes at the foot of the *aaya*. The act was arresting, yet simple. She fed the ritual fire, fed her household.

In the midst of all of this, a group of Australian tourists wandered in, looking for a meal and accommodations. In one turn of her skirt and rainbow-striped apron, the woman of the house shifted from ritual assistant to hostess and, in her best trekker's English, offered the tourists, "Beer maybe, and somethings food dinner?" The trekkers ordered a round of Star Beer and, after a quick glance at the menu, settled on *American Chop Suey—Jimmy favorit wit Pruple Hazes sauce (tomato catch-up)*.

"Hey missus," one of them called out after the woman, "Why is this place called Jimi Hendrix Restaurant?" But she was gone. The work of ritual, as well as running a restaurant, did not allow her time to offer an answer, even if she had wanted to.

One of the trekker's companions answered instead. "Ah, mate, I read about this place in one of the guidebooks. They say Hendrix really did come here."

"Far out, man," said Justin, calling out toward trekker territory from what had been staked out as the "researchers table." No matter how sincere his interest in shamanism, Bön, and sacrifices, my fellow student had grown bored with the ritual, its dizzying incantations and its exotic complexity. He moved away from Charles, who was deep in the throes of local place gods and the intricacies of offerings, to discuss Jimi Hendrix with the Aussie trekkers.

The night wore on. The trekkers went to bed. At about one in the morning, all of the men in the house ascended the ladder to the roof. Nyima took a camera. Charles took his notebook and a flashlight. The *aaya* took his frying pan, a small bell and drum, and a handful of juniper sprigs. Once the room had emptied of men, the woman of the house collapsed into a chair near me.

"Tired?" I asked the obvious.

"Tired," she said.

That night I felt the weight of being female, not just because of the missed opportunity to see a goat sacrificed, but because my exclusion from this event was symbolic of the larger challenge I'd set out for myself in Mustang. After all, horses were a man's business. Aside from this, I felt the literal and figurative weight carried by the local woman next to me. She was running a household and a business while her husband, so far away, labored in his own right, to earn a type and quantity of cash that was not available through local tourism or selling sweaters in India during the winter months.

For all the cultivated illusions of Mustang as a simple, subsistence-based, Buddhist place, everything I'd learned this evening revealed something quite different. The lives contained within the borders of the Jimi Hendrix Restaurant were at once bound to this place and, like the *aaya* himself, transcendent of it. I wondered, as I sat quietly, listening to the activity on the roof, if somewhere in Hong Kong a Mustangi man was listening for the *aaya*'s soundings. Could he hear them?

A bleat, followed by a muffled thud, signaled that the goat was dead on the roof above us. Blood spilled, as Charles explained, to wash clean the pollution of the last year, for good buckwheat and barley harvests this year, for the health and well-being of this family.

After the death of the goat and before the rounds of drinking, feasting, and singing that would last until dawn, I breathed in the night air and listened. The mistress of the Jimi Hendrix Restaurant had let her tired torso slump onto a dining room table. Sleep came to her for a few brief minutes. I settled on the thought of her rest, watched her eyes flicker under the spell of dream, and wondered where these dreams were taking her. On the opposite wall, in childlike capital letters, was painted the following:

> *If I don't see you in this world, I'll see you in the next. Don't be late.*
> —J. Hendrix

I FIRST SAW Sojun's prized horse on an early evening in Jomsom, after the dust and wind of midday subsided. I had been sitting on the porch of the Dancing Yak Lodge, watching long shadows fall across the Kali Gandaki valley, across the now empty airport tower, the Hotel Mona Lisa, and Om's Home. The Thakali ladies who sell vegetables and fruits by the airport each morning had retreated to interior spaces. From my place on the porch I could see some of the day's new foreign arrivals—German and Japanese, Israeli and American trekkers who now lounged in the solariums of airport hotels, watching the snowcapped pyramid of Nilgiri Himal turn purple in twilight.

A rattle of hooves and the distinctive jingle of a horse's bell broke my reverie. I looked up and saw a horse and rider moving toward me at a fast, extended trot, leaving a cloud of silty dirt in their wake. As the pair came closer, I recognized the rider. Sojun was a local businessman whose family owned a store in old Jomsom. Sojun himself ran a successful engineering business in Pokhara. He and I had met several times before, in part because he and Tshampa were collaborating on designs for the new nunnery in the Muktinath Valley, and also because Sojun was the son of one of lower Mustang's most renowned, and most recalcitrant, horse healers. Sojun's nonchalance, the ease with which he socialized across languages and cultures, was matched, measure for measure, by his father's surliness. Despite several attempts to spend time watching his father Mayala work on local horses, I'd never succeeded in sharing more than a few words with the old man in the months I'd been in Mustang.

That evening, Sojun pulled up his horse in front of the Dancing Yak. Even in the half-light of dusk, the animal looked impressively strong and well bred. The horse's coat was the color of red earth after a rain. Its muscles rippled.

"New horse?" I asked. Sojun used to ride a chestnut mare.

"Just bought it last month. A friend from Lo Monthang brought it down from Tibet."

"Beautiful," I said, admiring the horse's long, crow colored mane and tail. "Just like stories old folks tell about the Siling horses." "Right," Sojun responded. "That's why I wanted it. My uncle once had a Siling horse. This one is not from there, but it is from Tibet. My friend got it from some Khampa traders who work the trade fairs each summer, over the border from Lo Monthang. The king of Lo sometimes gets horses from the same men," he continued.

"Business must be doing well, Sojun. How much did you pay?" I asked.

"Enough," he said, slyly. "Enough. What are you doing out here, anyway?" said Sojun, changing the subject.

"Avoiding the noise inside, for a moment," I answered. Dinnertime at the Dancing Yak was always something akin to mayhem—the volcanic whir of pressure cookers, strewn potato peels, whining kids, grumbling guests waiting for their meals, and all manner of social callers.

I held out my hands toward Sojun's horse. The gelding sniffed my palms—a slow gesture of trust between horse and human. As I rubbed his muzzle, I noticed that the horse's forehead bore three small cowlicks, swirling clockwise.

"Even a *norbu* to bless this one," I said. According to Tibetan horse texts and local oral tradition, this was an auspicious sign, a precious jewel that would bring the owner of such an animal fortune and good luck. Sojun just smiled. I reached to loosen the horse's girth.

"Is Tshampa inside?" he asked.

"Yes, in the kitchen."

"I've brought the final plans for the new *ani gompa*," said Sojun.

"Go ahead inside," I said. "I'll take care of the horse."

Later that night, after Sojun had returned home, I sat talking with Tshampa.

"Have you seen Sojun's new horse?" I asked.

"The one from Tibet? Yes, I've seen it. It is beautiful. But do you know how much he paid for it?"

"I asked. He wouldn't say."

"Rs.115,000. That makes it the most expensive horse in Mustang. How much in dollars?"

"Almost $2000," I answered.

"That's more than a plane ticket to America," he said, not missing a beat.

"Well, it is nice. Those long legs, and very good markings."

"True, but those long legs and fine body won't last the winter—not the way Sojun rides. He's got good taste in animals, but he doesn't know how to care for them," Tshampa answered. "Besides, it was getting dark tonight. You probably didn't see the cowlick on its right-hind hock. Inauspicious. No, those pretty legs will give it problems. He might be able to afford the most expensive horse in Mustang, but what's the use of such an animal if you can't ride it?"

A few weeks later, I was passing through old Jomsom on my way to do some work up in the Muktinath Valley when I saw Sojun's father, Mayala, attending to a horse outside his house. As I drew closer, I recognized the horse as Sojun's. Knowing Malaya's ways, I approached the horse doctor and his charge slowly, and did not say much. The old man stooped in front of the horse and ran his wrinkled hands along it's right-hind leg. Malaya's touch remained light, but as he moved down the horse's gaskin toward its hock, the animal flinched in pain, pinned back its ears, and swished its tail across the old man's face, taking off his hat.

Mayala was unfazed. He walked into his house. In a few moments, one of his nephews emerged with a thick rope, which the young man wrapped around the horse's belly. Then, he picked up the horse's left front leg, bound it with the rope, and held both firm. Now it would be nearly impossible for the horse to move.

"What is he going to do?" I asked the nephew. After several failed attempts, I had been chastened against trying to speak with Mayala directly.

"Make a few cuts, let out the old air and blood. You'll see."

Mayala re-emerged a few minutes later with a small knife, blacked on the tip by fire.

"*Gen-la*," I asked, using the respectful term for "teacher" and finally getting up my courage to address the old healer. "Is it okay if I stay and watch?"

"Just be quiet and stay out of the way," Mayala answered.

Over the next hour, Mayala cut the hair away from four spots on the lame leg. He then made four incisions, each about a half inch long, though not too deep, and then let the wounds bleed for a moment. The blood ran dark at first, then vermilion as it oxidized.

"That's enough," said Mayala. "Boiled water with salt." The nephew dropped the opposite leg that he had been hobbling, untied the rope, walked into the house, and returned a few minutes later with a pail of steaming salty water. Mayala proceeded to drench the horse's new wounds in this mixture, his hands moving strong and swift down the length of the horse's leg. Once the bleeding had stopped, Mayala plucked four long hairs from the horse's tail, strung them through a needle, and then carefully stitched up the incisions he'd made with the animal's own hair. One more drench of boiling salt water followed by dabs of fresh, heated butter over the wounds, and the operation was complete. Malaya's nephew led the horse back toward Sojun's house, and Mayala stepped inside without a word.

Later that day, I shared this story with another local veterinarian named Karchung, a younger, soft-spoken man who was originally from Lubra, with whom I had an easy relationship. I had seen him perform a similar procedure on a *dzo*, and asked after Malaya's technique. Karchung explained that, from my description, it sounded as if the horse had strained itself while moving quickly, maybe over uneven ground, and that the result had been a separation of skin from muscle, muscle from bone, as well as a buildup of bad blood in the region. The incisions were meant to cleanse toxins from the blood of that area. The swift massage with boiled water and salt, as well as the stitches, were to rejoin skin, muscle, and bone and to prevent infection. Taken together with a protection charm and daily incense offerings, this should ensure recovery in a week or so, Karchung thought.

As in other moments when I witnessed and recorded such healing episodes, I was struck by just how different this system of knowledge was from the veterinary care I'd witnessed growing up in California. There was a poetry to how Karchung described the relationship between bones and tissues, one that recalled Tshampa's instruction in the nature of the Tibetan elements, and the ways the internal body and external environment are connected. I thought of the vet who had taken care of my horses, and wondered how he would have described the problem. Would he have even located the source of lameness in the same part of the horse's body? My quick look at Sojun's horse made me wonder about joint problems around the hock. But I was not even sure how to translate "joint" or "hock" into Nepali or Tibetan, and such a reading of the lameness seemed at least incongruent, if not unhelpful.

"Mayala might not know a lot about herbs, but he has very skillful hands. I'm sure the horse will get better."

"I wish he would talk more with me," I said, in an expression of fieldwork angst. Karchung simply grinned.

"Mayala is old, you know that. He's not sure what to make of foreign girls who start asking him lots of questions. Besides, he carries a lot of *drip* from all the animals he's treated," Karchung explained. The Tibetan word *drip* translates as pollution, defilement, or contamination. It has a physical dimension, but was also rooted in a sense of spiritual, even moral, impurity that causes weakness, sickness, and a vulnerability to various forms of external negative energies and forces. "Mayala has been doing this work for much longer than you've been alive," Karchung continued. "It is difficult, you know, dealing with sickness, sometimes even death, being with animals."

I was moved by this thought, and fascinated. What about healing animals made this an act that generated pollution? Was it that the Buddhist sanction against causing harm to other sentient beings produced a paradox when overlaid on local veterinary practice? Was it that Mayala could only conduct these physical operations, but that he was not skilled as a ritual specialist, capable of performing protection rituals and other purifying acts, like more literate healers such as my friend Tshampa? Why was it that caring for a human connoted compassionate medical duty while healing animals was even capable of rendering the healer marked, contaminated, sick?

A few days later I stopped by Sojun's house to see how the horse was doing. I found Sojun behind the counter of his shop, looking over a set of architectural plans.

"How is your horse?" I asked.

"Not so good. He was healing well for the first week after my father treated it, but that's because I was making sure to wash the wounds with salt water every day. We were giving the horse eggs mixed with grain, making sure he had plenty of water and that his corral was clean. But I had to go to Pokhara last week, and left our worker to look after the horse. Now the cuts are swollen. Pus is coming out.

"My father won't do any more for the horse. Said he's done all he can and that it was my responsibility not to leave the horse in someone else's care. What does he expect? That I won't do my business just because a horse is lame? Maybe in his day you could pass a whole season just watching a herd. Who has time for that anymore?"

"So what have you done with the horse now?"

"I told our helper to take the horse to the District Livestock Office. What else could I do? You know people generally don't like going to the vet here. We would rather use our local systems. Especially because my father knows a lot about horses, I don't like to go to the technicians. They do not understand horses and can hardly tell a yak from a *dzo*. They don't know enough about Mustang to be helpful to our animals. But I needed to do something. The horse had gotten worse while I was gone.

"The boy took the horse to the livestock office. They said we were stupid for having my father cut the horse. They said the cuts will do nothing, and that now they had to give antibiotic injections to heal the cuts. I have to bring the horse back four more times, for different injections."

"But they could not say what was wrong with the horse?" I followed.

"No. All they could say is that the horse was lame, that it hurt its leg. *Obviously*," said Sojun, annoyed.

"Are the shots free?" I asked.

"Yes. You just have to pay five rupees to register at the government office." Sojun paused. "I know the cuts will heal but I'm not so sure that the horse will ever be as good again. I guess the injections will stop the pus, but I worry sometimes about what those Western medicines do to the inside of the horse. They're so much stronger than the herbs *amchi* use, and I don't trust those *rongba* to know what they're doing. Sometimes they kill animals by giving them the wrong medicine."

Rongba were "people of the valley," and to those in Mustang and other high mountain areas, the term was the derogatory equivalent of being called *bhotiya* themselves, by people from the Hindu south. Both terms connoted a sense of distance and marked out the ways that geography—as a cultural construct as well as a physical reality—contributed to the partitioning of Nepal's people.

"I've heard about such problems. But I thought people liked Dr. Punel," I said, in reference to the head veterinarian at the District Livestock Office. I had met Dr. Punel on several occasions, and had always been impressed with his ability to speak across medical and social divides, to put people at ease when animals were in his care. The fact that he was from Manang, the district just east of Mustang, and that he was conversant in local dialects and customs, was critical to his ability to perform his job well. Even though he treated animals exclusively with Western remedies, the fact that he could explain things in local idiom, and that he was not dismissive of other healing practices, served him well.

"Dr. Punel is a good person and a good animal doctor. I trust him. Many people do. But his superiors keep calling him to Pokhara. They say he'll be transferred soon, probably to Beni."

"So what happened after the technicians gave your horse its shots?"

"The government technicians sent the boy home with some cream, and some other medicine, too. But I'm not using it because they didn't really say why I needed to," Sojun continued. "Sometimes, those government workers will just give you anything, just so you leave and they don't have to really help. I know they call people in Mustang *backward* for doing things like offering incense or making protection amulets—even the work my father does. But who is backward? I'm the engineer!

"These government workers, they're just small people with small salaries and small brains who don't know about Mustang. They think they're more *bikasi*, more developed than us, just because they wear rubber gloves and use syringes. I know Western medicine works," Sojun continued. "I know it can be beneficial. I understand science. But I still don't believe that just these shots can really cure the horse. Not the shots alone."

"How did the horse go lame in the first place?" I asked, shifting the subject.

Sojun blushed slightly. "I was on my way back from Lete to Jomsom. It was getting dark. I was in a hurry to get home, and was riding with a couple of friends. You know how it can be, when everyone is riding together. I wanted to show off my horse's gate, so I kept pushing. By the time we got to the Jomsom airport, the horse was limping. This sort of problem doesn't happen so much when you are riding by yourself," he confided, "because then you don't feel like you need to be the fastest.

"Actually, this is the second time the horse has had leg problems since I bought him. The first time was different, though. It didn't last long. That time, my father gave the horse a moxibustion treatment from the base of its tail straight up along the spinal cord." Sojun's description reminded me of acupuncture techniques. I wondered how these local systems of moxibustion and massage were related to the practices of equine acupuncture and acupressure, systems of "alternative" veterinary medicine now becoming popular in the U.S. and Europe.

"That time, the horse recovered quickly, no problems. But this time, the lameness was different. This time the bad blood had to come out. And the muscles needed to be rejoined to the bones and skin. There was a separation," said Sojun. "I've watched my father heal so many horses," he continued. "When I was young, I learned a bit from him before I went off to school and then university. I learned about *hre*. You know, the disease of the stomach, when we have to let blood from under the horse's tongue."

"I've seen that many times," I said.

"And problems when a horse's urine passage is blocked. Sometimes, if the problem is severe, we put dried chili powder up there. That always works. Really, all these treatments, they work very well," Sojun continued. "But these days, medicine is strange here. If a person is suffering, they go to *amchi* and lamas. Maybe they do a divination or sponsor a ritual. Some still call an *aaya* to do a sacrifice. But they also go to the dispensaries for *brufin* and other medicines," he said, referring to the local brand of ibuprofen. "They complain to the health post officers here, or go to hospital in Pokhara or Kathmandu—at least, if they have money. People want pills and injections. But for animals, I think most people trust Western medicine less. Who knows our animals better than we do?"

Sojun's opinion was echoed by many in Mustang, particularly in relation to the care of horses. But this question of "culturally appropriate care" also pertained to other animals. For instance, I heard tales about sheep and goats that had been poisoned because they were given the wrong doses of parasite medicine by government veterinary technicians. Many people I spoke with were quick to equate the ability to heal Mustang's animals with the healer in question being from Mustang itself. Although some people doubted the ability of biomedical drugs to heal their animals, or worried about these foreign medicines' side effects, the greater offense committed by the Livestock Services Office seemed to be the fact that its employees were outsiders.

Aside from these questions of more "routine" care or the occasional lameness, other veterinary issues brought these clashes of medicine and culture to the fore. The castration of horses had become a particularly fraught issue. For obvious reasons, the procedure pointed straight to the heart of Mustang *machismo*. The local system for castration involved offerings to the horse and an awareness of what they identified as the three channels of blood, semen, and life force. Once a horse was cut, the wounds were not stitched, for stitching up the horse could irrevocably alter its gait. A horse was given time to rest, its wounds were washed regularly and poulticed, and the new gelding was ridden lightly to prevent a tightening up of the horse's hind end. The operation was done with a sharp, heated knife. Government veterinarians, on the other hand, used shiny, sterilized clamps and stitched up the horse immediately after the operation was completed. On many occasions, I heard stories from local horse owners about government veterinary technicians who had destroyed a horse's gait or endangered its *sok*, its "life force," by performing a castration without regard for the horse's three channels, without making proper offerings.

Perhaps not surprisingly, the veterinary technicians also spoke to me about horses that had died of excess bleeding or infection from a locally performed castration. Indeed, even Tshampa admitted that the number of local practitioners who were skilled in performing this operation had dwindled. It was rumored that Mayala knew how to perform the operation. But it was dangerous. Now that he was older, he would no longer do it. I had also heard that Tibetan nomads sometimes came down to Lo Monthang to perform castrations. But, I learned, this reliance on Tibetan expertise had become more difficult after the closing of Mustang's northern border in the 1960s. Even after the border began to be more permeable during China's political reforms swept through Tibet in the 1980s, it remained difficult to find a person with the requisite skills to perform a castration. These days, everyone I spoke with about this delicate matter said that they, reluctantly, depended on the district veterinarian to do the deed. I did not know a single person who had taken his horse to be castrated anywhere but the livestock services office. Yet this did not mean that local Mustangis trusted the procedure. Indeed, the fact that my questions about castration so often prompted people to tell me first about the traditional practice, and only later about how the operation was performed today, reflected a certain set of cultural priorities, as well as a resignation to change.

Over the following week, I tracked Sojun's horse's progress, and even accompanied the family's hired help to the livestock services office when it was time for the horse's injections. The district veterinarian hadn't been in Jomsom since before the fall holiday season. I found two junior-level technicians lounging in the courtyard, sipping tea.

In the hour that followed, one of the technicians irrigated each of the four cuts with an antibacterial solution and then gave the horse several cc's of antibiotics right in the rump.

"That should solve it," he announced, confidently. *Perhaps*, I said to myself, recalling Sojun's remarks. After these days of lameness and multiple, perhaps conflicting, treatments, the horse's once glistening coat had lost its luster. Its head hung low, eyes dull. The gelding was skinny and unconditioned, half the horse it used to be.

"These people don't know what they're doing," the technician continued. "Silly superstitions. What good will cutting the horse's leg do? It just makes the lameness worse. Some people are learning not to believe these local things and to come here when something is wrong with their animals. But *so sorry* for this horse. Sojun is lucky that he's a rich man. At least he can buy another one. I guess it must be hard, though—being an engineer, developed, and having that crackpot shepherd for a father. But those old habits, people are losing them—slowly."

In the Shadow of Warriors

DURING MY FIRST TRIP to Mustang, Tshampa had alluded to the Khampas, and to the ways these Tibetan soldiers knew horses. Literally, a "Khampa" is a person from the eastern Tibetan region of Kham, which today maps onto parts of Sichuan, Yunnan, and the Tibet Autonomous Region of China. But the name "Khampa" had taken on a broader meaning in Mustang, and referred to all of the Tibetan men—regardless of their provenance—who fought against the Chinese occupation of their country, as part of the Tibetan Resistance movement. This movement was an organized military effort that began in the early 1950s, and reached an apex during the flight of His Holiness the Fourteenth Dalai Lama into exile in 1959. After this seminal event, the Tibetan Resistance soldiers regrouped outside Tibet's contested borders, and chose Mustang as their base of covert military operations against the Chinese People's Liberation Army (PLA) from 1960 to 1974.

Before my initial visit to Mustang, I had not heard of the Tibetan Resistance along the Nepali border after the Chinese claimed to have "peacefully liberated" Tibet in 1959. In the intervening years, I had read all I could about this movement. I wanted to understand more about how the Resistance had shaped Tibetan political history, and glean a sense of what the tenure of the Tibetan army in Mustang had meant for local lives. How did people from Mustang remember this time? What had they learned from it? How had they lived, then, in the shadow of warriors, and in the shadow of a war they did not choose?

The Resistance army was known in Tibetan as Chushi Gangdruk—a name that meant "four rivers, six ranges" and that referred to the vast grasslands of eastern Tibet where the movement had begun. Through my reading, I had learned that the history of the movement included years of covert Cold War–era funding from the U.S. Central Intelligence Agency (CIA). The Americans had gone so far as to take some of the Tibetan leaders of the Resistance—blindfolded, I might add—across the world for paramilitary training in the Colorado Rockies. Later, these Tibetans were parachuted back into embattled parts of central and eastern Tibet. Yet U.S. support for the Tibetan Resistance was neither uniform nor consistent, particularly from the mid 1960s onward. Several top-level U.S. diplomats feared that continued support for the Tibetans would not only jeopardize relations with China, but also with India. The CIA withdrew their support for Chushi Gangdruk in the late 1960s, before the United States rapprochement with China, which President Nixon facilitated between 1969–1971. The demise of the Tibetan Resistance movement was soon to follow, in 1974. These series of events contributed to what many Tibetans experienced as a betrayal by the U.S. of the Tibetan fight for sovereignty, and the sense that Tibetans were mere pawns in the Cold War game.

And yet, in the early 1960s, there was strong Tibetan, American, and Indian support for the reorganization of Tibetan military operations in the Himalayas—albeit for different strategic reasons. Although the Dalai Lama was opposed to the use of violence in the struggle against the Chinese, the Tibetan Resistance forces won tacit approval from the still-fledgling Tibetan government-in-exile. The Indians, for their part, helped the Resistance by harboring Tibetan refugees. The Indian army also indirectly aided the Tibetan Resistance by recruiting Tibetans into their covert military unit, which eventually became the Special Frontier Forces—battalions deployed in the Sino-Indian War of 1962.

After the Lhasa uprisings of 1959 and the flight into exile of the Fourteenth Dalai Lama, Chushi Gangdruk sought out Mustang as their primary base of military operations. On paper, Mustang appeared to be a nearly perfect center for the post-1959 Tibetan Resistance. It was, after all, a region that extended geographically into Tibet, whose northern border was near the Lhasa-Xinjiang highway. And Mustang was considered culturally and linguistically Tibetan, but located firmly within the borders of Nepal. In 1960 the king of Lo was paying a minimal annual tribute to the government Kathmandu. Significantly, he had only stopped sending annual tithes to Lhasa a handful of years previously.

Soldiers started to arrive in Mustang in late 1960. At that point, some of these cadres had been fighting the Chinese for more than a decade, since troops from the Chinese PLA first rolled into eastern Tibet in 1949. When the Khampa arrived in Mustang, they brought with them the violence and shellshock of war, the greedy and destitute outpourings of a people displaced, and the false hopes of victory against Chinese forces. A number of the Tibetan Resistance leaders had been monks before the Chinese invasion, and this, combined with the nature of their struggle, stirred sympathies in Mustang. But as a marginal region of a marginal country, Mustang and its people did not know what to expect either of the Khampa or of the Nepali government in relation to this covert struggle being fought in their midst, on their soil.

As it is remembered in Mustang, when the Khampa first arrived in 1960, they did not harm anyone. Some of them were so near dead with exhaustion that all they could do was maintain their discipline and establish a small base of operations. They had little save the clothes on their back, protective amulets, old muskets, and small stores of grain. But the soldiers boasted about guns and supplies that were coming from America, and said that these stores would be dropped from the sky into Mustang, and just across the border in Tibet—stories that, to most people from Mustang who remember this time, sounded too fantastic to be true.

Despite official directives from India and Washington to keep the Mustang base small, potential cadres began arriving in Mustang en masse. War camps sprang up throughout Mustang's high pastures. And things started going wrong. Supplies dwindled and were not replenished. By the winter of 1960–1961, no outside help had arrived—including the fabled assistance from America. It was said that one of the Resistance commanders radioed messages to their supporters in America and India: *We are boiling the soles of our shoes for soup.* But even if such a message was received, it did not seem to do much good during that first long winter. Nonetheless, new Resistance volunteers kept arriving in Mustang by the dozens.

Finally, by the spring of 1961, American planes loaded with supplies made drops inside Tibet, just north of the Mustang border. The air was so clear in these highlands that people in Lo Monthang could see the listless, billowing parachutes to which were attached boxes of munitions, food, and medicine. Even though these supplies were not sufficient to fully arm or feed the recruits, they were something. But these drops were only anodyne. No more airdrops were made until 1965, this time inside Mustang.

I imagine that the king of Lo—the current king's father—did not sleep well during those early Khampa years. As it is told now, more than forty years later, the king tried to accommodate the soldiers, where possible. When they had nothing, he gave them grain and animals, even some precious timber. In the years that followed, it was common to see gruff Khampa in their parachute silk and khaki cloaks herding pack trains up and down the Kali Gandaki, soldiers thinly disguised as itinerant muledrivers. In addition to staples such as rice and sugar, pack trains ferried noodles and biscuits, shoelaces, candles, and butter, watches, matches, and bolts of cloth from Pokhara. But this commerce wasn't as simple as supply and demand. Many people in Mustang remember it as a coercive trade.

The more stories I heard about the Khampa from friends in Mustang, the easier it became for me to imagine how their presence must have affected local lives, notwithstanding the sympathy Mustang's villagers had for the Tibetans' struggle. The Khampas' continued presence in Mustang caused great hardship, placing an insupportable burden both on natural resources and on the region's relations with Kathmandu. As an illustration, people in Mustang still spoke with resentment about the trees—rare in most of the district—that were felled to build the Khampas' base, high above Jomsom near Lake Tilicho, and the shrubs that were ripped out to feed their cooking fires. Caches of weapons had been stored under village homes, I learned. In the company of female Mustang friends, I was told stories that implicated many Khampa soldiers in the rapes and sometimes the marriages of local women. I knew, too, that some old Khampa had chosen to settle in Mustang permanently, after the demise of the movement, while many other former soldiers now lived in Kathmandu, Dharamsala, and other sites of Tibetan relocation. But I had come across very few artifacts that documented this period in Mustang's history, or that even treated these tragic and tumultuous events as part of Mustang's history at all.

I had brought with me to Mustang some books about this period of Tibetan history, and had, for the past few days, been reading John Avedon's *In Exile from the Land of Snows*. The book is a thoughtful rendering of the history and culture of Tibet, both before and after the Chinese invasion. Avedon's narrative was one of the first accounts that spelled out in impressive detail the plight of Tibetans against the massive force that was Mao's PLA, and that attempted to share something of how Tibetans were remaking their lives and worlds in exile.

I sat in the dining room of the Trekker's Inn in Jomsom, looking at the book's photographs of a war that most people in the world never knew had been fought. In one photograph, cool gray tones tempered the harshness of Mustang sun and wind. In the foreground, Tibetan soldiers walked north from Lo Monthang. According to the caption, they were on a foray into Tibet. I knew this wind so well, and now breathed the air they had breathed more than forty years ago. The stubble of spring grass they trudged over, the view from mountain passes—these too, I would come to know well in time. But what of the rifles they carried? What of the unresolved burden of their nation's future, slung across tired shoulders like their necklaces of bullets?

I was transfixed by all of the book's images, not just the few pictures of the Mustang-based Resistance troops. There, staring back at me, was the moon-faced boy who would become the Fourteenth Dalai Lama. He was bundled up in a worn, Tibetan-style tunic that shone like oilskin. I imagined that his shirt was slick with butter grease and spilled Tibetan tea, and that the boy's mother had dusted off *tsampa* flour from the corners of his Botticelli-esque mouth and wiped his face clean before the government search party that discovered him took the picture.

I flipped some pages and encountered Chinese commanders of the PLA, accompanied by Tibetan dignitaries, as they inspected a sea of PLA troops in Lhasa, circa 1953. The Potala palace loomed, dreamlike, in the distance. The red walls of Namgyal Dratsang, the Dalai Lama's monastery, floated on a cloud of whitewashed stone. Chinese cadres milled about in the picture, looking disoriented, while Tibetan noblemen, with their silk-covered hats and long-armed robes seemed a prescient augury of the destruction, foreign occupation, and internal conflicts that were to mar Tibet in the coming years. The nobles' robes were too beautiful for battle, and seemed no match for the well-worn uniforms of the PLA, already dusty and patched from the Long March.

In 1973, after more than ten years of surviving and fighting in Mustang, after CIA aid had dried up in 1968, and after increasing pressure from China, the Nepali army began to mobilize against the Khampa. But the Tibetans would not give up easily. Maintaining the struggle to free their country from Chinese control was an ideological and practical preoccupation, as was the political transformation of Tibet at the hands of Chinese ideologues, backed by the PLA. Losing American support had been a demoralizing blow for the Khampa, but they had begun this struggle without CIA assistance, and they were determined to continue on without it.

And yet the movement was not without its internal divisions. In the years leading up to the demise of the Tibetan Resistance's armed struggle, factions had developed within the ranks. Two leaders—Baba Yeshi and Wangdu—vied for power. Baba Yeshi, a former monk, retained a number of loyal followers, but by all accounts I heard in Mustang, Wangdu was the more popular leader. He also happened to be the nephew of Gompo Tashi Angdrutsang, a nobleman from Litang (in today's Sichuan Province) who had been a chief of Resistance operations in the early years, in Tibet. His name still inspired confidence and a sense of lineage.

In the autumn of 1973, Baba Yeshi was called to India where members of the government-in-exile asked him to withdraw from Mustang and let Wangdu take over as commander. Tensions between Baba Yeshi and the Tibetan government-in-exile had been swelling for some time, and the news of Baba Yeshi's removal from his post served to deepen rifts that had already been developing between Mustang-based soldiers who aligned themselves more closely with either Wangdu or Baba Yeshi.

Rumors flew. Some said that Wangdu was planning to regroup and transfer the soldiers still loyal to Baba Yeshi from Mustang to India. Baba Yeshi's supporters in Mustang were scheming to hold hostage those soldiers, loyal to Wangdu, whom they blamed for their leader's removal from duty.

Soon, Baba Yeshi surreptitiously fled Delhi for Mustang. Whether he was a wise man sure of footsteps and strategy, or whether he was a reckless man stripped of power, is still unclear. What is known is that Baba Yeshi reached Mustang, gathered up his supporters, and established a new camp southeast of Lo. Outright offensives between what were now two factions of Khampa soldiers broke the surface of a dissolving unity, even if their rationale for war remained unchanged. My friends in Mustang said, of this time, that the cadres stopped referring to each other as fellow Chushi Gangdruk soldiers. What was once a military collective became a menagerie, individuated by clan- and lineage-based alliances, regional dialects, and histories of conflict *within* this vast, diverse space now called Tibet. And so, the endgame of the Resistance echoed elements of much older Tibetan rivalries.

People say that Wangdu maintained military discipline during this time of dissension, and that he did not speak of surrender, even after he received word from Dharamsala that negotiations were underway with the Nepali government for a "peaceful" end to armed conflict. The Nepalis were working with the government-in-exile to carve out resettlement plans for the soldiers. But the Nepalis' actions were further complicated by Chinese pressure.

In November 1973, Chairman Mao threatened Nepal's King Birendra with Chinese military action unless the Nepalis put a stop to the Tibetan Resistance's use of Mustang as a base. Birendra thus declared all of Nepal's border areas "restricted zones"—an action that remains law to this day—and deployed some initial Nepali troops to Mustang. By March of 1974, the Nepalis demanded that the Khampa surrender their arms and dismantle all of their war camps in exchange for rehabilitation and aid—land and homes in which to resettle as legitimate refugees.

I can only imagine that when Wangdu heard this offer, perhaps a rifle strapped to his back and his tired eyes shaded by American sunglasses, he would have scoffed. What the historical record does tell us is that Wangdu requested that Lhamo Tsering, his confidant and an early engineer of the Resistance, come to Mustang and help think through options for disarmament. But Lhamo Tsering, then one of the Resistance's chief officers in Delhi, was arrested in Pokhara en route to Mustang. The Nepalis hoped his detainment would encourage a mass surrender. But Lhamo Tsering was still able to smuggle a message to Wangdu. In essence, that communique told Wangdu *not* to surrender at that point, and that the Nepali forces could not be trusted. All the while, Baba Yeshi remained in Kathmandu.

A few days later, the Nepali government presented Resistance leadership with an ultimatum. In no uncertain terms, they wanted the Khampa out of Mustang. The Tibetan government-in-exile knew there was little hope of getting most of their men safely to refugee settlements in India, or even achieving their acceptance as lay Tibetans seeking political asylum in Nepal, unless the fighting stopped. Finally, the Dalai Lama had no choice but to intervene. The government-in-exile cabinet ministers, who had been keeping many of the details about the armed Resistance from the Dalai Lama, were forced to reveal the full story of operations in Mustang. As a proponent of nonviolence to his core, the Dalai Lama was said to have been deeply saddened, if not shocked, by the extent of these military operations.

In response, and after realizing the potential bloodshed between Tibetan and Nepali soldiers, the Dalai Lama tape-recorded a message for the Khampa: twenty minutes of skillful persuasion, in which the soldiers' highest spiritual authority asked them to lay down their weapons. One can only imagine that His Holiness knew the message would be traumatic when it reached Mustang, and that, as the Tibetan spiritual leader's booming baritone voice sliced through the high mountain air, the soldiers would be overcome. After all, many of these men had once been monks, and undoubtedly all of them had dreamed of hearing his voice again. But the content of his message—one that called for peaceful disarmament and an end to this chapter of Tibetan history—hit hard.

In that place where historical memory meets imagination, I conjure visions of soldiers on that fated day: grown men bowed in the dirt, weeping, full of anguish, and others with their heads turned away from the tape recorder, trying to deny what they were hearing. Some soldiers could not reconcile the thought of disobeying the Dalai Lama with turning away from this fight for their homes, for their nation. Several soldiers slit their throats in response. Others threw themselves into the torrents of Mustang's rivers.

Many soldiers were convinced by the Dalai Lama's message. After the taped news reverberated in Mustang's canyons and came to rest in villages, high camps, and caves, load upon load of ammunition and weapons began making their way toward Jomsom, on the backs of mules, pack horses, and miniature donkeys. Wangdu did not want to submit to the Nepalis, but after several days, a group of his troops gave up their weapons. Others followed—ragged men weaving their way out of the hills. But what was supposed to have been a peaceful process, and one of amnesty, turned into more of a hunt. Nepali army and police routed out Resistance forces, arresting many in Jomsom. These Khampa soldiers who chose to disarm after hearing the Dalai Lama's message were then initially sent to detention centers in Pokhara.

Word of this betrayal quickly reached Wangdu. He began to rethink his limited options. As the story goes, the leader decided he would head west, toward the India-Tibet border, where one of the Resistance's radio reconnaissance teams had a small base. From there, he and his cohorts planned to reorganize and continue to fight the Chinese. It was a desperate plan, if noble. Several days later, forty armed horsemen rode west from Mustang, the Royal Nepal Army on their heels. For the next month they crisscrossed the border between Nepal and Tibet. When they reached the site of the radio operators, Wangdu sent a message to Tibetan Resistance leaders in India, proposing that he regroup in this area—a region even more remote than Mustang. They responded by ordering him and his remaining garrison to return to India. Wangdu did not heed this request. The group headed toward the Tinker La, a high pass that led into India.

Early in this march that would last a fortnight, fate further conspired against this last stand of soldiers. As the story goes, one of their mules carrying food was lost and Wangdu sent a soldier to retrieve it. This lone soldier, scared perhaps of what awaited him at the Tinker La, fled to Jomsom and, in exchange for reprieve, disclosed the guerrilla's planned escape route. Meanwhile, forty other men who were still loyal to Baba Yeshi had been commandeered by the Nepalis to track Wangdu and his men and help the Nepali troops plan an ambush. When Wangdu's weary men reached the Tinker La, everyone was disheartened. Nobody talked about the deserter, but the fact of his absence weighed on the group. They knew what it meant. The small party dipped down into a draw just before the last climb to the summit of the pass. A shattering cacophony of gunfire broke the silence. And then the five ponies belonging to Wangdu and his men were said to have returned, riderless. Several other men raced up to where their leader had disappeared over the ridge, just in time to see Wangdu gunned down by Nepali troops.

In a strange twist of fate, it was Baba Yeshi who positively identified Wangdu's body for the Nepali soldiers. The fallen leader's belongings were laid out for inspection in Kathmandu's Ratna Park, and visitors to the unusual shrine ran their fingers over Wangdu's amulet, wristwatch, rings, and wooden drinking bowl. Mustang's traumatic past was no longer a secret of the Himalayas.

The weight of this history felt heavy, even all these years later. Mustang was nowhere and everywhere in this story of the Tibetan Resistance. Staring back at me from the final page of black-and-white photographs in Avedon's book were Mustang's high pastures and mountain passes. Soldiers bundled for winter and for war walked through glacial patches of snow and ice, shrouded in morning fog. Tired legs moved over land that was not their own, in the name of freedom for their homeland. Even though the Khampa soldiers could feel a natural affinity among the villages of *tsampa* eaters in Mustang, these pastures and forests and hills did not belong to them. This, too, was an occupation. But nobody ever talks about it in those terms.

I was deep in thought when I heard somebody coming up the stairs of the Trekker's Inn. I looked up from Avedon's book. It was Yonten. A Tibetan, the son of a Khampa soldier, Yonten was someone I had come to know gradually, cautiously. He was tall and handsome and regarded as something of a ladies' man. His soft-spoken wife and their young son spent most of their time at Tserok, a Tibetan refugee camp south of Jomsom, across the river from the village of Marpha, while Yonten ran an antique store near the airport.

Yonten's family had been nomads from western Tibet. They had come across the border into upper Mustang when he was quite young, after his father joined the Resistance. Apparently, Yonten spent much of his youth in the palace at Monthang. He had learned about horses in part by helping the king's constable, a man named Pema Ngotug, whom I, too, would get to know in the coming months, as I traveled north to Lo. When Yonten learned that I was living in Mustang to study horses, he sought me out. He was eager to share what he knew about horse training, as well as colors and cowlicks—knowledge he'd picked up from his early years in Lo.

Yonten yawned and looked bored. "I ordered lemon tea," he said, by way of introduction.

"How's business?" I asked.

"Slow. Always is this time of year. But at least I'm not crouched in the dust like some of the others, selling Tibetan trinkets to tourists on the road. At least I've got this shop in Jomsom." Yonten's comment referenced the many refugees who would buy cheaply made prayer wheels, bowls, rosaries, and other knick-knacks in Pokhara or Kathmandu and later resell them as authentic Tibetan articles in the mountains.

"What are you reading?" Yonten asked. He spoke passable trekker's English, German, and Swiss but could read none of these languages.

"A book about the Dalai Lama and the history of Tibet. There are some pictures in here. Want to see?" Yonten nodded.

As soon as I opened up to the first page of the young Dalai Lama's image, Yonten's attitude changed. He grew quiet, contemplative. He took the book gently from my hands, touched it to his forehead, and then set the book down and continued flipping through images. I hadn't known Yonten to be particularly devout, but he showed the book as much respect as an old Tibetan grandmother might have. In Tibetan culture, writing is often a sacred act, and books are afforded the status of icons. One rarely sees a Tibetan put a book of any sort on the ground, particularly if it contains any Tibetan writing, images of high lamas, or deities. In general, this cultural habit reveals and enforces a connection between spiritual achievement and erudite learning, but there is more to it than that. A standardized Tibetan script was first developed as a vehicle for translating Buddhist texts from Sanskrit and Pali. In that sense, the act of writing—of forming Tibetan letters—is sacred at its core, and should be approached with right mindfulness and devotion. When Tibetans fled their country, they carted many texts with them, or, in some cases, buried them, when it became clear that these precious folios were being used for kindling and toilet paper by PLA cadres. Each year, in villages throughout the Tibetan cultural world, people hoist huge volumes of religious teachings onto their backs and circumambulate villages and fields—a means of earning religious merit and protecting the domestic domain.

I watched Yonten as he flipped through the photos in Avedon's book. When he asked me to, I read him the captions. When he came to a picture of rough-looking Tibetan Resistance soldiers who were escorting the Dalai Lama to India, he held up the book close to his eyes, scrutinizing the images.

"Do you recognize anyone?"

"That one," he said, pointing to a Khampa leading a horse. "He was here, in Mustang. My father knew him. And that other one, in the back there, behind His Holiness. It is hard to tell, but I think he was one of the soldiers who slit his throat."

"After His Holiness sent the tape asking the Khampa to surrender?" I asked. Yonten nodded.

"*Nyingje*," I said. The word means compassion in Tibetan, but it also implies a sense of mercy, humility, and empathy—marking a connection between the person who speaks the word and the object of this affection. I could think of little else to say.

As I looked at pictures, I wondered if any of these men were the leaders I had heard about. I asked Yonten.

"No," he answered. "No Wangdu or Baba Yeshi here."

"Did you know either of them?" I asked.

"I remember Wangdu better than Baba Yeshi. I was small at the time, and Baba Yeshi was called off to India and Kathmandu many times in those later years. I guess since I'm Tibetan I should be glad for any leader of the Resistance. At least they were trying to save our country. But I am more like Mustang people now, I think. Wangdu was a leader."

"And Baba Yeshi?" I asked

"He did well. He was strategic, clever. But people say he was not as kind. I know what people around here say about the Khampa—that they took things and sometimes were rough. They were fighting for their freedom. My father used to say that Baba Yeshi thought too much of himself. He took liberties," said Yonten.

"And Wangdu did not?"

"Wangdu, he was, well, such a man is hard to find. He was strong and smart—and excellent with a horse," Yonten added, for my benefit. "He knew how to talk, but he was also a good soldier. He was a headman in his blood." Yonten's comment struck me. According to local opinion, Baba Yeshi's failings seemed to be in his coarseness, egotism, and an allegiance to a vision, one that was often impractical. In the end he saved himself before his fellow soldiers, and sought amnesty in Kathmandu, where he lived until his death in 2001. Wangdu's strength was in his sense of the collective, the realization that as much as people needed a leader, they wanted someone they could admire, with whom they could share a drink and some humor at the end of a long day, a struggle. He died, tragically, among his fellow men.

"If you wanted to learn about horses, you could have asked Wangdu, too!" Yonten scratched his head and flipped the book, looking for more photographs. "He was excellent with horses. Knew how to cure the hot diseases and the cold, or to make a lame horse well again. Some of the other soldiers did too. But they would just take a horse from someone if they needed one. Wangdu would never do that. People gave him horses. I'm not sure, but I think I remember the king of Mustang gave him one once. Why aren't you in Monthang, anyway? You'll certainly learn more about horses up in Lo than you will down here," said Yonten. The comments hit a nerve.

"I hope to, soon. I'm still waiting for my permit for upper Mustang," I responded. Although my Fulbright grant application had clearly stated that I would need to travel to the restricted areas of Mustang to complete my project, my permit for passage to these areas, north of Kagbeni and on to Lo, was pending. When I had left Kathmandu for Mustang late in the fall, my file was somewhere in the bowels of the Home Ministry, waiting to be processed. Such a request was novel, and neither the Fulbright office nor their Nepali government counterparts knew exactly how to handle the request. I had been told to be patient, that the permit would come "slowly, slowly."

"Well, that is where you should be," replied Yonten. "Loba call the horses in southern Mustang 'chicken legs' because they're nowhere as good or as strong as the horses they have, and the ones that come from Tibet. These Thakalis around here don't know anything about horses, even though they are buying some of the most expensive ones around. The only one who knows anything is Mayala. But that's because, when he was young, he spent years up in Lo, and beyond, into Tibet, with the nomads."

"I've watched Mayala work on horses, but he isn't very friendly," I said.

"What to do?" said Yonten. "He's old. But there are still some old Khampa around. Do you want to meet one?" he asked. I nodded.

"A few of the old men at Tserok know a lot about horses. One even used to be a horse trader, bringing horses from Amdo and Kham to Lhasa. Before he joined the Resistance. He doesn't speak much Nepali, but I could come to translate. He can be a little difficult, but he likes me. And if we buy him some *chang*, he'll be happy and start telling old stories. Those Khampa don't eat so much. They used to go out to the grazing pastures or to battle for several days and would survive on *tsampa* and *arak* mixed together and stored under their saddles—but this one still likes to drink. I'll take you to meet him." We made plans to meet the next morning.

We sipped our sweet lemon tea. Outside, rain began to fall. The weather was unusual this time of year, but gave me and Yonten reason to stay where we were. And until the rain stopped, we talked about horses some more.

That night, while I ate dinner with Tshampa and his family, I asked Tshampa what he remembered of the Khampas' presence in Mustang.

Tshampa looked startled for a moment. "In the early years when many other refugees came pouring over the border, wanting to leave Tibet before the Chinese ate it up, my father also helped. It was his duty. They tried to take animals with them, but many died on the way or once they reached Mustang. Even though the grass was more plentiful then, there was still not enough. Animals died. People died. It was the saddest time I think Mustang has seen, but also a proud moment. We wanted to help, but how do you help when you're suffering too?

"Some of our people still have trouble talking about that time. Those Khampa liked to carry knives. They ran off with quite a few daughters, and nuns. Why do you ask about all this?"

"I'm going to Tserok with Yonten tomorrow, to meet an old Khampa. He says the Khampa knows some things about horses."

"Those old men don't know much anymore," said Tshampa. "They've lost their memories to *chang* and *arak*, most of them. And they're more Mustangi than Tibetan at this point. After a while, you become a part of where you live, even if it isn't your birthplace."

I thought about Tshampa's statement. "But if the Chinese left Tibet, would they go back?"

Tshampa shrugged. "It is difficult to say. The older ones, perhaps. But all the people who were born here? Who are they, Tibetan or Nepali? Both. But where would they choose, maybe not here or not Tibet. Maybe America," he said.

The next day, with morning sun on our faces and a stillness to walk in, before the midday wind, Yonten and I headed toward Tserok. The Tibetan clipped along and I hitched the skirt of my *chuba* to keep up. We walked in silence mostly, past the fields near Syang where I'd worked with Karma, past Marpha's apple orchards, the trees now bare. The shops and hotels that lined Marpha's flagstone streets were still shuttered and dark. Chickens scampered and pecked at pebbles. We walked on, through the town and over the bridge to Tserok.

Every time I had been to this refugee settlement it had depressed me. This time was no exception. Tattered and faded prayer flags strung from tall polls fluttered in the light morning breeze. Though built in local architectural style—with flat roofs and whitewashed sides and mud floors—Tserok's dwellings retained an institutional feel: two rows of dwellings, facing each other like barracks. I could tell they had been built in haste, even though they were now well worn by more than thirty years of occupancy.

I followed Yonten toward one of the houses. His wife squatted in the courtyard, plucking lice from another woman's head. She nodded when she saw us.

"You've come," she said, in her own Central Tibetan dialect. "Have you eaten?" These were simple sentences, but I took some pleasure in the fact that I could understand her much more easily than I could follow local Mustang banter. She spoke with a crispness that reminded me of the tapes of Tibetan language I had listened to before I left for Nepal.

"Have you seen Norbu Wangchuk?" Yonten asked. "The American wants to meet him."

"He's probably sleeping. He and the others played *sho* until late last night. Drank a lot of *chang*." *Sho* is a Tibetan gambling game, played with stones or shells and dice.

"Why does she want to meet him?"

"She wants to ask him about horses."

"Horses?"

"Yes, horses."

"Are there no horses in America?" Yonten did not answer, but just ushered me inside.

While the old Khampa slept, Yonten and I ate a meal of curried potatoes and rice with our hands.

"Tibetan salt," Yonten said, licking his fingers. "Have you had it before?"

"I think so. It definitely tastes different. Where do you get it from?"

"Oh, here and there. It's more expensive than the Indian salt, but it tastes much better to us."

"Karma uses it to make butter tea," I said. "I've seen it in the kitchen." Yonten reached into an old Nescafé can and pulled out some salt crystals, the color of faint rose quartz. He placed the coarse lumps in my hand. The salt smelled like the mountains over which it had been carried, and like the ancient sea from whence it came. Tibetan salt was preferred for its taste and nutritional value throughout the Nepali Himalayas, but the incursion of Indian salt threatened the viability of what remained of the ancient exchange of salt for grain. The Nepali Ministry of Health and development agencies praised Indian salt because, aside from its cheaper price, it was iodized and therefore curbed goiter. At that time, Tibetan salt cost more than double, measure for measure, than the packaged Indian variety. But its value could not be measured in rupees saved. Much more than a seasoning or a vehicle for improving public health, Tibetan salt has been, and remains, a medium of exchange and a marker of identity. It is also considered medicinal.

"In Tibet, horses and yak are fed Tibetan salt regularly, to keep them healthy," Yonten continued. "In Lo there are some places where there is still salt in the earth. Down here, some people still feed horses and other animals Tibetan salt, too, once or twice a month. People who don't know what they're doing will feed horses Indian salt, but that is not good for them. Horses that come from Tibet who are then fed Indian salt have a difficult time. They lose their hair and become skinny. So, if you want a healthy horse, feed Tibetan salt. If you want a fast horse, feed the horse tea, *tsampa*, and brown sugar. At least that's what the Tibetan nomads say."

I had heard similar things from Tshampa before: *Let the horse drink some* arak *before a race. Mix eggs and honey into a horse's grain to make the horse fat and its coat shiny. Don't let a pregnant mare eat green grass with frost on it, because the gestating foal will get cold and the mare might miscarry. Don't feed buckwheat to a pregnant mare either, for buckwheat is a cold food. Feed corn in the winter to increase a horse's internal heat, because corn comes from hot places. Mix tsampa with tea, brown sugar, and the liquid left over from making chang. This will keep the horse healthy through the long winter. Feed late-blooming grass in the fall. Always dry hay in the indirect* sun. *When the dry hay begins to smell like beer, never feed it to a horse. For very good horses, mix buckwheat with hot water, lentils, and the thin grass that yaks have trampled on. Make this into a cake, cover it with fine silk during the day, and then feed this to the horse at night. This is what nobles feed their horses.*

These recipes and instructions read like edicts, and although I had seen very few Mustangis pay such close attention to the elaborate instructions, there was poetry in these ideals.

After our meal, Yonten leaned back, rested his head on a stack of saddle blankets in the corner, and closed his eyes. Soon, he was snoring, his breath thick and sweet against the cold winter air, now that the fire had been reduced to embers. I sat quietly and wrote in my journal, until Yonten woke—a waking as impromptu as had been the nap.

"Norbu Wangchuk should be awake by now." Yonten yawned and rose. I followed.

The old Khampa lived in one of the smaller houses of the settlement, and he seemed to live alone.

"Wangchuk-la," Yonten called, "The sun is risen. Have you?" Wangchuk did not respond directly, but ushered us in and motioned for us to sit on a worn Tibetan carpet. He wore a tassel of red string around his head, the signature headpiece of men from Kham.

"Tashi Deleg," I offered, and then paused before continuing. I had hoped that Yonten would jump in and introduce me, but when no such introduction was forthcoming, I bumbled through my awkward Tibetan sentences. "I'm here in Mustang to learn about horses. Yonten said you knew a lot about horses. That you used to be a horse trader in Tibet."

Wangchuk looked at me sleepily and mumbled "Mmm? Horses? America?"

Although Yonten and I usually spoke in Nepali, he turned to me at that moment and said, in English, *"The old man, he's happier to talking if we go to restaurant, has some beer. I suggest."* I realized that I had been rushing things.

"Okay, let's go," I responded, also in English.

Yonten then properly invited Wangchuk and we all headed out, toward Marpha. We walked slowly, taking measured steps across the suspension bridge that spanned the river. I paced myself behind the two men. The old Khampa seemed frail at that moment, unsteady on his feet. It was difficult to imagine him as a courageous soldier.

Wangchuk led us to a small restaurant, identified as a place of business only by the stainless steel cups and plates stacked neatly in a corner and several tables lined up against the far window. Yonten ordered a pitcher of *chang* with two glasses. I asked the Thakali woman running the shop for tea. She nodded. Dabs of butter lined the rim of the pitcher, marking the *chang* as an auspicious substance. The woman plucked a bit of butter from the vessel and placed three small dabs on each glass, as was local custom. After all, the thick barley beer was the libation of ritual, of offering, even here, on a cold winter's morning, with nothing much to celebrate.

"Drink, drink," the woman motioned to Yonten and Wangchuk. They drank, and the gesture was repeated twice.

"She wants to know about horses," Yonten said, after they had slung back their third cup of *chang*.

Wangchuk sat for a time in silence, scratching his head and picking dirt from his fingernails. Then, he began to speak—slowly at first, in measured Tibetan, and then more fluently, as I imagined the *chang* began coursing through his veins. I nudged Yonten to translate.

"Many years ago, before the Chinese, there were businessmen who were very good at selling horses in Lhasa," the old Khampa began. "I learned from them. When a person who didn't know about horses came to Lhasa looking for an animal, some of these smart people would take one of their older horses and poke it in the mouth with a sharp stick, over and over. When the potential buyer tried to check the age of the horse, the animal would refuse to give the man its head. Then the horse trader would say that this was just a feisty horse full of energy and very young. This way, the buyer could not look at the horse's age and would end up buying an old horse. You always have to check a horse's teeth, and also the roof of the mouth, to know if you're getting a good animal. If the horse is old, the teeth will look like an old man's"—Wangchuk smiled wide, as if to demonstrate—"and the roof of the horse's mouth will be more black than pink. These are the things anyone should know," he continued. Wangchuk seemed to come alive as he spoke about the old business, the cunning of it all.

"Suppose you want to sell a thin horse," the Khampa continued. "Then, the morning before a man comes to see the horse, feed the horse yeast and lots of green grass. This will make the horse's stomach swell up and make it look fat. Then men will want to buy it. But then, in a few days time, the horse would look its skinny self again."

"Would this not harm the horse?" I asked.

"Not usually," answered Wangchuk. "But sometimes it would make the horse sick in the stomach—sometimes so sick that the animal would die. But that was also good for business!" I tried not to register my shock, as the old man continued.

"Two friends might work together, to trick someone into paying more for a horse than it was worth. One friend would pretend to be a buyer, while the other friend offered a horse for sale. They would talk loudly in the marketplace, and the one friend said he would pay an outrageous sum for the horse—just so this talk would catch the attention of some-one passing by. You see, Tibetans are always thinking, *I need the best horse*. So, this fool would think to himself, *this must be a great horse, if this man would offer so much money for it*, and he would outbid the sneaky friend. The friend would haggle for a while, to see how high the price would go. But the two friends would never let the bargaining go on for too long, and the man being tricked would always 'win' the bidding. Then, everyone would share a drink to mark the trade. The gullible man would go off with his expensive horse, and the two friends would split the profit."

I was amused by these stories, if a bit disconcerted by the glee Wangchuk seemed to take in swindling, his recollections of the con.

"What else did you do?" I asked.

"If a horse is really slow," Wangchuk continued, "then we would put a small nail on the inside of the stirrup and then the horse will move very fast when the potential buyer is watching or riding it. Then, we'd remove the spike after the person bought the horse. Then we'd watch him try to make the horse move, and laugh and laugh!"

"*But this risky businessman,*" Yonten said to me, in English, "*is always bandit. Horses, gold, jewels, no matter.*"

I was taken by these descriptions of horse-trading antics, but these stories were not really why I had come to Tserok to meet this Khampa. I wanted to learn what the old man knew about horses, but I was also curious about his place in the Tibetan Resistance, about what it meant—or had meant—to be a Khampa in Mustang. I wanted to ask Wangchuk this, but did not know how. Would he take offense?

"*When did Wangchuk become a soldier?*" I asked Yonten, also in English. "*Is it okay to ask him that? When did he come to Mustang? How come he decided to stay?*"

"*Those are more difficult things to be asking. I try.*" Yonten said. He took a long drink, ordered more *chang*, filled Wangchuk's glass.

"About Chushi Gangdruk, *gen-la*," Yonten began, shifting his tone, and now speaking in a low voice. "What were those years like for you?"

Wangchuk seemed undaunted by the line of inquiry, and, if anything, grew more thoughtful as the two men continued talking. I listened carefully, and followed Wangchuk's recollections as best I could. After some time, Yonten turned to me and paraphrased, in Nepali.

"When Wangchuk was first in Lhasa, after coming from Kham, where there were already many Chinese, he would sometimes escort Dalai Lama from the Potala Palace to the Norbulingka, the summer palace. Whenever this happened, they used the finest horses, two of each, and their colors matched. Two horses, bays, two grays, two chestnuts, and two roans all carried the nobles. They rode slowly, since they were important men."

Wangchuk nodded his head as Yonten translated, and stared out the window, as if he could still see this procession in his mind's eye. Then, Yonten switched to English.

"*I learned new thing, too,*" he began, "*Wangchuk remembered day His Holiness left for India. He said beautiful things, but to say in English difficult. That night, many people and so much confused. Nighttime they escaped. His Holiness dress like Chinese soldier. Wangchuk was told but he didn't know whether to believe. He was Chushi Gangdruk—Tibet army, you know—for long time. But this night was new kind of fear and duty. He was told stay near*

Lhasa, with other soldiers. Then His Holiness Dalai Lama made escape to India, but many of friends, other soldiers, not returned. Not long and he came India then Mustang to fight still. In the end, Nepali army made many difficulty. He gave up guns. Stayed here. Now many years home is Mustang, but still Tibet something there too. In dreaming, he is in Kham."

PART III

To see the greatness of a mountain, one must keep one's distance.

To understand its form, one must move around it.

To experience its moods, one must see it at sunrise and sunset, at noon and at midnight, in sun and in rain, in snow and in storm, in summer and in winter, and in all the other seasons.

He who can see the mountain like this comes near to the life of the mountain, a life that is as intense and varied as that of a human being.

—Lama Govinda

Royal Mustang Excursions

TSHAMPA AND I continued with our work into the winter, but as the months passed, there developed between us the dual sense of comfort and restlessness. I began to spend more time with Jomsom's other healers and to travel north to the Muktinath Valley. There, I met other local veterinarians and observed, eyes refreshed, the complex beauty of a culture not my own. I watched as Sonam, a lanky herder from the village of Putak, plunged his moxabustion irons into hot coals and coaxed the "excess heat" out of a yearling's hind end, and then returned a porter horse to soundness. There was gentleness in this act, even as the smell of scorched hair and blistering skin wafted through crisp mountain air. Some days, local men would demonstrate their horsemanship for me. They would race up and down the stretch of packed earth just below the Muktinath temple complex, limber in the saddle. Their calloused hands would reach down and pretend to snatch up *kathag* scarves from the ground as their mounts galloped underneath them. After such equestrian displays, the men would speak to me of summer horse races, and the joy of winning. I took notes on these acts and their meanings and made sketches of Sonam's treatments and the young men's acrobatics. But in my journal, I admitted to a certain weariness. What would become of these notes, these renderings? The anthropologist in me knew that all, for now, was in the gathering. But the writer in me longed for a sense of purpose— an overarching narrative that I could not yet sense.

After one such trip to Muktinath, I returned to Jomsom to find a letter waiting for me. The note from the Fulbright office in Kathmandu confirmed my sense that it was time to head back to the city for a spell. The issuance of my research permit for upper Mustang was still mired in

Home Ministry bureaucracy. Signatures and lobbying were required. This brief directive made the decision to leave Mustang for the deep months of winter easy, necessary even. Tshampa and Karma sent me off with a *kathag* wrapped around my neck and dried apples in my pockets.

I departed Mustang in late December with the hope that I would return to the mountains in early spring, permits for my travel to upper Mustang in hand. In the meantime, I would pass a couple of months in Kathmandu getting to know as many Loba as I could, continuing with language study, and speaking with other foreigners and Nepalis who had spent significant time in Mustang District. I knew that many people from upper Mustang, including the king and queen of Lo, passed much of the winter in the capital's more hospitable climes; other Loba transited through the valley on their way to trade in India. I was interested in speaking to those somewhat separated from daily life in Mustang, even if only temporarily, seasonally. What did they make of the movement between worlds?

I was also anxious to begin building rapport with some of the people who I hoped would lend my time in Lo a sense of form, and a semblance of home. And, after several months in the mountains, I was also looking forward to reconnecting with urban Nepal, seeing friends, and regaining a sense of privacy and anonymity that was not possible in Mustang. My friend Ken had offered me his apartment in the city while he made a trip back to the States to visit family. The thought of having a "room of my own"—at least for a short while—sounded incredibly appealing.

Early one morning after my arrival in Kathmandu, Manjushree Thapa, a young Nepali writer, met me for coffee. Manjushree and I sat in the courtyard of a hip Kathmandu café. We gulped caffeine greedily and spoke about novels, finding common ground in our tastes and experiences.

Manju and I had both spent our college years in Rhode Island—she at the Rhode Island School of Design. More importantly, we shared a connection to Mustang. Manju had spent two years living in Mustang in the early 1990s, working for the Annapurna Conservation Area Project, and she had published a collection of essays on the area called *Mustang Bhot in Fragments*. When I had discovered it in a Kathmandu bookshop,

Manju's slim book had been a gift. She had written of her time in Mustang with humility, and with attention to her place as a young woman bridging worlds. Although she was born in Kathmandu, Manju spent much of her young life in the United States, the daughter of a diplomat. English was her first language. Now that she had returned to Nepal, the pages of her book spoke of her personal struggles with being Nepali, finding a sense of self, purpose, and place within her country. Even before meeting her, and despite the differences in our experiences in Mustang, I felt a certain affinity.

Through conversations with both locals and foreigners traveling through the area, Manju's book articulated the cultural dissonance I had also felt among my agemates in Mustang and those of elder generations, as well as the separation—geographic, economic, and cultural—between lower and upper Mustang. Manju's vignettes also spoke to the paradoxes and failures of development efforts in Mustang—stories charted, by turns, through the various attempts by locals, lowland Nepalis, and foreigners to engage in the tricky business of engineering change, both technological and social.

I had searched Manju's book for details about horses, and had discovered with interest passages in which she described issues surrounding contested grazing lands. There were problems that evoked questions about the borders between private and public space, but that also spoke to the small details of subsistence: the price of hay, the human costs of a recent flood.

In arranging to meet Manju, I had hoped to hear more of her impressions of life in upper Mustang.

"I'm sure that people have told you that the king is an excellent horseman," said Manju, after I briefed her on my own research interests.

"Yes. I hope to meet him," I said.

"He is not that keen on speaking Nepali, but he does love his horses. The *raja* was always kind to me," Manju responded, referring to the king of Lo by his Nepali title. "But I think all of these changes have been difficult for him. There has been so much politics to deal with, so many expectations—not just from his people, but also from other Nepalis and foreigners—and a lot of empty promises in these past few years," she continued.

As in other moments, the mere mention of the king sparked a sense of longing in me—raw, romantic, deeply curious—and also an inkling of just how much I did not know about Mustang.

"While you're here in Kathmandu, though, you should talk with the junior *raja*, or *gyalchung*, as they call him locally," she went on.

"I would like that."

"Sometimes the *gyalchung* calls himself Ashok, his Hindu name. But his real name is Jigme, just like the king." Jigme was not alone in his bifurcated identity. Nation-building efforts in the previous thirty years had caused many Mustangi children to be given Nepali names by their schoolteachers in order to foster in these young citizens a greater sense of national identity. Hindu names were also easier for *rongba* teachers to pronounce.

"Jigme is pretty unassuming, for a *gyalchung*," Manju went on. "He was always helpful when I was working in Monthang. But he doesn't go to Mustang all that much anymore, mostly in the summertime. He's been running a carpet factory near Boudha for several years now." Manju leaned back in her chair and dropped her eyes.

I wondered, not *if* she missed Mustang, but *how* she missed it. I wondered where Mustang lived in Manju and how it had shaped her. How did her time there push the limits of what she knew and understood of herself, and her country? As I sat across the table from this young writer—Nepali, but still self-admittedly finding her way in Nepal—I thought about how the elements carve us, like sculpture.

"Jigme and his cousin Tsewang recently opened a trekking company," Manju continued. "Royal Mustang Excursions, that's what it is called. They started this venture recently, to help create local employment from the tourists passing through Mustang. You've probably realized that most of the economic benefits from tourism aren't reaching Lo," said Manju, leaning in toward me.

"I have. Most of the trekking groups bring in their porters, guides, and cooks from outside Mustang, right?"

"Yes, and a lot of the pack animals that are used for tourist trips to Lo come from lower Mustang. Even though people in Lo have started charging for hay and grazing rights for the horses and mules, the costs to them still outweigh the benefits."

"What about the money that is supposed to be going to upper Mustang from the government, through ACAP? Do you think that money will ever materialize?" I asked.

Manju sighed. "I had a lot of hope that ACAP would be helpful in upper Mustang, but the situation is pretty inflamed just now. There is not a lot of trust."

Manju also affirmed my notion that the government was supposed to give ACAP sixty percent of the money from trekking permit fees, but that most of that money was not reaching Mustang. The government contends that they never formally committed to such an agreement and that funds must first go through the King Mahendra Trust for Nature Conservation. They take their cut, then pass it on to ACAP who take their cut in the Kathmandu and Pokhara offices before sending money to Mustang. As it was then, there was hardly enough money left to pay the staff. "The worst part of this is that most Loba know this—even the old villagers. It doesn't make the local ACAP staff's difficult job any easier," Manju continued.

"What about the king or the *gyalchung*? Can't they do anything about this?" I asked.

"They're in a really difficult position," she said. "I suppose they could, but it is always doubtful that the government would actually listen to them. And as it is, the relationship between ACAP and the royal family of Lo is already a bit strained," replied Manju.

"I can imagine."

We were silent for a time. Manju stirred milk into her coffee, listless, before scribbling the *gyalchung's* phone number and address on a scrap of paper. "I'm sure he would meet you."

"Ok, I'll call."

"Since you are interested in horses," Manju continued, "you should also meet Raju Bista. Technically, he's the *gyalchung's* nephew, but in age they're more like cousins. Raju lives in the village of Ghami. He's spent more time in Mustang than Jigme or Tsewang," said Manju, "and he loves horses. Sometimes he comes to Kathmandu." I said I would try to contact him as well.

I called Jigme the next day. My brief, if bouncy, introduction was met by
a thick, resonant voice. I told him I was interested in horses and that I
would be traveling to Lo soon. We spoke in Nepali at first, and he
answered my queries in a tone that I would come to know as the pitch
he reserved for strangers, the pitch of a carpet salesman.

"I don't know much about horses. My father is the real expert—"

"Yes, I've heard. I hope to meet him," I said.

"Well, he loves his horses. Maybe he will have time to talk with you
when you get to Monthang."

"Jigme-la, would it be possible to meet you?" My voice cracked. I was
more nervous than I thought I would be.

"Of course. Please, come to my home," he offered. The crackling of
Kathmandu phone lines muffled his voice. Despite the distraction, we
arranged to meet for dinner in a few days.

On the evening of our engagement, I bicycled northeast out of town,
toward Jigme's home. By the time I reached his neighborhood by the
Boudha *stupa*, the dusk sky was an aqueous blood orange, deep cerulean
at the edges. Fruit vendors wheeled their basket-heavy bicycles home,
their unsold tangerines the same color as the sunset. An unseasonable
shower earlier in the day had washed away the pollution, leaving the
Himalayas sparkling in the distance.

Boudha, or Boudhanath as it is sometimes called, takes its name from
the *stupa* at its center: a monument to the Buddha. Long a place of pilgrimage for Nepalis and Tibetans, Hindus and Buddhists, the Tibetan diaspora and the rural to urban migration in Nepal have transformed Boudha.
When viewed from the air, Boudha reveals itself as a perfect *mandala*, a
cosmic map, and a way of conceiving the universe. As the story goes,
toward the end of Shakyamuni Buddha's life, his disciples asked what they
should do with his body once he passed away. The Buddha answered by
taking a begging bowl in each hand and turning them over, one atop the
other. His message was an elemental one: emptiness upon emptiness.
What becomes of this human form is of little consequence. It is a vessel,
nothing more. But upon this acted metaphor was built many an edifice.
The *stupa* was born. Here at Boudha, great whitewashed mounds are

crowned with iconic technicolor renderings of the Buddha's eyes, staring off in the four directions, and aflutter with thousands of prayer flags. Its eggshell sides are painted with arcs of saffron and marigold. Only a century ago, the eyes were majestically painted in lapis lazuli and gold leaf.

At Boudha, pilgrims' feet shuffle along slate, welcoming the day and walking the evening down. Travelers from places like the high valleys of Humla and Dolpo in the west and Walangchung Gola in the east circle the *stupa* beside each other. The distances between their homelands are charted in the varied hues of women's aprons and the inflections of their Tibetan dialects, as they pray, gossip, and laugh their way around the *stupa*'s base, earning merit and passing time. Tibetan grandmothers walk the circle, their silver plaits interwoven with pastel ribbons and joined at the bottom like clasped hands, while men of all ages cluster in Boudha's many tea stalls and beer parlors, sipping fermented millet out of plastic jugs, lengths of metal piping as straws.

On this cool winter evening, I circumambulated the shrine, spinning the dented prayer wheels that belt its girth. Tibetan and Newari traders clapped closed the wooden windows of their shops.

I was early for my meeting with *gyalchung* Jigme. I propped myself on one of the corners of the *stupa*, facing the Tibetan Buddhist monastery behind which he lived. I sat, letting the edge of day slip away like a memory. How does one greet a *gyalchung*? I wondered.

I walked through the gates of the large Sakya monastery as the monks were sitting down to dinner. The doors to the main temple had been bolted shut, but activity burst forth from the kitchen. Geysers of steam released from pressure cookers. Novice monks crashed tinny pots against each other. The smell of *dhal* and garlic rose up toward the night sky. Beyond the *gompa* stood the building to which Jigme had directed me when we spoke on the phone. The second floor was well lit, and I could see the outlines of people through the window. I ascended the stairs and rang the doorbell.

I was greeted by a stout young woman named Tuli who was the cook and maidservant to the queen. "Tuli *didi*," I whispered as she led me down a corridor toward the sitting room, "What should I call the *gyalchung*? Do I call him Jigme? Ashok? Something else?"

"Most foreigners just call him Jigme. Some of the Nepalis who come to visit call him Ashok. But everyone from Mustang calls him *gyalchung*— little king. You can call him what you like, though. He's friendly. Don't worry," she smiled.

Tuli motioned for me to slip off my shoes and pointed to a Tibetan tapestry hung over a door. "Go on in," she urged. Upon entering I was met by a handsome man in his late thirties, his hair as dark as India ink and just as slick, his eyes like almonds. *Gyalchung* Jigme's chiseled profile had an aristocratic air, but his direct, curious gaze met mine, dissipating my nervousness.

"Welcome," said the *gyalchung*, in English. "Come sit down. Tuli will bring tea," he continued, switching to Nepali.

"*Gyalchung*-la, it is a pleasure to meet you," I offered, with respect. "I have heard so much about you and your family, and about Lo. I hope to go there soon."

"You said on the phone that you would be traveling there as soon as your permit was ready. When will that be?"

"I'm hoping to have a permit by early spring, but it might take longer," I said.

Just then, the curtain to the room parted and in walked a tall man, younger than Jigme but strikingly similar in profile. When he spoke, his voice bore a similar resonance, but he spoke in pitch-perfect English, mastered in a Darjeeling boarding school. This was Tsewang.

"Are you the person who's come to Mustang to study horses?" he said, bypassing small talk.

Yes," I answered.

"Well, you are talking to the wrong people. We both know how to ride, but you should be talking to the king, or to my cousin, Raju."

Tsewang and Jigme quickly began rattling off the names of several other individuals for me to consult with about horses. It was clear that my research in Lo would be fruitful, and that I would want to spend time in villages throughout the restricted area, not just in Monthang.

"Those are the experts," Jigme continued, "but really everyone in Lo knows more about how to care for horses than people from lower Mustang—the Thakalis and the people from the Baragaon area. They can go to the government clinic if something is really wrong, but we have to be more self-sufficient."

"Most people know how to take care of the hot and cold diseases, and to bleed a horse from its tongue, but not much more," said Tsewang. As he and Jigme spoke, I thought about the fact that even though it seemed like the average horse owner, whether in Lo or in Jomsom, knew how to solve the same sorts of problems, they all vied with each other for who knew more.

"The only person in lower Mustang who really knows anything about horses is Mayala, but that's because he spent so much time in Tibet, with the nomads," said Jigme. "Sometimes my father even calls him to help if one of his horses is really sick."

"I've tried to talk with Mayala. He's not that friendly."

"No. He's tough," said Tsewang. "But he knows a lot."

"More than Tshampa Ngawang," Jigme added. "You said you'd studied a bit with him."

"Yes."

"He's a good *amchi*, but he doesn't know much about horse care, really, even though he has borrowed some of my father's horse books." It was as if Jigme could see straight through to the ambivalence I'd felt during my stay at the Dancing Yak.

The more the three of us spoke, the more I got the feeling that these two men were separated from Mustang life in a way that I had not originally anticipated. Jigme's knowledge of Mustang seemed to me whole, and yet abstract, as if he were piecing together fractured memories of his childhood with the current events he heard in passing from other Loba who came to pay their respects to him and his family. I had a difficult time imagining him settling a domestic dispute or mitigating between villages about land ownership, as his father was reputed to do.

At that moment, Tuli came in with three steaming plates of *momo*, Tibetan dumplings. She winked at me, and smiled. For as hospitable as Jigme and Tsewang were being—and as accommodating to my questions—at that moment I felt like getting up and following Tuli into the kitchen.

"We have not seen as much economic and social benefit from tourism as we thought we would," said Jigme, as if responding to a script.

"I know about the government money, the problems—"

"Those won't be resolved anytime soon," Tsewang interjected. "But that is one of the reasons why we started our trekking company. Some people think they're preserving Lo by putting so many restrictions on travel there, but it is just an excuse to make money at our expense." Tsewang went further to explain to me some of the problems between ACAP, the government, and the local people, all of which I had heard from various sources.

"ACAP is trying," Jigme added. "But they don't have much funds. Some people in Lo are not happy."

Jigme sipped from his cup of tea while Tsewang picked at the remains of his plate of *momo*. After a time, Jigme changed the subject.

"We can certainly help you when you come to Lo. I can introduce you to my father. Is there anything else I can help you with?"

"Well, there is one thing," I said. I sensed that Jigme wanted to get on with his evening, but I asked anyway. "When I was still in America I started studying Tibetan language with a monk from Sikkim. He was a good teacher, but I could only take lessons for two months. I really want to learn how to speak Tibetan, especially the local dialect from Lo. In lower Mustang I can get along with Nepali, but I know things are different up north. Is there anyone you know who could work with me on the language?"

Jigme and Tsewang bantered back and forth for a few minutes in their local dialect of Tibetan. As soon as they seemed to agree on something, Tsewang rose to leave.

"We've thought of someone. He's a monk at the Sakya monastery here and he's worked with other researchers before. His name is Wangdi. Tsewang has gone to fetch him."

I checked the clock on the wall. It was already nearing nine, late by Nepali standards.

"Won't we be disturbing him? I can meet him another time," I said.

"He won't be disturbed," said Jigme. "He'll be happy to help."

A few minutes later, a tired looking monk with large ears, a broad fore-head, and a long face came into the room, trailing behind Tsewang. When he saw Jigme, he bent low and took off his woolen cap, whispering a polite greeting to his *gyalchung*. He turned to me and we agreed to meet three days a week for language lessons in his quarters just outside the Boudha gate. He had worked with other foreign scholars, and spoke some English and German, as well as fluent Nepali. The match seemed perfect.

The moon had long since risen by the time I took leave of the *gyalchung* and Tsewang. Wangdi and I walked out together before heading to our respective homes.

"What did you think of the *gyalchung*?" said Wangdi once we stepped outside the *gyalchung's* compound.

"He seems very nice," I said, not sure what Wangdi expected me to say. "What do *you* think of the *gyalchung*?" I responded.

Wangdi laughed. "Sometimes foreigners get nervous around him. Others think they're special just because they get to meet him. But really he's just a man, in *samsara* like the rest of us." I was struck by Wangdi's candor, and immediately took a liking to him.

"He has a good heart," Wangdi continued. "But sometimes it is diffi-cult for him to know what to do. Things are changing in Mustang, and not everyone believes the royal family has the right ideas for Mustang's future. I am loyal to them, and they have been good to me. But in Lo there is *tension* sometimes." Wangdi had shed all traces of the demure monastic I had seen in the *gyalchung's* drawing room. "But you're proba-bly not interested in politics. Just horses, right?" Wangdi snickered, glee-fully, with a sense of humor and irony that I would come to greatly enjoy.

"Right!" I said, "See you next week." I cycled toward town by the light of the moon.

HEAT AND DUST

THE SKY had just begun to lighten as I left my apartment near the Bhat Bateni temple and walked east. Wangdi and I had arranged to meet near the tourist buses promptly at six-thirty and travel to Pokhara together.

The madwoman who made her home near the temple had already begun her morning ablutions, worn and dirty hands purifying this corner of Kathmandu. An "untouchable sweeper"—barefoot with her *saree* rolled up, revealing thick, varicosed ankles—coaxed the street clean during these dry months of winter.

I kept walking. Fog clung to the ground and thickened the air. The doors to neighborhood tea stalls had just begun to open. Portable gas stoves hissed at the hands of the old men who tended them. There, breath and steam and boiled milk melded, an atmosphere at once warm and cold. Vegetable sellers wrapped themselves in shawls and squatted close to the ground, eyes peering over piles of damp spinach, and eggplants glossy with dew. The night dogs slept near garbage piles, too docile, like vampires.

In Ghaididara, the pot-bellied owner of a shack that sold tandoori-style chicken wrapped in yesterday's newspaper had already begun to knead dough for the day's *naan*. Bats hung from telephone wires near the police headquarters, their small bodies the color of brackish water. Bamboo shoots, thick as oboes, spilled over the cement wall that surrounds the Nepali Royal Palace. Taxi drivers slept in their cars, mouths agape, chins tilted back, feet propped up on the dashboard.

I turned the corner onto Kantipath and the quiet of morning dissipated. Rows of buses were lined up head to tail like a train without tracks.

Drivers blessed their buses for a safe journey, splashing holy water on bumpers, stringing marigolds from rearview mirrors. Ticketmasters hawked last-minute fares and helper *bhai* tossed bags up to the tops of the buses. Even though high tourist season had passed, the buses to Pokhara were crowded with Nepalis who could afford the extra rupees that bought them velour seats and bus stereos blaring the latest Hindi film soundtrack.

Wangdi waited for me on the corner, just where we had planned to meet. His long, thin face looked flushed, an uneven watercolor wash of pink against the brown of his skin. He raised his hand and waved. Even though I was on time, I knew from experience that Wangdi would arrive before me.

"So cold," said my friend, as greeting. He blew into his palms and rubbed them together. "It will be warmer in Pokhara."

"And the air will be better, too," I answered. Kathmandu in the winter made most people's lungs ache, as the cool air sank down into the valley, layering inverted pollution atop the city dwellers. On most days, though, the haze dissolved under noontime sun, leaving only pale light and exhaust.

During my language sessions with Wangdi, we had developed an easy rapport. We spent more time chatting in Nepali about horses, politics, and history, though, than we did on my acquisition of Lo's dialect of Tibetan. But what language I learned was useful, and nicely couched in the context of questions I wanted to ask people in Lo.

As we passed time together three afternoons a week, I learned that Wangdi came from a poor family in Lo Monthang. He had spent much of his youth as a shepherd in the pastures surrounding the walled city until his family decided to make him a monk at Monthang's Chöde Monastery. Wangdi excelled at his religious studies and despite his lack of formal secular education he was recognized by the abbot and later the king as a young man with a mind for scholarship. And so Wangdi was sent from Lo to the Kathmandu monastery belonging to Sakya Trizin Rinpoche, a revered Tibetan lama with family ties to Mustang. Wangdi settled into city life and continued his studies.

Wangdi had gained a reputation as a translator and guide for both foreign and Nepali social scientists, archaeologists, anthropologists, and historians interested in Mustang. He chose to live outside the monastery in a small apartment that afforded him some space to entertain and educate guests. In some senses, he was a monk on the fringes, never fully able to turn away from the householder life. Wangdi's father had passed away some years ago, and his mother died the same year I met him. His younger brother had a slow way about him, and his younger sister was married to "a lout with a drinking problem," as my friend described, clearly bitter. Wangdi had taken on the responsibility of educating his nieces and nephews, buying the family clothes, and sending cash when he could.

Each winter Wangdi's sister and many other Lobas traveled south from Lo Monthang to Pokhara in order to trade sweaters and other goods in India. Horses and mules were brought along to transport supplies, but yak never left Lo, as they suffered at the lower altitudes. In the lean times of winter, their sandpaper tongues scoured the frozen ground for stubble in pastures north and west of Monthang. Cows, sheep, and goats nibbled the soles of old shoes, plastic bags, and the grains spent from making *chang*.

These days, fewer and fewer people and animals wintered in Lo. These annual migrations south were just one illustration of how life in Mustang was irrevocably changed after the Chinese occupation of Tibet. Historically, many people from Lo had traveled north to Tibet each winter. There, on the vast, high altitude plains of Tibet, the pastures were not abundant, but they were significantly better than the gullied valleys of Lo. The closing of the border by the Chinese in 1960 forced Loba—and others like them across northern Nepal—to change their seasonal migrations. Without access to these Tibetan pastures, people in Lo now faced a perpetual shortage of winter fodder, which, in turn, compromised and diminished the herds that remain crucial forms of wealth and sustenance in these tough trans-Himalayan environs. This loss of access to grazing land, combined with the hardship of the Khampa years, had made the delicate job of stewarding a marginal landscape all the more difficult. Now, for the three months of winter, many Lobas lived as itinerant herders in Pokhara, negotiating with local farmers to allow their highland horses and mules to graze on what was left of harvested rice paddies. After the Tibetan New Year, the Lobas loaded up their animals with a year's supply of rice, sugar, oil, and lentils, and began the long trek north again.

As a Loba who had spent most of the last fifteen years living in Kathmandu, Wangdi saw clearly the ways in which upper Mustang's relative remoteness, lack of educational opportunities, and the cost of life in a high, dry place had kept many people hovering just above abject poverty. His sister and others like her lived marginally, balancing the little their land produced with itinerant labor. Like many others, Wangdi resented the ways things had turned out since upper Mustang was opened to foreign tourists. He saw that the lives of most people in upper Mustang had not improved. Yet Wangdi blamed this failure as much on the lack of business imagination and inability to see past "old traditions" of many Lobas as he did on Thakali and Tibetans who had the good fortune of living on the trekking trail, and the government who perpetually neglected and yet profited from its highland populations.

During one of our language lessons, Wangdi had mentioned that he was going to see his sister in Pokhara and asked if I wanted to come along. It was a chance to learn more about what horses meant to local livelihood, how they defined Mustang life and were cared for. Now, on this day of departure, Wangdi teased me: "You sure you're ready to go spend time with the Lobas? You know, they're not as civilized as those people you've been hanging around with recently, " he jested.

"Of course I want to go meet the Lobas and see the horses at Kaji Pokhari. Why else would I have gotten up so early?" I said, smiling.

"Well, get ready for rocks in your rice," said Wangdi as we boarded our bus. This was a signal of rough existence, a life meted out in handfuls of government subsidy grain to people on the margins.

Although Wangdi was just thirty-five, he traveled like an old man. Before we settled into our seats, he produced a handkerchief from the folds in his robes and dusted off both of our seats before laying the small piece of cloth on his headrest. "Lice," he muttered. Although the bus would stop for tea and a meal along the way, Wangdi refused the roadside fare, instead nibbling on Tibetan bread and hard-boiled eggs that he had carried from home.

The bus wound its way out of the valley, past petrol stations and barbershops and through suburban towns: homes with tin roofs; homes made of bricks, red earth, and thatch. The bus lurched past rice paddies, planted yet parched. Terraces textured this land, so worn by human labor.

Although the journey between Kathmandu and Pokhara measured only about 125 miles, it would take us six hours to get there. Aside from walking through the hills and mountains, there is no better way to educate oneself about rural Nepali life than to take a bus trip. As Wangdi dozed, I watched women squatting by the banks of rivers, kneading and slapping clothes on flat stones, beating them clean. Others stooped over piles of rocks, pounding large stones into small stones with sledgehammers. They were making gravel for the stretches of highway washed away each year by monsoon. We passed groves of conifers and clusters of thick bamboo, evergreen hardwoods and unwieldy poinsettia bushes. I watched as barefoot children, limber as gymnasts and browned by the sun, climbed up into trees to cut fodder for their livestock, sickle blades of roughly smithed metal arched like moons. Sometimes grandmothers did the same, though to a slower rhythm.

As we rode along, I recalled that first bus trip I had taken to Pokhara with my college peers. Although I was staring out the window at the same landscape, I could read it differently now. I had more Nepali words to describe what I saw: *kachiyaa* for the sickle and *sal* for the trees; *kipat* for communal lands that had become threatened by Nepal's ruling elites through *birta*, land grant practice; *Muluki Ain* for the laws of caste and class that divided Nepalis into haves and have nots, the "enslavable" from the "non-enslavable," and *janajati* for the country's indigenous and ethnic folk. Still, much of what passed before my eyes was a window onto a world I had hardly begun to know—and one that was distinct from the worlds I was getting to know in Mustang.

As we neared Pokhara, I marveled that Mustang was also a part of *this* Nepal. Its fluted cliffs and dry air were so different from this heat-soaked tropical landscape. I wondered what it meant for someone from Mustang to adjust to life here. The chill of the Kathmandu morning seemed yet another world away.

"How do people from Mustang stand the heat?" I asked Wangdi as we sipped sodas during one of many roadside stops. "The air is so different here."

"Oh, people get used to it. Before, some Lobas were scared to go south because they heard they would get sick. Sometimes they did. Hot diseases, from the bugs and the water—the different elements. But now they've gotten used to it. No choice, really. The horses don't like it much either, but what can you do? People from Monthang used to think Jomsom was far away. Everything changes. People. Environment. Ideas. Ten years ago there were no mosquitoes in Jomsom, but now they come in the summer."

"How different is life in Lo now from the way things were when you were young?" I asked.

"That's a big question. Sometimes I don't think I know how to answer it, since I don't really live in Mustang now. But in general, there's more desire, more inflation, more people disobeying the king and doing what they want." Even though I had yet to meet the king of Lo, I had heard about such shifts from other Lobas I'd met in Kathmandu. Lo was experiencing a sea change. I could see it reflected in the eyes of *gyalchung* Jigme as much as I could hear it in Wangdi's assessments.

"When I was small," Wangdi continued, "people didn't travel as much—especially after the Khampa came to Mustang. We made do. My younger brother was a horse shepherd in Monthang for seven years, just like my father had been for much of his life. Until recently, Loba did not like to go south because besides the heat and dust there was the language problem. Not many people spoke Nepali. Sweater trade in India was difficult, too, because people did not speak Hindi. Sometimes, even though we think we know what we're doing now, we can still act like *leba jangu*, green brains, stuck in the past." In Tibetan, being a "green brain" implies intellectual laziness and stubbornness. Today it has also come to imply the generation gap and a lack of modern sentiment.

"But Loba are getting smarter," Wangdi continued. "It is not an easy life in Monthang or in Pokhara in the winter. But even though it is hard work, this migration is good in some ways because it is allowing people from Lo to expand their minds in more directions. The same is true about tourism. Even though we haven't gotten much money from tourism, it has been good for people in Lo to meet foreigners. Before, people were busy during the harvest and then bored or just gossiping about each other for the rest of the year. Now things are different, people are thinking differently."

The bus honked and swayed as it pulled into the Pokhara station: an unpaved plot, littered with old tires and bus skeletons. Men loitered near makeshift teashops constructed out of scrap tin and blue plastic tarps. They clutched signs and business cards for tourist hotels beside Phewa Lake and waited for the afternoon arrivals.

I'd spent enough days stuck in Pokhara waiting out canceled flights to Jomsom that I had begun to dread the place. No matter how comfortable I became speaking Nepali, no matter how at home I felt in Nepal, I would remain a target for the crowd at the Pokhara bus stop: a tip to be earned, a scam in the making. But when I arrived in Pokhara with Wangdi, things were different.

"Come, follow me, before the flies land on us!" Wangdi said as we grabbed our bags and headed out of the bus park. I did as I was told, and watched out of the corner of my eyes as the men who commanded the tourist racket wondered who I was and what I was doing with a monk. Some whispered in Nepali, speculating on the nature of our relationship. Was I buying him a ticket to America? Had I fallen in love with him? Was he using me for a visa?

A few called out.

"Eh, madam? Like Buddhism? I take you special temple."

"All American likes monks, no? I have special monk price, special monk hotel." More than anything else, the comments made me realize something of Pokhara's provincial nature. In Kathmandu, the sight of foreigners in the company of Tibetan Buddhist monks—not to mention motorcycling monks or monks wearing Rolex watches—was passé, just another fragment of Kathmandu's postmodern montage. Here, the sight still gave people something to talk about.

Wangdi walked quickly toward Mahendra Chowk, an intersection marked by a statue of Nepal's King Mahendra. Pigeons squatted on the

monarch's head, preened themselves from their perch on his hat of pea-
cock plumes rendered in stone.

Once we'd distanced ourselves from the bus station, Wangdi hailed
a taxi. We climbed in, our bodies sinking into a lumpy back seat,
springs poking through in places. As was Pokhara fashion, the inside
door panels of the taxi had been covered with laminated posters: a
Swiss chalet near the passenger's seat, rows of flowers in the Luxem-
bourg Gardens in back.

We drove on. Every once in a while, Wangdi would give the taxi
driver directions until we finally pulled off the paved road onto a pot-
holed dirt path.

"Here," Wangdi tapped the driver on the shoulder. "We'll walk now."

Out beyond the bazaars and the bus stops, the tourist hotels that line
Phewa Lake, Pokhara shed its city garb and became more like a village,
stitched together by fields and kinship. A pair of old women watched us
pass, their eyes shaded from afternoon sun by matching dishtowels
folded atop their heads. A Brahmin schoolmaster passed us on his bicycle, his white shirt miraculously clean. Bony, boyish knees poked out to
either side as he pedaled.

"See that field over there, and the little house next to it?" Wangdi
motioned southeast. "That's where my sister lives. The fields just beyond
the house are filled with Mustang animals."

"But I don't see anyone from Mustang," I said.

"We will, soon enough." Wangdi was right, of course. As we neared
the house, the monk called out in his native tongue, signaling our arrival.
In a few minutes, half a dozen Loba children surrounded us, their cheeks
still chapped from the Mustang wind and sun. Wangdi reached down
and patted each one on the head. These were his nieces and nephews, as
well as the children of his neighbors. A woman poked her head out from
the house. Her face was as long as Wangdi's though more wrinkled and
worn. Nyima Wangmo, Wangdi's sister, smiled beautifully and then covered her mouth in shyness.

"Come inside," she welcomed us.

I listened to Nyima Wangmo and Wangdi catch up as we ate a simple
meal of corn mash and chili paste. I could not help thinking that this was

a woman who had taken her share of beatings, physical and emotional. She had a moth-like fragility to her.

"When did you get here from Monthang?" I asked Nyima Wangmo.

"About a month ago. We'll stay for another two before heading home," she said as she poured us cups of lukewarm salt-butter tea.

"Do you live with the same people every year, or do you move around?"

"That depends on how much they want to charge us for rent," she explained. "Right now we pay 400–500 rupees per month—a lot more than last year." Although a small sum by most standards, this was a lot of cash for people who depended as much on their own harvests and barter as they did on hard currency for survival. "It keeps going up each year," she continued.

"Do you have to pay the owners of the fields, too, for letting the horses graze?" I asked.

"We don't pay per animal, but if the animals go into a field that has been planted or roped off, then we have to pay 100 rupees an animal for each day they do this, and double at night because they can eat more," Nyima Wangmo answered.

"But even though we don't pay rent for the grazing land, the quality of the land and grass keeps going down, and the places we are allowed to graze our animals keep getting smaller. This year is the worst year I can remember. When we first started coming to Pokhara, our animals could graze in the whole area behind the houses. Now there are more houses and some places are fenced off and filled with water buffalo, gardens, and some new rice paddies." Nyima Wangmo looked tired as she spoke. She rested her back against the walls of her small, makeshift home and wrung her hands in her lap.

"So we have to move farther away each day for grazing," she continued. "Now we have to travel an hour away just to graze the horses. The men are taking turns sleeping out there with the horses some nights because they have to go so far to find good grass now, and it is too much work to come and go."

"That sounds like difficult work," I responded. "How many people are here to watch the animals?"

"Oh, in our party, about ten. But not all of us can watch the animals. Some of us have to watch the children!" As if on cue, her daughter and son wandered in, accompanied by their cousins and friends. While Nyima Wangmo looked after the children, Wangdi suggested we go see the horses.

"It will take us some time to find them," he said, "and there is not much of the day left. Tokme Bista is here, too. We'll go see the animals and then talk with him," Wangdi suggested. Tokme was known as an excellent, thoughtful shepherd who loved horses. He often spent the winter in Pokhara with the animals instead of in India.

I followed Wangdi out of the house. We walked along irrigation ditches and rice paddy walls in search of the horses. In time, Mustang's shaggy ponies came into view. Some looked mangy, and none of them looked very healthy. A few were pregnant, their bellies bulging with the weight of new life.

"Will they give birth here or in Monthang?" I asked, stroking one pregnant mare's neck.

"The lucky ones will wait until Monthang. It is difficult for them to walk, but it is more difficult for the foals to survive their first weeks down here. Too hot, and the water is no good."

Wangdi and I found Tokme resting under a tree, out near the harvested rice paddies dotted with Mustang's horses. He wore a "Ford Mustang" baseball hat—the gift of a tourist—and sported a faded T-shirt with an image of a prancing black stallion on the front. He smiled widely when I told him that I was interested in what he knew about horses.

"If you want to know about horses, you should come to Lo," said Tokme. "This place is just like a horse hotel. None of us are at home here. The horses don't like the water or the grass. They get skinny."

"Do they get sick here often? What do you do if that happens?" I asked.

"They do get sick. Sometimes the chemicals that farmers put in the fields to kill bugs that eat their rice end up killing our horses, or at least giving them stomach problems. I can take care of some of the problems, but not all of them. If a horse needs its tongue bled or if it eats a poisonous grass in Lo, I know exactly what to do. But I don't know as well what to do here," Tokme explained, "because it is not my place. If a horse gets sick here, sometimes it dies and sometimes the government veterinary technicians can help." I noted that location could influence the treatment and outcome of a sickness as much as the skill of a healer. Furthermore, the skepticism that people from Mustang felt for government veterinarians seemingly transformed into a certain kind of trust when they were out of their element in the lowlands.

We chatted with Tokme until near dusk, and then started a slow walk home, through dry fields and along paddy walls.

"What was it like when you were watching horses in Monthang? When you were small," I asked Wangdi as we walked along the raised earth edges of parched rice paddies.

"In summer, when the grass was good, I would watch the horses all day," Wangdi began. "During the first month of summer, we would bring the horses to the grazing area at the beginning of the day and then take them home at dusk. During the second month, we would bring a tent and stay out with the animals. But we only watched the horses that did not have foals, and no stallions. That would have caused too much trouble.

"During the first and second months of summer we would sometimes take the horses east about an hour outside of Monthang to let them lick salt from a place that was like a dried ocean," Wangdi continued. I had heard of this custom before. The Lobas' horses were running their rough tongues and warm muzzles along the bottom of the ancient Tythes Sea that rose up eons ago to form the Himalayas.

"This was also the time that we would collect our wages from the villagers. They called us 'salt and butter beggars' because that is what we got in exchange for watching the horses."

"How many horses did you watch?" I asked.

"Between two and three hundred, probably."

"And in the winter, what would happen then? I know the yak used to go to Tibet, but what about the horses?"

"After the fall harvest, the community responsibility became a household responsibility. Each family looked after their own horses. This worked, because we needed horses to help with harvest and threshing the grain. It was cheaper because people could feed their horses hay from their own fields, instead of having to pay someone to watch them eat out in the pastures. If it were late summer now, people would be picking grass from their fields to give to their horses, and make hay. They would be picking a grass called *yurma* from the barley crop. It has whisker-like threads that turn to flowers with white blossoms if they are not picked, but if they are, they can help feed animals when we most need hay.

"Other grasses are also picked, like the *gyal-leh* that grows at the edges of fields. We pick these and dry them for hay," Wangdi paused. "But these days, ACAP has tried to tell us that we shouldn't pick these grasses from the barley fields to feed the animals because they think it decreases the harvest. But they can't tell the difference between the barley and the grasses that grow near the barley. They don't know our systems. Actually, most of the men in Monthang probably couldn't tell the difference between the grasses and the barley stalks either. Mostly, women do this work."

If it weren't for the humidity that lingered in the air and the *saree*-clad women carrying water jugs on their heads in the distance, I would have thought I was in Monthang, so intricate and local was Wangdi's knowledge.

But, then, Wangdi no longer lived in Monthang. To what extent did his recollections speak *only* of how things used to be, of what people used to know? The dry rice fields and scruffy ponies seemed out of place, yet signaled how things were now. I was beginning to feel an even greater sense of urgency and a deepening desire to visit Lo myself, and try to patch together this tapestry of change and continuity that was, and is, Mustang.

Am I a "Conservation"?

AFTER MY TRIP to Pokhara with Wangdi, I returned to Kathmandu and continued with the routine of interviews, language lessons, and the seemingly interminable wait for my upper Mustang permit. I still was planning on returning to Mustang just after the Tibetan New Year, when many locals would also be heading back after a season of sweater trade in India. But for the time being, I awoke each morning to the tinny clatter of door-to-door salesmen peddling pressure cookers, temple bells ringing, and the soft winter calls of spiny babblers, a local bird.

One morning that winter, the phone in Ken's apartment rang at six-thirty sharp. A glint of sunlight had just begun to come in through thin cotton drapes. I picked up the receiver, still in the haze of sleep.

"Namaste. Sienna, is this you?"

"Tshampa-la?" I responded, recognizing his voice over the crackly phone line.

"Yes. I came from Mustang two days ago and then on the night bus from Pokhara. I came to visit an old friend. She's the one I've told you about, from the Peace Corps, the one who sponsors my daughter. I want you to meet her. Come to the big *pipal* tree near the sleeping Vishnu temple, up at Buddhanilkhanta. She stays near there. We will go for tea."

"Okay, I will be there soon," I answered.

"Come quickly, don't delay," commanded Tshampa. "We do not want to keep her waiting."

I did as instructed and went by taxi to the temple. A thick fog curled around the gate that kept non-Hindus out of the complex. I glimpsed Vishnu's supine form: cold, smooth stone surrounded by a moat, thick and green with algae. Several devotees wrapped in pale orange robes dotted the statue's forehead with vermilion powder and sprinkled marigolds on his feet and hands. Tshampa stood in front of the *pipal* tree. This giant sacred fig was a tangled mass of vines, trunk, and branches whose canopy spread nearly thirty feet in diameter.

Tshampa seemed overly excited to see me. "My friend is staying in a big house near here," he said. "It is not far." I followed Tshampa through the early morning fog, down the narrow, meandering lanes that led away from the temple, past family plots of rice and maize and a smattering of brick homes, both small and grand.

As we walked, Tshampa recounted the news from Mustang. He'd bought a new gray gelding with a white star and very auspicious cowlicks. It had snowed on *tshong gyug*, the local version of Tibetan New Year, signifying a fortuitous beginning to the next twelve-month cycle. The Eco-Museum had closed for the season as tourists had dwindled. These days, Karma was weaving blankets while Tshampa ground raw plants into new batches of medicine, the two of them working together in their sunny courtyard, sheltered from Mustang's terrific winds. Tshampa spoke about the ongoing construction plans for the new nunnery that was being built in the Muktinath Valley. He had been commissioned to carve and paint the nunnery's altar, and would spend a portion of the winter instructing young people from lower Mustang in woodcarving.

"We're getting close," said Tshampa, pointing to a large compound surrounded by bougainvillea vines. The home was a classically Rana-era construction. The Ranas were a family who had ruled Nepal for just over a century until 1951. They were an oligarchic lot who had also coveted certain symbols and forms of Western civilization, mostly filtered through their own encounters with the British Raj. Their palatial residences tended toward architectural excess, even as they were strangely, sometimes coldly, beautiful. Doric columns supported elaborate pediments and façades, entrance halls were sculpted in mosaic and marble, plush Victorian chairs sat conspicuously in Baroque dining rooms, and clawfoot bathtubs were present even in the eras before indoor plumbing.

"Whose house is this?" I asked Tshampa as we neared the gate.

"An old British lady. She's lived in Nepal for many years, but I don't think she speaks Nepali. This is where my friend stays when she comes."

We rang the bell and a dapper Nepali guard let us through the main gate. "Come right this way," he directed in British English.

"This is the day watchman," Tshampa whispered to me as we walked toward the front door. "My friend told me the old lady has two guards, a gardener, a driver, three women who clean and cook, and one person who knows how to make foreign food." Tshampa nicked off a count for each servant on his fingers. "Can you imagine? There is only one of her!"

The door flung open and a handsome woman in her late thirties greeted us. "Tshampa-la!" The woman threw open her pashmina stole and enveloped Tshampa. I could see him turning red beneath her embrace. Although he had many foreign friends, Tshampa, like most Nepalis, was not accustomed to Western-style greetings. He pulled away, and for the first time I had known him, he seemed shy.

"You must be Sienna," said Molly, Tshampa's old friend.

"It is great to meet you. I've heard a lot about you," I said.

"Oh no. Is Tshampa telling stories again?" she laughed. Tshampa and I followed his old friend through a cool entry hall bedecked with Nepali artwork and into a parlor. An electric heater buzzed in the corner—a relative luxury in the damp Kathmandu winter—and plush Tibetan carpets lined the floor. Molly motioned for us to sit, and we made ourselves comfortable on the rattan sofa.

"I'm not sure if Tshampa explained this to you," Molly began, "but I'm working for an education program at the World Wildlife Fund. I'm based in Washington DC, but one of the benefits of the job is that I can keep coming back to Nepal." We chatted in Nepali, for Tshampa's benefit, and I was impressed at her command of the language, for all the years since her Peace Corps training. Although it had been three years since she had last come to Nepal, she had lived here for much of the 1980s and seemed to possess both a deep knowledge of, and affection for, the country that had been her adopted home.

We sipped tea and chatted for a bit, before the conversation turned toward the specific reason for this visit. Molly and Tshampa had been discussing a fellowship program sponsored by the World Wildlife Fund for citizens of its member countries either to pursue advanced degrees in the West or to conduct research in their home regions. Molly thought that Tshampa should apply, with the hopes that such a grant would allow him to visit other *amchi* outside of Nepal, to learn more about how Tibetan medicine was being practiced in other parts of South Asia, and to understand how the challenges of being a traditional doctor in the modern world related to the need to conserve and protect the medicinal plants on which this medical system depends. But the application needed to be in English. Tshampa would need help to apply.

"Of course I'll help him with the application," I said immediately. At the time, I had no idea the time and effort this project would entail. Nor could I fully envision the transformations this fellowship would have on Tshampa's life and our working relationship, if he were to be selected. I did feel nervous, though, knowing that despite our successful working relationship, I had never collaborated with him on a piece of writing in English. I knew he would benefit from a chance to travel and do his own research about Tibetan medicine, *amchi* history, and medicinal plants, but I was also apprehensive about the effects that receiving the grant's relatively large stipend might have on his relationships with others from Mustang, or the impact it would have on *my* connections to others in Mustang. After all, it was a small place: people liked to talk, and gossiping about money earned, money wasted, and connections to foreigners were local pastimes.

The fact that he could have the opportunity for further study and for expanding his own vision seemed like reason enough to help. Finally, the filial obligation I felt, stemming from my time at the Dancing Yak, made it impossible for me to consider *not* helping Tshampa.

"The application is due in two weeks, so you will have to work quickly," said Tshampa's friend.

"Well, Tshampa, when do you want to start?" I asked.

"Morning. When we are alert. I'll do a ritual tonight, so we will start well and with the Buddha's blessings first thing tomorrow. I think we will be successful."

The next morning, my doorbell rang directly at seven. "Good morning!" Tshampa called out. "Ready to work?"

I showed Tshampa into the room where I'd set up my computer and grabbed my Nepali and Tibetan dictionaries, as well as some literature about Tibetan medicine. While I arranged myself at my computer, Tshampa organized a number of his own medical books on the table, along with reports and articles that had been written about him over the years. "I thought these might help with the English," he said.

"Good idea. Let's start by reading the directions for the application together," I said, flipping open the pamphlet his friend had given me. The instructions spoke of advanced education for conservation leaders in developing countries and promoting multidisciplinary approaches to conservation, natural resource management, and environmental policy as well as about "indigenous knowledge." I read aloud, translating this as best I could into Nepali.

"What do they mean by *conservation*?" Tshampa interjected. "Am I a *conservation*?"

"No." I couldn't help but chuckle, as telling as this malapropism was. "Conservation is not a person. It means using natural resources—things from the forest, water, medicinal plants—in a way that allows them to return for generations, and not get depleted because they are used too much or in the wrong way. *Amchi* medicine is similar to what they mean by 'indigenous knowledge.' I'd say you are a conservation*ist*, someone who helps to protect these things and who teaches others about conservation—like the way you instruct people who help you to gather medicinal plants."

"Sure. Of course I am. Is that all they're asking? That seems simple." There was ground truth to his assessment. To him, conservation seemed something inherently personal, even intuitive. But his initial comments also bore the marks of romanticism: the tendency, sometimes shared by professionals in the fields of conservation and development, to view so-called indigenous knowledge and traditional practices as inherently environmentalist in orientation, and also unchanging.

As we sorted through the application details, our discussion turned toward the relationship between conservation and development. Tshampa struggled, at first, to understand the connection between the concept "conservation" with what he understood *bikas*, the Nepali word for "development," to mean. Like other Nepalis, Tshampa connected "development" to material improvements like drinking water taps, paved roads, and dams, as well as to the waste and corruption sometimes associated with international aid. I tried to make concrete links between these abstract concepts, and to intuit how the idea of Tshampa's vocation would be evaluated by the selection committee.

"You need to explain why this project will help you be a better *amchi*. Will it help the whole environment of the Himalayas—people, plants, everything? You need to show how these things are related," I said.

"I also need to tell them how things have changed in my generation," answered Tshampa. I agreed.

"*Amchi* aren't just in Nepal," he went on. "Borders don't make sense in that way. Just like plants don't play politics." We looked at each other and started to laugh.

"Sure. But seriously, you do have to listen to politics, and politics are connected to conservation and *amchi* tradition. Think of *amchi* medicine in Lhasa now that the Chinese—"

"Ate Tibet."

"Yes, exactly."

"Or what about the ways that Nepali government health posts don't see *amchi* as real healers, even though government health workers never show up, just take their salaries, and go back to the lowlands?" said Tshampa.

"Right. But we have to think about how this relates to what the sponsor wants to hear in this application."

"Keep reading."

"*The primary factors in selection of scholars and fellows are demonstrated academic excellence in an area related to conservation or natural resource development; a comprehensive, clear, and feasible proposal including multidisciplinary study in your own country or region; and the integration of the proposed program into your academic and professional field and long-range goals,*" I read and again did my best to translate. It occurred to me that

Tshampa would not have any advantage in this respect. Although he had received a classical Tibetan education and was literate in Nepali, he had never attended a school, as such. If selected, he would be the first such didactic scholar to successfully apply for this fellowship. Most of the other applicants and recipients had been enrolled in postgraduate degree programs and had used the funding to return to their home countries to pursue thesis research. "They want to know how your research project will relate to your profession—what you've been trained for in your life."

The idea of a profession *per se* was also still new to Tshampa. "More words for the same thing," he said, frustrated and excited both.

"Maybe you should start by telling me what you would do if you could spend a year learning more about Tibetan medicine and *amchi*, and making a path for *amchi* development as you and other *amchi* think it should happen. I will write down what you say, and then we can go back over it to make sure we answer all their questions," I suggested.

"Good. I'll start, then." Over the next several hours, Tshampa spoke of his concern for the *amchi* tradition, by which he meant knowledge transmission as well as the quality of diagnosis, treatments, and medicines themselves now that raw materials and ready-made compounds were becoming expensive, Western medicine was available, and everyone needed cash to survive. He spoke about gathering plants with his father when he was young, and how the availability of plants, as well as local peoples' knowledge about them, had declined in recent years. Tshampa told stories about the great medical institutions in Tibet, the history of Tibetan medicine, and the book he wanted to write about the life histories of old *amchi* from Mustang. His prayers to the Medicine Buddha were interspersed with poetic descriptions of blue poppies and other rare medicinal plants, as described in Tibetan medical texts.

Tshampa went on to talk about his views of the differences between Western and Tibetan medicine. Although his exposure to Western medicine was limited, he conjectured about the ways each system could teach the other new things about mind and body, consciousness, and liberation from suffering. Tshampa said that, if granted this fellowship, he would spend time in Dharamsala, studying at the Tibetan Medical and Astrological Institute, to expand his own knowledge, in addition to conducting interviews and doing archival work. He also planned to visit Ladakh, Sikkim, Bhutan, and, if possible, Tibet. Without a sense of how *amchi* in other parts of the Himalayas were living and working, including a sense of the challenges they faced, how would it be possible to share knowledge and make a better future for the system of Tibetan medicine as a whole? He described with passion how these efforts at organization were the only way that Himalayan healers stood a chance of preserving their tradition and gaining governmental recognition for their contributions to health care, let alone to Nepal's diverse cultural heritage.

I remained quiet, but my fingers flew. I had never typed so fast in my life. In those kinetic hours, Tshampa spoke his vision through me. For the first time, I gleaned some sense of the true nature of translation: always an interpretation, and yet also always something bigger than oneself and the limits of one's own knowledge. After Tshampa finished, I scrolled through this massive brainstorm.

"Now, Tshampa, what I need to do is whittle. As you do with wood. We need to take all these ideas and make them into three pages in English."

"Thank you." For the first time in our relationship, Tshampa looked at me as a confidant. For that brief instant, we were equals.

I spent the next week refining Tshampa's words, snipping and cutting his fragments of clarity and strategy into a proposal under the title *Tibetan Medicine in the Himalayas: Sustainable Medicinal Plant Collection, Cultural Preservation, and Local Education*. We spent another week quibbling over details, correcting misunderstandings, and gathering letters of recommendation from Nepali and foreign scholars who had known Tshampa for years. We made photocopies of articles that had been published in academic journals and glossy travel publications that mentioned Tshampa, as well as copies of independent study project reports written by students who had worked with Tshampa. Finally, we delivered the application to the WWF office in Kathmandu, where they would send it to Washington DC. Tshampa handed the package to the office secretary. His hands shook.

"Good luck," said the secretary.

"Thank you," said Tshampa, regaining his composure. "I think we will be successful. I saw it in a dream."

One morning later that spring, before my return to Mustang, I received another phone call.

"Hello. Is this Sienna?" I recognized the lilting soprano as the WWF secretary. "This is the World Wildlife Fund Nepal Program calling. Miss Sienna, I wanted to inform you that we were just notified by Washington DC about the scholarships. We have sent a letter to Jomsom, but we wanted to let you know that Dr. Tshampa Ngawang received the award. His fellowship period can begin as soon as next month, if he likes."

"Thank you for calling," I hung up the phone and started jumping up and down. I had not felt this giddy and proud since I opened up my own letter of acceptance from the Fulbright commission the year before telling me that I could return to Mustang.

As the news settled in, I slowly began to gain a sense of the weight of this responsibility, not only what it meant in terms of Tshampa's accountability to his benefactors, but also what it would mean for us, for our friendship, and for his family. I would move on, back toward Mustang and eventually up to Lo. And Tshampa, upon hearing the news of his award, would pack his bags with changes of red and gold clothes, handmade medicines, Tibetan texts, and his Nepali passport, and head off on what he would come to call his "research pilgrimage." This scholarship presented Tshampa with a once-in-a-lifetime opportunity. In many senses, the award seemed to cement a certain karmic connection between me and Tshampa, as if the writing of this application and the news of his award left each of us filled, ready to move on from each other, as much as it also deepened our bond.

But Tshampa's scholarship also meant that the work of running the Dancing Yak would be left to Karma and her hired help. The clinic would be empty as well, his patients unseen for months at a time. Tshampa was moving forward with his dream, but it was unclear what this would come to mean for everyone else involved. And, although this scholarship would continue to bear fruit for both of us, opening us up to new types of collaboration, these projects and possibilities would leave our early conversations about horses feeling distant, primary, small, and yet somehow the most beautiful of them all.

Muledrivers and Kings

S EVERAL WEEKS after I got the call about Tshampa's fellowship, I found myself sitting in a dingy restaurant across from the Pokhara airport. A chilling drizzle fell outside. I had been stuck in Pokhara for three days already as bad weather had prompted a string of canceled flights to Jomsom, otherwise I would have enjoyed the cool rush of rain. But this weather meant more Pokhara days, indeterminate and languid, as I waited for the skies to clear and the tarmac to dry.

It was now March. Losar, the Tibetan New Year, had come and gone, and I was still awaiting my permit for upper Mustang. But I decided that I had been away from Mustang for long enough. I had spoken with *gyalchung* Jigme and Tsewang before leaving. The king and queen of Lo had already returned to Monthang, but Jigme said that his father would most likely be returning to Kathmandu later in the month, and that, if my timing were correct, it might be possible to meet the king of Lo as he and his entourage traveled south to Jomsom. Hearing of a possible chance meeting with the king was enough to make me pack my bags.

As it was, I had spent that morning being harassed by the Everest Airlines staff, trying to secure a seat on the proverbial "first flight"—which could be tomorrow morning, or in a week's time. Precipitation progressed from drizzle to downpour, dampening my spirits. The bored men who manned the ticket counters were hopeless against a swelling tide of unsatisfied customers. Rain dripped in through the shoddy building, concrete threatening to return to water and sand. Nothing would happen today, I decided, but I couldn't bear the thought of returning, defeated and alone, to my hotel room.

The wife of a friend from the Muktinath Valley ran a small inn across the street from the airport, and I decided to head there for a cup of tea and some company. When I arrived, the restaurant was empty save for a toddler asleep on one of the low mattresses that lined the room—a space that no doubt doubled as a bedroom for the family. I seated myself near the window and took out my journal, expecting that someone would show up eventually to take my order and chat.

The child's sleeping form and soft breathing lulled me, after the chaos and frustration of the airport. Hesitantly, I rested my head on a plastic placemat and closed my eyes. Sleep soon took over.

I don't know how long I napped, but I slept deeply. When I awoke to the smell of Surya cigarettes and heavily sweetened Nescafé, a small puddle of drool had formed on the placemat and my head felt as if it had been suctioned to the table.

"Did you sleep well?" a male voice asked in Nepali, before I'd even looked up. I couldn't answer immediately, but righted myself, brushed back my hair, and tried to focus on the man leaning back in his chair at the other end of the room. His beige trenchcoat hung open at the waist, revealing neat blue jeans and a pair of cowboy boots tipped with silver and well oiled, as if they'd come straight from Texas.

"Is it still raining?" I asked.

"Just sprinkles, but the planes still won't fly. You're trying to get to Jomsom, aren't you?"

"Yes," I said. My eyes began to focus on the handsome man across from me. His voice seemed familiar, as did his face, at once round and angular, framed by raven-black hair, thick as a horse's mane. "Have we met?"

"No, but I've heard about you…and you've probably heard about me. I'm Raju Bista. I'm from Ghami."

"The cousin-brother of Tsewang and *gyalchung* Jigme? The one who knows horses?" I asked.

"Yes, the very one," Raju smiled. He seemed proud like his royal cousins, and yet somehow more approachable.

"I would like to talk with you about horses sometime. Are you traveling to Mustang now?"

"No," answered Raju, "I just came down from Jomsom a few days ago. On the last flight before this bad weather started."

"Lucky you."

"When you come to Lo, we'll go for a ride and visit some of the old guys who know about horses. I don't know that much, aside from what they've taught me," said Raju. I had the feeling he was being modest. I had heard from many people that while Raju knew how to treat basic equine illnesses, his real strength was in training horses. He was good with feisty animals—the type with more will and strength than most people could handle. In the parlance of Western horse culture, these horses would have been called "projects." Raju was discerning, too, when it came to bloodlines, and he tended to buy his horses from Tibet and sometimes breed his own.

"That would be great," I answered. "I hope to be in Lo all summer."

"That is good timing. The horses will be fat, and you will be in time to see Mal." Tshampa had told me about Mal. As far as I understood, this was a ritual bathing and bloodletting ceremony for horses that was performed near special lakes and rivers in late summer, after which horses were given several weeks of rest. The ritual occurred throughout Mustang, but I had hoped to witness this custom performed on the king's herd. This was wonderful news. Now, all I needed to do was get to Lo.

"Where are you going now? Kathmandu?" I asked.

"Soon. I have some business to take care of here in Pokhara first. You'll meet Tsewang in Jomsom," Raju paused. "There is trouble in Jomsom these days."

"What kind of trouble?"

"The *case*," he said, his brow furrowing. I had heard about this lawsuit through snippets of Nepali press. One of the king's sisters had charged the king and his immediate family with stealing some of her property and denying her a portion of her inheritance. In turn, the king argued that his estranged relative and her family had forfeited their claims to Mustang property years ago, when they moved permanently to Kathmandu.

"The other side of the family has already taken the case to Jomsom court. Now they're making a decision—tomorrow. But it won't end there. Whoever loses will appeal. The case will probably go to Kathmandu."

"Who, exactly, has brought the case to court?"

"The king's oldest sister and her son, Ngawang. She was married to a Tibetan who died a while back. They sold off their property in Lo and bought a hotel in Kathmandu years ago. Now they say that the king's family owes them money and land. They say that they owe them nothing, and they owe the crown they 'borrowed' for Ngawang's wedding and never gave back."

Raju looked agitated as he spoke. The terms of the dispute seemed at once medieval—crown jewels and all—and also consistent with the ways social relations, migration, and new economies were impacting life in Mustang. I wondered what had motivated the king's sister and her family to leave Mustang in the first place, and how this rivalry played out in Lo's villages.

"Who do you think will win the case?" I asked. "Do you think your side of the family will get the crown back?"

"I doubt it. Ngawang is a smart businessman. He deals in antiques. I heard they're moving to America and making a Tibetan shop there. Maybe they already sold the crown to some rich foreigner."

"And the property?"

"I don't know if the king will win. Lawyers and judges can be bought, you know."

"So why is there trouble in Jomsom?"

"Ngawang is on his way to Jomsom. You've probably seen him at the airport. He's been waiting because of the weather, too. He doesn't have many supporters in Mustang, but those who are his friends have come down from Lo to back him. The king has also called his supporters. Tsewang radioed me from Jomsom yesterday and said it was like a storm brewing. Dust and men everywhere. There will be fights."

"Is Jigme in Jomsom? The king?"

"Neither of them are because it's too difficult for the king. He will stay in Monthang, and it would be too dangerous for Jigme. That's why Tsewang is there. He's the representative. Jigme will come soon, though."

"Once the dust has settled."

"Exactly. Besides," Raju continued, "this problem won't end in Jomsom."

The next morning I woke before sunrise. The pre-dawn sky was clear and I had the feeling that flights to Jomsom would run. But I had only succeeded in talking my way onto the second Everest Air flight, and therefore had to hope that the weather held until mid-morning.

The airport buzzed with activity by 5:30 AM. Bags were checked and the radio tower whirred, sounding fair weather in Jomsom. I scanned the grounds for Ngawang. If Raju was right, then he had to be here some-where. I assumed that he had managed a place for himself on one of the first flights, and so waited in the departure lounge on the edge of my seat, scanning the passengers.

I found Ngawang, or the person I assumed had to be Ngawang, look-ing sleepy and sipping a cup of tea out of a plastic cup. His features were unmistakable: he was tall like Tsewang but he had a round face like Raju, and his wide forehead looked just like pictures I'd seen of the king. Ngawang's refined presence and the way he carried himself spoke of aris-tocracy as much as it revealed a mountain-born person who had spent many of his formative years in Kathmandu. He wore an expensive gold watch and polished leather shoes that I imagined would be scuffed and dusty by the end of this day.

Had I been bolder, I would have gone up to this renegade member of the royal family and introduced myself. As it was, I chose to remain quiet, and in so doing, chose sides. Although I probably should not have worried about it, I was concerned that trying to connect with Ngawang would in some way harm my burgeoning relationships with the members of the royal family who actually lived in upper Mustang. Although I had not yet met the king, I felt a strong sense of allegiance to him, not only because of our shared love of horses, but also because he had weathered more changes in the last decade than most people lived through in a life-time. There seemed much to admire in a leader who was still so inti-mately tied to his land, his people.

I observed Ngawang from afar that morning, and watched him saunter onto the airplane bound for Jomsom. He seemed haughty to me, as if a trip to the mountains was somehow beneath him. And yet I knew that these negative first impressions had more to do with my own sense of allegiance, however romantic or naïve, to the king and *gyalchung* than it did with any real knowledge about this antagonistic strain coursing through the royal family of Lo. Whatever my thoughts of Ngawang, one thing was certain: the eighteen-minute flight separating Pokhara from Jomsom not only divided worlds, but also marked rifts in human relationships.

By the time I landed in Jomsom on the second flight from Pokhara, the street in front of the airport was thronged with people. I could see the dust and nearly taste the tension. Somehow it felt strange that neither Tshampa nor Karma was there to greet me. Tshampa had just left for his first foray to India on his scholarship and, undoubtedly, Karma was somewhere in the crowd just outside the airport. From my place on the tarmac, I could see the army captain pacing back and forth in the radio tower. He looked nervous, which was not like him. The few Nepali policemen who usually guarded the entrance to the airport were nowhere to be seen. The women who sold apples beside the airport had abandoned their posts, their neat pyramids of fruit left to gather dust in the mid-morning sun.

I had never seen more horses in Jomsom than I did that morning: bays and chestnuts, grays and roans haphazardly hitched to hotel signs and fences. They, too, looked nervous. And, judging by the fine weave of their saddle blankets, the horses had all come from Lo. Several muledrivers had stopped their teams in the middle of Jomsom Airport to watch the action. Strings of tawny mules faced south, loaded with empty beer bottles. They were the only living creatures who did not seem interested in the unfolding drama, as even the dogs had stopped to bark and sniff at the pant legs of the pulsating crowd.

A group of Loba had gathered in a circle near the gates to the airport. Everyone was shouting and pushing, fists clenched. It was clear that they had been here for a while, gathering resentment and tension around the two families members standing at the eye of this storm.

I had come to know Tsewang as an educated, mild-mannered man of refinement, and imagined this was why he had been chosen as the representative of the king's side of this dispute. In this sense, Tsewang lived up to his family's expectations, as did Ngawang. As fist fights brewed around them, they stood their ground, slinging words instead of punches. But the words did fly, bellicose, with rough undertones and sharp edges.

I stood on the fringes of the fray, watching. Local shop owners and people passing through from Baragaon were sidelined during this show-down in Jomsom, their mouths agape. It occurred to me that this was one of the only times I'd ever seen Jomsom dominated not by tourists and Thakalis but by the rough and resilient faces of Lo.

As much as this was a showdown of power within the royal family itself, the fact that the dispute had made its way to Jomsom also revealed the ways in which power and influence were shifting throughout Mus-tang. In previous generations, this conflict over power, property, and resources would have played out most likely in the villages of Lo. Hear-ing Raju mention that it would most likely end up in a Kathmandu court-house made me wonder what the ramifications would be for the king's authority and his side of the family in Lo. Was this case, with all its polit-ical and geographic trajectories, serving to undermine his local powers?

As I stood watching, I heard my name being called over the din of sharp Tibetan words.

"Eh, Sienna!" Across the circle of protest stood Pushpa Tulachan, hugging his video camera to his chest with one hand and waving to me with the other. Pushpa was a Thakali filmmaker who had been born in the village of Tukche, in lower Mustang, and who was now pursuing a Ph.D. in anthropology, focused on the impacts of tourism in upper Mus-tang. We had met during my stay in Kathmandu in the winter, and had immediately hit it off. I knew that Pushpa had returned to Lo around the Tibetan New Year after having gone to Benares with some of the sweater traders. Apparently, he had traveled down to Jomsom from Lo Monthang to watch the action unfold. Now, Pushpa looked tired, as if he had been up most of the night.

"Come over here!" Pushpa motioned. I edged my way around the crowd toward him.

"What's happening?" I asked. "Has the judge made a decision?"

"Yes, he ruled in favor of Ngawang. It just happened a few minutes ago. Tsewang immediately appealed, so the case will probably go to Kathmandu."

"Aren't you scared to be wandering around with your camera?" I asked.

"Not really. Even if they get really angry, none of these Loba will hurt me. None of them have guns or anything. Not like L.A.!" he laughed. As a graduate student at the University of Southern California, Pushpa had been living in South Central Los Angeles before returning to Nepal to do his fieldwork. "Tsewang asked me to film some of this in case they need it as evidence in the future. But," he continued, "things have gotten quite ugly."

"Can you understand what they're saying?" I asked.

"Not really, but some of the people I was standing around with were translating. Basically, it's what you would expect from an old family feud. But the police have already arrested about five Loba, all supporters of the king's side. They almost arrested Tokme, and they beat one Loba up pretty badly."

"On what grounds?"

"They said they were causing a 'civil disturbance,' but they weren't causing any more disturbance than the supporters of Ngawang who showed up. All of them are drunk and angry, and there are just more people on the king's side. It's easy for the police to look at these Lobas and call them 'uncivilized.' They think they can bully the Loba just because so many of them are poor and don't speak Nepali well."

"What will happen to the people they put in jail?" I asked.

"Oh, they'll probably be let out in the morning. I doubt the police would be able to keep them locked up for long. The king's secretary, Chandra Thakali, is well connected with the local government and army. He'll probably get them out."

"And the court case itself? What are people saying?"

"Well, there is not much support for Ngawang and his mother here. They're seen as outsiders—people who left Mustang for a better life. They don't have much popular sympathy, but they have money and influence in Kathmandu on their side. Honestly, both Ngawang and the king's side of this argument probably have some truth to them."

Pushpa and I grew quiet and simply watched the argument between Ngawang and Tsewang continue, unresolved, until the afternoon winds began to stir. Then, nature forced this very human rivalry to subside. The noble factions sought shelter in restaurants at opposite ends of Jomsom Airport. Soon, the streets were empty, a relative peace was restored as wind howled in the canyons, as the muledrivers turned south again, gritting against the dust.

The weeks after the royal spar passed quietly in Jomsom. I kept up with my interviews in Tshampa's absence, and felt a rekindled affection for Karma and the Dancing Yak, now that she was on her own, with Tshampa in northern India, pursuing his own research. One day I was sitting at the Hotel Marco Polo, drinking tea and talking with Nirmal Gauchan, when their hotel manager rushed in, looking excited.

"The Mustang *raja* has come. He's here, just across from us, at the Laligurans Hotel!"

I nearly leapt out of my seat, but Nirmal did not look surprised.

"Yes, I heard the king would be coming down. He has to go to Kathmandu to deal with his court case. What a mess. You were here when they made the decision, right?"

"Yes," I answered. "I guess this means their appeal was accepted."

"I would assume so. The king would not be making the effort to leave Lo otherwise. He's getting on in years and doesn't like to leave Monthang once he returns after the winter," said Nirmal. His brow wrinkled and he stared past me, toward the door to his hotel.

Although Nirmal and the king led very different lives, Nirmal respected the *raja* and felt strongly about his providence over Lo. As a politician, but also as someone who had a real emotional attachment to this place, Nirmal did what he could to maintain good relations with the Loba. Although he clearly identified as Thakali, the fact that his mother had come from upper Mustang helped him maintained a sense of allegiance to people from the kingdom to the north.

"You have never met the king, have you?" he asked me.

"No. But I've wanted to for months."

"Well, what are you waiting for?"

"I can't just walk in on the king, can I?"

"No, I suppose you can't just do that. But you know Chandra Thakali, right? The king's secretary? I'll find him and ask him to make the introductions. I'll come along. It has been too long since I last saw the king." Nirmal rose and donned his *topi*, the signature Nepali hat that marked him here in Jomsom as an official, and headed off to find Chandra. "I'll be back soon."

For what seemed like an eternity, I sat in the dimly lit kitchen of the Hotel Marco Polo, peeling potatoes with Laxmi, Nirmal's wife. Finally, the door swung open and Nirmal called out for me.

"Let's go. The king is just across the street. Chandra has told him that we'll be coming. I have a *kathag* for you. You know, it is best not to keep the king waiting."

I felt giddy as I brushed the potato peels from my lap, straightened my *chuba*, and went off to meet the king of Lo.

I suppose most kings travel with an extensive entourage. King Jigme Palbar Bista was no exception, though I imagine that his council was a bit rougher around the edges than most royal brigades. No less than a dozen weathered men sat in the dining room at the Lalugirans Hotel, where the king was staying. I did not recognize any of them. Nirmal greeted most of them by name, and Chandra introduced me to Pema Ngotug, the king's constable and the caretaker of his horses. He was a burly looking man with gigantic hands and a long, full face. Gyatso, an *amchi* like Tshampa and the son of Tashi Chusang, the royal physician and astrologer of Lo, was also there. I was immediately struck by his kindness, his lilting laugh. Lhakpa, a helper at the palace in Lo, looked in my direction and said he had heard about me from Raju and Tsewang.

"You're the one who likes horses, right?" he asked. I nodded. Turning to Nirmal, I whispered, "Where is the king? Is he here?"

Just then, I heard footsteps coming from the kitchen. Pema Ngotug rose and Gyatso bowed his head. The king entered the room. My sense of nervous giddiness dissipated, and was replaced by a quiet awe.

The king was exquisite. His worn face was the color of honey. A piece of fine turquoise hung from one ear, and he had large and lovely eyes. I bowed and extended my *kathag* toward him, and mumbled a greeting in unsure Tibetan.

"She's the one who likes horses," Pema Ngotug offered.

"Have you been to Lo Monthang?" asked the king.

"No, but I will be going there soon, later in the spring. It has been difficult to get my permit," I said.

"Yes, difficult," answered the king. He looked tired.

"I have heard that you know a lot about horses, Your Majesty. I have been studying some of the horse books here and have learned what I can. But everybody tells me that I should speak with you and visit Lo if I really want to learn."

"Who are you studying with here?"

"I have lived with Tshampa Ngawang, and studied with him. Also with Karchung and Mayala. I've learned what I can."

"Tshampa Ngawang. He has some of my books, right?" said the king, addressing Chandra Thakali. The secretary nodded.

"We have more uses for horses in Monthang than they do down here," the king continued, addressing me. "We depend on them. But I don't know much about horse care. Pema Ngotug and a few other old men in Lo know much more than I do. You should talk to them."

"I would like that. I would also like to learn from you." The king fell silent for some time, turning his *mala*, or rosary, through his hands, counting beads and reciting prayers under his breath.

"Well, when you come to Monthang, you will visit me. Pema Ngotug loves horses. He will also share what he knows."

"Thank you," I answered.

We drank tea and the men in the room chatted. I listened, and answered the Lobas' questions when asked. Gyatso smiled warmly and complimented me on my Nepali.

"How long have you been in our country?" he asked.

"About six months."

"And you learned Nepali so quickly! They teach students how to learn well in your country," he said.

"I learned to speak Nepali here," I answered. "But I am still trying to learn Tibetan. It is more difficult. I've begun to study some of your dialect with a monk at Boudha, Wangdi. But it is not easy."

"You will learn," said Gyatso. "Give yourself time. And when you come to Lo, I can help you." I sensed this *amchi's* sincerity, and would look forward to meeting him again.

"Thank you." I answered, and prepared to take my leave. The king had been quiet as Gyatso and I chatted. I stood, bowed toward the king, and said farewell, addressing him with the honorific forms of Tibetan as best I could.

"You have come from so far," he replied. "My family will do what we can to help you. How old are you?" he asked.

"Twenty-two," I answered.

"*Nyingje*," he said. It was a Tibetan endearment, one that I understood. "You are young." I carried the sweet, grandfatherly gesture with me as we parted company.

Woodsmoke and Radishes

A southern wind churned up the sky as I rode north from Jomsom toward Lubra. Nilgiri Himal yielded its summit to a patch of clear, thin atmosphere in an otherwise stormy sky. Rain clouds gathered and chilling sprinkles spat on the dusty ground. These drops would turn to snow by nightfall, if they did not become hail first. I rode slowly, despite the weather. Hurrying through this afternoon, with its chill and rainbows and iridescent streaks of light, was not possible. I would get to Lubra when I got there.

My horse stopped to drink at the crossroads of the Kali Gandaki River and the Panda Khola. He gulped, not minding the rain, and I took pleasure in the pause. Lubra was a mere bend in the river away. Truly alone for the first time in weeks, I simply stared at the cliffs, these welcome markers of familiar territory. The vertical canyon walls that form one side of the valley were scarred with bedrock ripples. At one point in time, this rock had been ocean floor. The opposite side of the valley was dotted with juniper trees and dwarfed pines, hardy shrubs and shale, providing Tibetan blue sheep places to forage and take shelter during the winter. Cairns marked the landscape, some adorned with the horns of blue sheep and yak, while others were splashed red with natural pigments.

I continued toward the village and crossed the river. Early in these lean months of spring this fording was still possible at any time of day. In summer, the river swelled with glacial melt and monsoon rains, washing out bridges and making the task of crossing the river treacherous. I heard few sounds, save the trees and the water, as I turned east and guided my horse through the maze of river stones to the village's entrance.

Looking toward the outcropping of small houses and buildings, I felt an odd sense of homecoming. Even though Lubra was not a village where I had conducted any formal research, it had become something of a haven over these past six months. I was traveling to Lubra to see Palsang, a woman first introduced to me by Charles Ramble. Charles had met Palsang and her husband Tsewang Tenzin when he first came to Mustang as a young graduate student. Their house became his fieldwork "home" and he had continued to return, year after year.

From the first time I met Palsang, I felt a deep affection for her. She had a lively sense of humor and a deep knowledge of this landscape and its people. I came to cherish the days and nights passed under Palsang's roof. Mustang's history lived in her. Just sitting around her hearth, listening to her talk down her day, was a lesson in Mustang's culture, its complexity. Palsang was always warm and welcoming, She easily made me forget my foreign-ness and allowed me to become her friend.

Like several other villages in Mustang, Lubra was a Bön settlement, not a Buddhist one. Since I was now in Bön territory, I led my borrowed horse around the cairn announcing the entrance to Lubra, in a counter-clockwise direction, instead of the clockwise fashion that marks a Buddhist's circumambulatory path. The horse's bell jingled, signaling my arrival as I passed under the canopy of an ancient walnut tree and through the main cluster of dwellings, toward Palsang's house. Sangye, the mother of the house where my friend Sara had lived when she did her research here, called out to me in welcome. A few children gathered round, skittering and laughing and grabbing for my hand.

I found Palsang standing on the roof of her house. As I approached, all I could see of my friend was her stiff, woven apron folded into a triangle and wrapped around her waist in the convention of Mustang's women. The tip of this striped outer garment stuck up like the feathers of an exotic bird. As I moved closer, I saw that she was fixing a plastic sheet over her kitchen's open skylight, anticipating a night of snow.

"You've come? In this weather?" she gestured toward the menacing sky. "Are you crazy?" she joked. I laughed out loud at her endearments. Had I had caught cold? Had the journey been terrible?

"Oh! My aching bones! My sore feet! This is no place for people to live," I giggled. Her laughter echoed mine with a boisterous burst of joy.

"Come in, come in. You must be hungry," she called as she climbed down from the roof. "What kind of host am I? I haven't even made tea."

"Palsang, I just got here. There is plenty of time for tea," I said, grasping her hands. Warm palms, cold fingertips.

Once inside, I sat down near Palsang as she stoked the fire, poured water into a soot-stained pot, and set it to boil. Smoke filtered up through a chimney—one of the few in this village, and a novelty still in some of Mustang's villages. Further north, in Lo, wood is replaced as a fuel almost exclusively by animal dung. Chimneys are rare. Inside such houses, air grows thick with smoke, eyes sting. One struggles to see, let alone breathe, as plumes of smoke make their way through skylights and small windows.

A wooden cabinet was propped up against the wall near the hearth. Dingy tin jars whose painted logos—Nescafé, Mechi Tea—had been all but worn off rested on the shelves. Other recycled plastic containers—vessels that once held hand lotion or *ghee*—now bore the distinctive marks of food and fire: grease around the edges, a plastic lid deformed by flame. Palsang's house smelled of cumin and wild garlic, woodsmoke and radishes.

It was here that I came to feel most at home in Mustang. Although much of this had to do with Palsang's kindness and affability, there was something about her, and her home, which ignited in me deep childhood memories. Sitting in her small kitchen with her stove puffing, I felt the same sense of warmth and calm that I had experienced as a very young child, when my father was out working at an archaeological site and I passed hours in the company of Chumash women and girls, talking and making tortillas. Also, as an only child, I have always tended to gravitate toward relationships that filled some intuited need for a sibling, and Palsang was such a person. She was sisterly. Her friendship helped me to negotiate a new sense of internal balance and belonging, now that I had uprooted myself, chosen to leave my home and natal family, and settled, for the time being, halfway across the world.

The tea water gurgled and Palsang grabbed one of the jars. She pinched out a loose-leaf handful of tea, tossed in some sugar, and reached for a crinkled Mylar package of Everyday dairy powder, one of Nabisco's Third World synthetic milk products. Cows, though kept in Lubra, do not produce much milk in the early spring, when pasture is at its most lean and stores of hay have been all but depleted. Palsang ladled some of the white powder into the tea. She stirred with as much grace and flair as a French waiter pouring wine.

I had come to Lubra this time for a women's prayer ritual, or *matri*. This *matri* was a day of feast, some rest, and much prayer for Lubra's women. On the day of the *matri*, the village monastery would not be filled with the sound of many chanting *nakpa*, or householder priests, as was the convention during other religious gatherings. A few of the *nakpa* would attend to read scripture, but the voices coming from the monastery would be resoundingly female. Young and old, turning prayer beads, singing songs and their Bön *mantra—Om matri muyi sa len do—* the equivalent of the ubiquitous Buddhist *Om mani padme hum*. I arrived in Lubra with the expectation that I would wake before dawn with Palsang and head to the village temple, where I would sit, pray, gossip, eat, drink, and, for a time, *not* think about horses.

"How long will you stay?" Palsang asked. I shrugged. "A couple of days or so. I'm not sure. I'll be here through the *matri* ceremony, but I might stay a bit longer. I need a break from Jomsom. Too many men there— and they sure like to talk."

"See, that's what happens when you wear a *chuba* and start pouring tea," Palsang joked. "All the boys will come after you!"

The first time I went to Lubra, Tshampa had interrogated me. "Why go there? They don't have *amchi*, and the only person from Lubra who worked with animals moved to Jomsom decades ago," he had said. But I had been curious, and had gone anyway. My friend Sara was living in the village at that time, and I had also wanted to visit her. Charles had given me Palsang's name as a potential home in which to stay, and we had immediately enjoyed each other's company. I had returned to Lubra again for the *do gyab* ceremonies later in the winter, and had since taken to visiting Palsang whenever I could.

That evening with Palsang, endless cups of sweet tea led to peeling potatoes, crushing dried chilies, scooping out rice for the evening meal.

We worked alongside each other, saying little. Tsewang Tenzin came home late, but still in time for dinner. He had spent the day in Jomsom selling homemade *arak* liquor—Lubra's specialty—and was now hungry, exhausted. Five-year-old Chimi Dolkar, their youngest child and the only daughter, squirmed against Palsang and whined.

"The girl can't stand bedbugs," said Palsang. "What was she thinking being born here?" Bedbugs and fleas were rather permanent fixtures in Mustang homes. Even in winter, when most other life had slowed, these nearly invisible critters wiggled their ways under socks and sleeping garments, in search of warmth like the rest of us.

Palsang soothed her child, scratching her small back. "You should see her in the summertime. She hardly sits still."

Tsewang Tenzin got up and prepared to take his leave of us. "Stay warm and sleep well." He was off to a neighbor's house for a nightcap and some village politics, Palsang explained.

"He'll be gone a while," said Palsang.

"Tsewang Tenzin is a fine worker," said Palsang. "He is strong, and a good person. *Nyingje*, I am lucky to be married to him." I agreed. Tsewang Tenzin's crooked-toothed grin and flyaway hair, his small, leathery hands and stilted walk always struck me as a rather goofy example of Mustang machismo. Palsang, on the other hand, had a cultivated manner to her, elegance. But he had a sense of humor to match his wife's, and he seemed like a loving father. I had always seen Tsewang Tenzin treat Palsang with affection. As in many Tibetan households, he conceded to her on most things.

"Of course we bicker. Who doesn't? But we don't fight that often any more, now that we're old timers!" Palsang and Tsewang Tenzin had been married for about twenty years.

But, as I had learned, Palsang did not go quietly into marriage. A "stolen" bride, she had been kidnapped by Tsewang Tenzin and a band of his friends and male relatives when she was just nineteen.

"Tell me again how you were married," I asked.

"One day I was out working in our family's fields, and I heard a band of people riding very quickly on horses. They were making all sorts of noise. I didn't know what was happening. I guess I should have been more prepared. After all, I was not the first woman to be stolen for marriage like that. It is an old custom, but it used to happen more in my mother's generation than it did when I was a young woman. At the time, I thought, *maybe these men are coming for someone*, but I didn't know they were coming for me!

"I remember them riding up and dragging me. I started kicking and screaming. What was going to happen to me? I had never really met Tsewang Tenzin before, but I had seen him at festivals. I knew that some of the men thought I was beautiful. I used to have such long, thick hair— all that changed when I started having babies, though. Anyway, I knew that Tsewang Tenzin was not the only one who liked me. Other young men had flirted with me before, so I guess in some way I was ready for being married when it happened. But flirting is different, too."

As Palsang spoke, her expressions became animated, her gestures lively. Something of that initial shock seemed to live with her still, after all these years.

"They put me on a horse and started to ride off. I fought. We were riding quickly to Lubra. I could tell that much, but everything was happening so fast.

"At some point I jumped off, and the horse dragged me for a while because nobody would stop. I hurt my tailbone and was dirty and dusty. But I survived the ride."

Palsang explained that, for some couples, such marriage captures are mere drama. Friends help lovers act out this ritual of union as a way of legitimizing an already established intimacy. In other stolen-bride scenarios, a woman spends three nights in her husband's family's house. After the third night, her father or uncle comes calling. If the woman is unhappy, she walks outside and returns to her natal home. If she is happy with her mate, she simply stays inside.

"In the end, things worked out. Tsewang Tenzin listens to me. There is love between us," said Palsang. "And things could have been a lot more complicated. I could have been married to brothers."

Fraternal polyandry has been a standard, culturally sanctioned form of marriage throughout the Tibetan-speaking world, including Mustang, for centuries, particularly among nobles. With limited arable land, brothers who married one woman were able to maintain a family's land base and accrue more wealth. In an ideal situation, one or more brothers might spend several months of the year away from the village, trading or engaged in other economic activities, while another would remain at home and share domestic work with his wife. Children born of such families would refer to all of their "fathers" as just that, only making a distinction in accordance with age: *little* father, *big* father.

Women of Palsang's generation and older were often chosen as brides for such unions. These days, however, the numbers of people choosing polyandry—or allowing their parents to match them in this way—was on the wane. This shift in social attitudes has many possible sources, from the current generation's exposure to Bollywood movies with their images of monogamous love, to increased urban migration and a growing sense among young people that a small family served their interests best. Many people I spoke with considered polyandry out of a sense of vague cultural pride—tradition seen through the muslin of memory, a beautiful obscuration. But when given a choice about who and how they would marry, few saw the custom as appealing, either in terms of love or property. As one young Loba I had met in Jomsom explained to me, "It takes so much labor to work the fields. This is labor we don't have anymore, now that so many people are leaving and making money outside Mustang. Even if I wanted to marry with my brothers it wouldn't work," he continued. "The one brother I have who is still in Mustang is a monk, and my other brother has gone off to Japan." The exodus of people from Mustang to America and Japan that I would witness in the coming years had yet to begin in earnest, but I could hear the murmurings of migration now.

Palsang laughed, bringing me back to the present. "*Ah mo*! Tsewang Tenzin has difficulty enough getting under my *chuba* after a day of hard work. What if I had to fend off brothers!"

"Have you ever used birth control?" I asked. Though many young local women had heard of condoms, pills, and IUDs, few women I spoke with in Mustang said they used them. Nonetheless premarital sex and friendly promiscuity is not frowned upon nearly as much in Tibetan culture as it is within Hindu communities in Nepal.

"You mean have I ever taken medicine so I won't get pregnant?" asked Palsang. "No, I've never tried that. But I think it is a good idea. It is not smart to have children when you are too young. You simply don't know what you are getting into. I had my first child when I was twenty, the year after I got married." I knew that this child had not lived and didn't push Palsang to talk about it.

"It is terrible that *rongba* girls get married when they are eleven, even younger sometimes, and then they get pregnant when they are still children. I thought I was going to die of the pain the first time I gave birth. It gets easier. That doesn't happen in America, does it?" she asked. "People having children when they are so young? Doesn't everyone in America get married when they are old ladies? They take medicine so they don't have babies and then they have to take more medicine so they can have babies, right?"

"Sometimes that is true," I said. "But some young women are having babies when they are thirteen or fourteen in America, too."

"Why? Are these girls poor? Maybe they don't know any better. But how could they not know about medicines in America? If I know about it then they have to know, don't they?"

"Not always, Palsang." I was amazed at her perceptiveness. She had no context with which to comprehend the pregnancy experience in the United States. Yet she had an uncanny ability to imagine places beyond her experience, and to not merely understand, but to intuit their meaning.

As we talked into the evening, Palsang prepared a soupy concoction of umber clay and water, swishing a rag through the mixture to smooth out lumps of earth. The natural paint stained her fingers a deep orange. Careful not to drip on the floor, she applied paint to the edges of the main sitting room, her legs folded up under herself as she shuffled along near the wall. The house should be clean before the *matri*, she explained.

"So you've never used a condom?" I was curious.

"You mean one of those plastic things? No! They just seem so silly, like putting on clothes before you take a bath."

I couldn't help but laugh. While condoms were available through health clinics in Jomsom, their specific usage was not always clear. A grandmother once enthusiastically told me how much she enjoyed using them to carry *chang* or *arak* into the fields. "They're great. You can tie them off with string and carry just enough out to the fields to warm you up, but not enough to get you drunk," she said, quite pleased with her adaptation. It was clear to me that *not* having children was as big of a problem as actually becoming pregnant. Nepal's infant and maternal mortality rates were higher than in most countries in the world. Mustang women's perspectives on pregnancy were markedly different than anything I had previously known.

"Condoms can do more than stop pregnancy," I said. "They can also stop diseases."

"Health workers have come and told us about them," said Palsang. "Some people have gotten sores or fevers. I don't think anyone has ever died from that sort of thing here. Life is so hard that most people will probably get sick and die of something else before that would ever happen."

While this was perhaps true, something in Palsang's response to the question of condoms worried me. The threat of HIV infection seemed to be becoming greater. Though the reported cases in the high mountains of Nepal were still relatively low, this statistic seemed illusory. I thought about the men from Mustang who spent their winters migrating south, to India, for trade. I imagined that these men, while away from their wives for three or four months each year, sometimes took pleasure and comfort in the arms of women, including commercial sex workers. I did not feel a moral judgment about such acts of seeking affection—particularly since concepts of loyalty and fidelity were different in this cultural context. Yet when I looked at Palsang, I thought of how vulnerable local women may be, despite their magnitudes of strength.

As if reading my thoughts, Palsang said, "I know things are changing. There are new problems, new things to be worried about. You say that I'm not an old woman, but much of what my mother knows, what she has taught me, will die with me. And Chimi will have to learn things that I don't know anything about. She is learning from me, too, but there is so much that I cannot teach her." Palsang sat down next to me. As her daughter slept soundly in her arms, I felt Palsang struggle with the thought of Chimi's life, her trajectory. Carefully, so as not to wake her child, Palsang carried Chimi into the adjacent room and laid her to rest in the family bed. Outside, moonlight flooded the night sky.

Palsang returned to the main room of the house and sat down beside me. She pulled a letter from one of her two boys out of the folds of her *chuba*. I had seen them before, but only in pictures. "My oldest son is very bright," she said.

"Like you," I returned, causing a blush to spread across her face. Palsang knew she was smart, but still called herself "stupid" when faced with a notebook or a letter from her sons like the one she now held.

"I'm nearly illiterate," she said. "That makes me slow." Even though I knew Palsang to be a woman of confidence, something about her inability to decipher much of the world of script stopped her short. To this I found I could console her, or at least identify. So much of my time in Mustang was spent deciphering the language and its fluctuations, working with it like clay, struggling to coax out meaning and form.

"You do much besides read," I offered. "How would Lubra function without the women?"

"It wouldn't," Palsang said plainly, pulling out a stack of photographs from inside a copper pot. The first depicted a young Palsang and Tsewang Tenzin, newly married, in front of a painted backdrop of tropical fruits and palm trees. In another photo they stood, stone-faced and stiff, in front of a faux Potala Palace. Palsang's face was fuller then.

"I was beautiful then, wasn't I?" she said.

"Still are," I nodded.

We passed over blurry pictures of village rituals; a smeared portrait of Chimi, age three; a horse Tsewang Tenzin bought that died last winter; a mass-reproduced picture of one of the preeminent Bön lamas, high on a throne in Dolanji, India.

"Do you ever go to Dolanji and see your sons?" I asked, knowing that they attended boarding school there. Dolanji, in Himachal Pradesh, is the seat of the Bön community-in-exile. Many of Lubra's young people had been sent there to receive monastic and Bön-oriented lay educations.

"No. Tsewang Tenzin goes to see them and brings them back for vacations sometimes. If I went, who would take care of all this?" A flick of her chin indicated her house, the low bench on which I sat, the slightly tilted shelves brimming with pots, pressure cookers, and bags of grain, a few spoons. The storeroom door creaked and I heard it as this home's answer. Palsang was needed here.

"Can I rub your hands?" I asked. Some of the cracks in her flesh had not healed since the last winter. They were a village woman's hands, battered by the sting of a burning kettle, nearly immune to snow, and adept at picking lice out of children's scalps.

I greased my own palms with apricot oil. In Lubra, the oil is wrenched by hand from the pits of local fruit. I reached for her hands and began to rub. A pail of embers burned between us to keep us warm, but soon the oil became another kind of fire. Her hands radiated their own warmth. *Heat is the echo of your gold*, I thought, remembering a line of poetry from a very different time and place: Philip Larkin in Providence coffee shops.

"How is your stomach these days?" I asked, remembering there was fire inside her, too.

"Sometimes it feels like fire on my insides," she said, motioning to her abdomen. "But lately it has been okay. I'm not supposed to drink any alcohol when it hurts, though. And you know how hard that is in this village." I did know. Lubra was renowned for its local spirits, and refusing to drink was nearly impossible, especially during rituals.

"I brought some more medicine for you."

Once, after Palsang suffered a serious bout with gastric pain, she showed me some crumpled foil packages. "I ran out of medicine, and I won't buy it in Jomsom because everything there is twice as expensive as it is in Pokhara or Kathmandu," she admitted at that time. I scrawled the brand names in my journal. On my return to Kathmandu, I showed this strange and private poetry to a chemist, who filled the order.

"You shouldn't have spent money on medicine for me." But she took the aluminum packets and the bottle of antacid anyway, stuffed it into one of the copper pots that sat like roosting pigeons on her shelves.

"I miss my sons," Palsang said, changing the subject as I continued to massage her palms.

"You know," she paused, sipped a glass of warm, homemade *arak*, "I had four who died. One lived for a few years. The others died early. That was before children began getting injections. They had spots all over them, like many other children in the village. Everyone said that it was nobody's fault, but we still did many different rituals because we thought one of the village gods must have been angry, for so many children to die. We even took some to the hospital in Jomsom, but all the doctors could do was give them some medicine for their pains. They said it was too late." I had heard from others about this measles epidemic.

"It wasn't that difficult for some women to lose their babies. It had happened to them before. But these were my first four. People in the village began to wonder if there was something wrong with me. Maybe I was cursed, they thought. But then I had my boys and now things are different. They are growing—far away, but they are growing—and I have Chimi and Tsewang Tenzin here.

"I am glad for my three children, but sometimes I can still feel the lost ones," she said, rubbing her stomach. "Now they don't die so easily. They just go away. When you have children, you will know." Tears formed, so transparent against Palsang's burnished face that all I noticed was a flicker of light from the candle reflected on her cheek.

"I wonder if my sons could name all the houses in Lubra," she whispered. "Could they do that? There is a lot to forget here and not much to remember. Their old mother—"

"You aren't old," I interjected.

She wiped her eyes and seemed to fold up her last thought, tucking it away into the stack of pictures.

"Let me comb your hair," I said. Palsang shifted her back toward me. My fingers navigated Palsang's tresses. Knots begot knots, leaving coarse, black strands wrapped around my knuckles. I worked slowly with a comb, untangling the mass. A braid, half-finished, had been twisted into an awkward bun some hours before and tied up in a bandana after the midday meal. Since then, it had spilled out from her kerchief as she trudged down from her buckwheat crop.

Once her hair lay flat against her back like a horse's mane, I divided it into three sections, plaited it loose. She neither answered nor resisted.

Chimi Dolkar pushed open the door and waddled in, naked from the waist down, a stained T-shirt resting just above her belly button. "I itch," she sniffled, sleepily. Palsang stroked Chimi's cheeks, as ruddy as her own, and scratched her back as lullaby.

By the time I finished with Palsang's hair, my friend was nearly asleep, her breathing deep and resonant in the room. A slight nudge and Palsang darted awake.

"Can I get you some tea? You must be hungry," she mumbled. It was late and I needed nothing except her company.

"I will wake you up early tomorrow for the *matri*," said Palsang. I wrapped my hands, glossy with oil, around Palsang. I felt a paradox of emotions come over me. I knew that I was comforting her, yet at the same time I felt her rescuing me from my own waves of loneliness and isolation. If it is the only thing I do here, I thought to myself, I will know Palsang, and she will know me. Lifetimes in her fingertips, woodsmoke in her hair.

A Ritual, A Birth

IT WAS STILL DARK outside when I heard the front door of Palsang's house creak open. Through sleep-soaked eyes I could sense her walking past me, the faint glow from an oil lamp piercing the pre-dawn pitch. Palsang's *chuba* hung loose at the waist, untied. I got up, put on my own *chuba*, and stumbled into the kitchen, my mind still heavy with dreams. Palsang had gone outside to gather up some wood. I prodded the fire awake, aware that Tsewang Tenzin and Chimi were still sleeping in the next room. It must have been about five in the morning.

My friend and I worked in silence, making tea and straightening up. We kneaded coarse wheat flour and water into dough, rolled it out, and threw the flatbread on a cast-iron skillet to bake. Palsang nodded in approval at my efforts at bread making.

"You make bread better than you make rice," she snickered. I could not help but laugh, too. On a previous visit to Lubra, Palsang had gone up to the fields and had left me alone in the house for a morning. I thought I would surprise Palsang and make her lunch. How hard could it be to cook rice and make some curried potatoes over an open flame? After all, I had helped Palsang and other local women prepare identical meals countless times.

When Palsang returned to cook a midday meal, she was pleasantly surprised to find the task finished. That is, until she opened the rice pot and discovered a coagulated, sticky mess. "Is this rice?" she had managed, nearly doubled over with laughter. The potatoes were edible, but even the young blacksmith boy, who, because of his low social status within the village, was used to being fed leftovers in exchange for work, balked at the glutinous mass that ended up on his plate.

Now, in the cool predawn hours, I whispered, "I promise I won't make any rice while I'm here!" We both laughed, quietly but with fervor, and then tucked the memory away as if it were a dream, waiting for the sun to rise.

Bread made, Palsang rooted around to find a clean towel in which to wrap our food. She then blanketed the fire's embers in ash, grabbed a basket, and threw in our belongings: thermoses of tea, flasks of *arak*, our stiff and heavy pancakes, some dried apricots, and a few bags of instant noodles to cook in the *gompa* kitchen for hungry and cranky children. Palsang had a childish grin on her face, and I imagined she took pleasure in this shift from her daily routine. We left the house, lunches packed and *malas* dangling from our wrists, ready for the day of prayers and prostrations.

As we walked down the path from her house to the monastery she said, "You know, sometimes I think it is confusing, all these differences between Buddhism and Bön. I was raised a Buddhist, but when I married Tsewang Tenzin and came to Lubra I switched to Bön." Such conversions, if one can call them that, are relatively common in marriages involving people from Lubra. Other Bön families exist throughout Mustang, but entire communities that identify themselves as Bön practitioners are less common.

"There are differences between the two," Palsang continued. "But many Buddhist teachings are a lot like ours. I am glad that my boys are being educated at Dolanji and learning about Bön there. I hope Chimi will grow up and know something about what it means to be Bönpo. But really I don't think the difference matters that much, so long as there is *dharma* in you. That, and pay attention to the gods of this place," said Palsang. Through my fieldwork I had come to see Mustang's landscape as sacred, embodied, and animate. Palsang's mentioning of the local gods echoed the sentiment that spiritual duty lived in the elements here as much as it resided in a more uniform cosmology—whether labeled Buddhist or Bön.

Palsang and I approached the village monastery. Other women called to each other as they left their houses. When I stopped listening to understand and instead listened for cadence and rhythm, the women's voices tethered the line between prose and song, lines like boats adrift, loosened from their moorings. It is funny to think they were actually saying things like: "Dawa, do you have the dried cheese?" "Sangye, I can't find the wool I set aside for wicks. Can you bring some?" and "Takla cut his hand yesterday. Ask Sienna if she has medicine."

We entered the courtyard just outside the temple. None of the village lamas attending the ritual had arrived. The women, young and old, wandered in, their arms and backs laden with thermoses and baskets of food. They shed their slippers at the door and knelt, performing three prostrations as is custom when entering any sacred space. There is poetry in this movement: hands rise to forehead, drop to mouth, rest at chest, acknowledging body, speech, and mind. I followed Palsang. The wood, polished by years of use, cradled me as I dropped to the floor. Knees bent, I could feel the warp and weft of planks beneath me. I slid my hands across the floor and rested my forehead on the dusty surface. A pause, a breath, and I continued.

Lubra's women took their place in a line along the wall. The way they sat had a meaning and an order to it based on age, religious practice, and social status in the community. Chomo Kandro, the eldest woman in Lubra and one of the village's only *chomo* (a word that roughly translates as "nun") sat at the head of the row. I had not seen her for some months, when I had spent the day with Sara who had been recording her life history. Kandro looked at once old yet sturdy, a survivor of so many Mustang winters.

Once they finished their prostrations, the younger women moved between the main temple and the kitchen, stirring pots and pouring tea. Palsang took her place somewhere in the middle of this female hierarchy, and discussion began about where to put me.

"How old are you?" the woman asked me.

"Twenty-two."

"And you're not married?" another woman asked.

"No."

"*Nyingje.*" Some of the women wondered aloud how it was possible that my parents let me go so far away from home on my own. After some bantering, I was seated several seats down from Palsang, next to a very pregnant young woman, Monlam. We were about the same age, and she told me that she had returned home to Lubra to give birth. Her body heaved, lowered itself, and leaned awkwardly against the wall. I could not imagine a comfortable way to sit cross-legged while pregnant.

The morning had not really started, but as I watched the lineup and sipped my sweet tea, I remembered the *do gyab*, a ritual that occurred before fields were planted in late winter. Then, I had listened for hours to the women of the village as they sang *om matri mu yi sa len do*. Now, as I tried to find my place, I was glad for the half darkness of the *gompa* and for the order of these women, the structure it implied.

"Are you the one who lived with us last year?" Chomo Kandro asked me, craning her neck to peer down the row. She looked small in her heavy winter cloak, smiling in the corner. I realized that with cataracts getting the better of her vision, the female elder had mistaken me for Sara. Palsang and several other younger women piped in and corrected Kandro's mistake. "No, this is See-na." I smiled at the sound of my name pronounced in thick Tibetan accent. "She came for the *do gyab*, remember?" Kandro nodded and then began to chant. With that first *mantra* she seemed to lose the weariness of age. Her voice was clear, sonorous. We followed her, singing up the sun, ticking time on our prayer beads, sipping tea. The line of women broke at times to nurse babies, visit the monastery's pit toilet, refill thermoses, and direct children up the hill to the government primary school. The *matri* was a fluid event, at once focused and flexible.

At about ten the male lamas arrived. Though officially winter had passed, days were still short and these householder priests seemed in no hurry to venture outside their houses until the sun had risen over the steep walls of the valley. The men all looked slightly hungover as they wandered into the *gompa*, prostrated, and settled into making *torma*, ritual barley cakes, to place on the altar. The oil-stained, wooden shrine was bare, save a couple of empty butter lamps and water bowls, a few handfuls of scattered grains. Lama Tsultrim, the most gregarious of the bunch, teased me.

"Why have you come here? Lubra is no good!" he said in sarcastic, schoolboy Nepali. He sat down across from his wife with a happy *humph* and began making butter ornaments with which to decorate the *torma*.

"I've come here to see you, Tsultrim," I jested. "Why else would some-one come to Lubra?" We had developed an easy rapport during my *do gyab* stay, one that I enjoyed.

Tsultrim then explained that the delicate forms he was coaxing out of a cold and cumbersome lump of fat would represent a village *yidam*, or tutelary deity, that on this occasion was represented in its wrathful form. "We have all kinds of gods...too many. They make my hands tired!" joked Tsultrim.

For the next hour or so, the *gompa* bustled with activity. One group of mothers busied themselves by cleaning the silver and bronze goblets used for butter lamps while others acted as *torma* prep cooks: dolling out flour, pouring water as the lamas made dough.

In time, the *torma* were finished and placed on the altar, the men took their seats, one of the women poured everyone a glass of liquor that was as pink as cotton candy, and we resumed our chanting. Switching bev-erages marked hours: sweet tea at dawn, Tibetan tea by mid-morning, hard local liquor for much of the day. The afternoon wore on in a cross-hatch of prayer and silence, food and drink. I wished, for a moment, that someone I knew from home were with me. Surrounded by a sense of female community, I felt a sudden longing for my college roommates.

I also wondered what friends from home would make of this experi-ence. Would someone fresh to this place, unfamiliar with its languages, be able to decipher the rhythms, if not the meanings, of this ritual? My own cultivated comfort here was still so limited, as was my understand-ing. What I saw of the women then, what the women saw in me, remained at a certain level opaque and mysterious, for all that we could and did share.

Time wound on toward afternoon. Monlam, my pregnant neighbor, took her leave as soon as she could. Needing a break, and unable to drink any more liquor, I followed her up to the roof of the monastery. The ritual was nearing completion. Monlam seemed so full of life, and so overwhelmed by the birth waiting to happen inside her, that she could do little but lean up against the low wall along the roof and stare out at the cliffs across the valley.

"I think the baby is coming soon," she said.

"Are you nervous?" I asked.

"Not really. My mother is here, and I know that other women will help me if I need it. That is why I came home."

When I reentered the temple, the lamas were packing up their books and instruments. They teetered, drunkenness and exhaustion overtaking them, and then stumbled home.

Late afternoon light filtered through the monastery windows in shafts thick with dust. Most of the women sat in a semicircle, counting a pile of dirty rupees on the floor in front of them. They explained that this was the *matri's* "kitty" and that each woman was now responsible for paying her family's dues to a community fund established some months ago that helped to reestablish the ritual within the village. Some of the money collected that day was offered directly to the monastery, while other funds were used for food and supplies.

Earlier that morning I had asked Palsang how much I should give. As always, she had advised me honestly and well. One woman looked at my contribution, however, and said, "You are from America. This is like two rupees of your money. Why don't you give more?" I felt a cringe in my stomach. This was certainly not the first time that the disparity in wealth between Nepal and "A-mee-ri-kaa" had been an issue.

My presence in this tiny community represented chasms of economy and power, true. Yet I felt confronted with a strange inversion of tradition. I wanted nothing more than to give responsibly, to honor the *matri*, and my inclusion in it, with the integrity this ritual deserved. But my presence was not simple, and, as much as I felt "at home" here in Lubra, I could never be an "insider." Some of the women in Lubra, like many other people in Mustang, knew that foreigners sometimes donated absurd amounts of money because they simply did not know better, or because they thought their philanthropic largesse would balance the proverbial scales of global inequality, or at least earn them some merit. Some Lubra woman saw me, and in some sense quite appropriately, as just another *chikya*, an outsider who had wandered in. Others, like Palsang, had come to know me more deeply, as an individual, and responded to me as such.

"You know she is a student and young," Palsang interjected. "She doesn't have much money. Not all America is rich." This proved to be an unexpected entrée into a larger conversation, one that enlivened the late afternoon.

"Do you know that in America it costs many people 100,000 rupees each month just to rent a house?" Palsang continued. Once, she had asked me how much I paid for rent before I had left the U.S. for Nepal. I had described to her the $1500-a-month sublet that my college boyfriend and I shared in Somerville, outside of Boston, and had answered, in turn, her questions about how much I made from piecemeal editorial assignments, research work, and babysitting. Although she could appreciate the sense of economy, the simple amounts of these transactions were quick reminders of the differences between us.

Palsang's enticing comment invited the women of Lubra to begin firing questions at me: *How much do potatoes cost in America? What about rice? Clothes? Why do you need to pay rent on a house when you can live with your parents or build your own?*

A breath, a sip of *arak*, and the conversation dovetailed from money to family politics. I was inundated with questions: *Why did children not stay in their family homes until they got married, or even after? What do you mean you don't have any brothers or sisters? Did they all die? Your parents are separated? Ah mo! How terrible that must have been! Why didn't they just sleep with whoever they wanted to and stay together?*

I answered the Lubra women's questions as best I could. I figured supermarket prices into rupees and tried to encapsulate the strange triangle of money, social value, and cultural economies, as it exists in America, to these talkative, tipsy women. I realized that I understood their ritual economy just about as well as they understood my family life in the U.S., but the awkward conversation seemed, in itself, to close a bit of the gap between us.

Soon, we all began to gather up our belongings, file out, and return home. We did our prostrations and turned to leave, facing the altar, walking backward to the door so as not to turn our backs on the gods. Spilled *arak* in small pools on the floor reflected the day's last light.

When I woke the next morning Palsang was gone. Chimi nagged me for tea and biscuits. I fed her and then sat back, pulled out my journal, and began scribbling about the *matri*. Palsang hurried into the house an hour later.

"Where did you go?" I asked. It was still early and I had not expected her to be up much before me.

"Monlam started giving birth at four this morning. We have been helping her."

"Is the baby born?"

"Yes, a boy. You can come see if you'd like," said Palsang as she rushed around her house, gathering up a few eggs, some roasted barley kernels, a few rupees—always an odd number, for luck—and a blessing scarf. She placed these offerings on a plate and prepared to leave. I leapt up and followed after her to Monlam's home.

Men were nowhere to be seen and the village was quiet. A few girls hovered about the edges of the house, awed by the mystery of birth. A half dozen women sat chatting on the roof. Monlam lay crumpled in the corner, spent. Her mother knelt beside her, massaging her back and buttocks with heated oil.

"I knew he was coming," she said to me, by way of greeting. The woman's bent form was a beautiful paradox of weakness and utter strength—the epitome of birth. Her belly sagged, moist with sweat and oil. Streaks of blood ran along Monlam's legs and down her feet like veins and arteries exposed.

Wool blankets swaddled her child, so puckered and new. His grandmother kept watch on him and made sure to keep his eyes shaded from the harsh Mustang sun.

"Was it difficult?" I asked Monlam, not really knowing what else to say. Monlam just nodded.

"Her water came at night, after we had all gone to sleep," said Monlam's mother. "Then the pains started. I heated water and cleaned and made a woolen string to tie off the cord. We were ready. She was so big that we knew the baby was coming soon." In other parts of Nepal, particularly in regions where infant mortality remains exceptionally high, international health programs and Nepali non-governmental organizations had collaborated to produce and disseminate "birth kits": a sterile razor blade, anti-bacterial wipes, latex gloves, a plastic sheet. Though health workers had on occasion visited Lubra, I saw no evidence of such supplies that morning. The tools of this birth were more local: boiled water, wool twine, a sharpened steel blade, incense, and collective women's experience.

When I peered in on the baby, I noticed that he had also been rubbed down with oil. "What do you need to do when a baby is born?" I asked. I realized that I knew more about what people in Mustang did when a horse foaled than how they guided human births.

"Sometimes we mix some different herbs with milk or butter and a little *tsampa*, then we feed a bit of it to the baby. And oil is very good for taking away a woman's pain—especially apricot oil from Lubra. It is the best."

"People say it is good luck to have a daughter first, so that you will have someone to take care of you when you are old," said another woman, echoing common Tibetan folklore, "but I was just glad if my babies were born healthy and lived."

The cut umbilical cord had been stuffed into a plastic instant noodle container and would be kept for the first few weeks of its life, to cure the infant of "mouth diseases"—problems that a Western doctor might have called thrush. It looked gray and lifeless now, even though it had been a conduit for life just hours before. The placenta, I was told, had already been tossed into the Panda Khola.

"A lama told me once that it is auspicious if you have good dreams before you give birth," said another woman. Monlam whispered that she had paid a call on one of Lubra's lamas, and had asked for blessings and prayers.

Birth in the Tibetan context can be associated with *drip*, pollution or defilement, and so it is often followed by purifying rituals. It is unusual, I also learned, for men to attend a birth. Some Mustang men I asked about childbirth looked shy and said they would be no help to a laboring women, while others claimed it was bad luck for a man to participate. And, despite the sophistication of some aspects of Tibetan medicine, including embryology, this healing practice had very little to offer a pregnant woman aside from a few dietary and behavior suggestions; birthing complications remained superficially accounted for in many Tibetan medical texts. But when one considers that many *amchi* and scholars of Tibetan medicine were also monks or householder priests, this social fact is less surprising.

As it was, no *amchi* would visit Monlam and her new child. Birth was not an "illness" in this culture, but just a part of daily life. Monlam would stay at home for a few weeks to recover, and after some time, one of the village priests would name the boy. If he were to suffer a sickly infancy, perhaps the lama would rename him with a blacksmith's appellation to throw off the demons and guard against further sickness.

When I asked Monlam how long she would stay in Lubra, her mother answered in her place. "What good would it be if she went to all the trouble to give birth at home, and then rush off to her husband's home without my grandchild being blessed and named by our lamas?" said the elder Lubra woman. As Monlam's mother spoke, her daughter, now a new mother herself, closed her eyes and, like her child, fell asleep.

The next morning, Palsang stuffed dried apples from last year's harvest, a buckwheat cake, and a boiled egg into my bag. I was heading north to Kagbeni and then on to the Muktinath Valley for several days. The ride to Kagbeni would only take me an hour or so, but as usual, Palsang tried to guard me against hardship and hunger. I left the village quietly, glad for having come.

The Panda Khola valley glistened under a clear sky after a night of soft rain. It seemed the snow that ushered me into the village was the last of the season. A blessing scarf slung around my neck, I crossed the river and headed up the trail, making good time, happy to be alone again. Some switchbacks later, I passed the chorten at the edge of Lubra, a spiritual as well as geographic marker that is home to one of Lubra's village gods. I dismounted. *So sooo*, I yelled, tossing a rock onto the pile and leaving Bön territory as I had entered it: passing the cairn counterclockwise.

In the distance I heard bleating goats and could see the faint outlines of two children's frames. These were prepubescent shepherds, holding hands and leaning up against one of the many low rock shelters built to block Mustang's cool, early spring wind. I kept riding. Out of the corner of my eye, I spotted a lone goat quite near the trail. Her legs were folded under her and she looked as if she could have been hurt. I moved closer and dismounted again. Far from injured, I discovered that she was actually in labor. Two tiny legs had already emerged from her womb. The creature struggled for breath, and in her panting pushed her offspring free. The mother goat looked up at me and bleated. The animal seemed beyond this world and yet completely grounded in the messiness of life, the sanctity of birth.

Part IV

Man knows that there are in the soul tints more bewildering, more numberless, and more nameless than the colours of an autumn forest...Yet he seriously believes that these things can, every one of them, in all their tones and semi-tones, in all their blends and unions, be accurately represented by an arbitrary system of grunts and squeals. He believes that an ordinary man can really produce...that which denotes all the mystery of memory and all the agonies of desire.

—José Luis Borges

རི་མོ་པ་བསྟན་འཛིན་ནོར་བུ།

SOMETIMES a single piece of paper is worth more than gold. To some people, this cliché might inspire visions of lucky lottery tickets, the giant checks that contestants win on game shows, or even a Green Card. In my case, the invaluable paper in question came smelling of cardamom and dirty hands. It was written mostly in *devanagari*, the Nepali script, save for a precious word that was not even written in English, but in Latin. There, in the middle of the paper that eventuated in a special stamp into my passport, was the word *gratis*.

After six months and not a small amount of diplomacy on the part of the Fulbright office, I had been granted my research and travel permit to upper Mustang. Although restricted area travel permits were available for purchase by tourists, they came at the steep price of seventy dollars per person, per day. When planning my fieldwork, I realized that I would need an extended amount of time in Lo Monthang, and the daily cost of the permit would make this research financially impossible. The *gratis* research permit would now enable me to travel and conduct interviews as I saw necessary, over a four month period. The research permit would also mean that I did not have to travel in a group, and that I could stay in local homes. The one stipulation was that I would still have to be accompanied by a government liaison officer, but I would be able to arrange these services locally, in Jomsom. Finally, I would be allowed past Kagbeni. Finally, I would see Lo Monthang.

There was, however, an added element to this glorious news. In early May 1996, I returned to Kathmandu from Mustang for a brief visit to collect my permit—and my mother and stepfather. They had planned to visit me in Nepal and travel north with me to Lo Monthang. My stepfather,

Macduff, is a professional photographer, and we were to collaborate on a story about our trip for a travel magazine. Months before, when we had begun to plan this family excursion, I had assumed that by the time they arrived in late spring, I would already be familiar with Lo and deep into my research there. But government bureaucracy had forced a change in plans, and now I began to mentally prepare myself for the fact that my first trip to upper Mustang would be in the company of my mom and Macduff.

I had my reservations about this. For all its beauty, Mustang is not an easy place. Although both my mom and Macduff were seasoned adventurers, I knew that much of my energy would need to be directed toward them on this first trip. Yet I also missed my family deeply and was ready to share something of the life I was making for myself here, on the other side of the world. And, I reasoned, even if they accompanied me on this first trip, there was a season of fieldwork ahead of me once they returned to the U.S.

By this time in late spring, the streets of Kathmandu were enveloped in an unrelenting cloud of dust and pollution. It had not rained since February, and monsoon was still a solid month away. Dry heat beat down on the city. Papayas and lychees seemed to rot in front of their vendor's eyes. Women shaded themselves under umbrellas. Even those bicyclists who wore masks against the particulate haze sputtered and coughed at traffic signals. Everyone had pollution headaches. The Bagmati, a tributary of the sacred Ganges that flows through Kathmandu, looked more like a swamp than a river, its banks parched and its flow more sewage than stream.

But when I stepped outside the Nepali Home Ministry the day I got my permit, nothing could bother me. I looked north toward the mountains and even though I could not see them, I knew that I would be back in the high country soon, and that I would finally get to see the place I'd been dreaming about for years now. I envisioned Lo Monthang's bright barley fields and perfectly blue sky framing the walled city that was to be my home for much of the summer.

The permit had come through just in time. My mom and Macduff were due to arrive in Kathmandu in a week. Jigme and Tsewang's travel outfit,

Royal Mustang Excursions, was making all the arrangements for our three-person trek. Amchi Gyatso would travel with us as our guide. Although I did not yet know him well, Gyatso would soon become a confidant. As with Tshampa, Gyatso and I could laugh and laugh. But whereas Tshampa had heady ambition, Gyatso was lighthearted and affable. Over the coming months he would become both a brotherly companion as well as a key informant. His father, Tashi Chusang, was one of the last of his kind: a deeply knowledgeable *amchi* who had been trained not only by local healers in Mustang, but also by practitioners who had studied at the great medical institutions in Tibet. Tashi Chusang and Tshampa's father, Pembar, had been contemporaries and friends. Now, Tshampa and Gyatso were both struggling to determine how to keep their medical tradition alive in Mustang, and to pass on their knowledge to a next generation of *amchi*. Although I was still mostly focused on veterinary care, and on horses, I was becoming more curious about Tibetan medicine—how it was practiced in Mustang, and how these practices were changing.

For these reasons, I had asked Jigme if Gyatso could travel with us. Although Gyatso did not speak any English, he was more knowledgeable about Mustang's history and culture than most of the young Lobas Jigme was cultivating as trekking guides. I could serve as a translator for my parents, and so the arrangements were made.

For better or for worse, my parents and I had decided to time our visit to upper Mustang in accordance with Tempa Chirim, an annual three-day festival in Lo Monthang. Commonly called "Tiji," the festival involves rituals and masked dances performed by the monks at Chödyi, Monthang's Sakya monastery headed by Khempo Tashi Tenzin, a senior monk whose moral and religious authority in Lo was second only to the king. This late spring celebration served as a festival of renewal, as much as it involved a dramatic, almost violent, set of exorcism rituals, in which effigies of nefarious spirits were burned, ancient muskets were fired, and local gods were honored and appeased.

As an internationally renowned photographer, Macduff was chronically "on assignment." Having an opportunity to shoot images of an important festival, as well as to capture Mustang's natural beauty through

the lens of his panoramic camera, served as justification for the particular timing of this trip. The Tiji festival would certainly give Macduff
something to photograph, but, as I learned before our departure from
Kathmandu, we would be far from the only group of foreigners in Lo at
the time. Charles Ramble and a group of other European Tibetologists
were to attend the event as part of a summer research trip. Wangdi, my
language teacher and friend from the Sakya monastery in Kathmandu,
would travel with them as an assistant. A delegation from the World
Wildlife Fund Nepal Program would also be in attendance, as would
another professional photographer who was working on a story about
Mustang for *National Geographic*. In addition, a group of American
Himalayan Foundation executives would be helicoptering to Monthang
just before Tiji was scheduled to begin. They were courting the king
these days, trying to will him toward several projects they wanted to
fund, especially the renovation of Monthang's two ancient temples,
Thubchen and Jampa. In addition to these visitors, several other groups
of tourists would likely be in attendance.

In the center of this show, surrounded by villagers and foreigners,
would be the king, queen, and royal family. Gyalchang Jigme had been
assigned the job of accompanying the "big people" in the helicopter up
to Monthang from Kathmandu, a task that he seemed to take on with a
telling combination of hope and resignation. He explained that in addition to the festival, ACAP had arranged for other activities as well for the
tourists to take part in. These involved a tug-of-war, a volleyball game,
and a "traditional" horse race.

Jigme recounted these plans over dinner. He and his wife Droyoung
had invited me and my parents over to a pre-trek meal at his quarters
near Boudha. We ate *momo* dumplings and julienned radishes, served in
elegant Chinese bowls. The pace and sensory assault of Kathmandu
proved jarring for my mother. Although she is an avid traveler, fear and
disorientation could creep up on her. Sitting around the low tables of
Jigme's dining room, she seemed at peace for the first time since her
arrival. Seeing her relax settled me, in turn. I had told Macduff that Jigme
enjoyed scotch, and Macduff, whose Scottish roots were justification for
his being something of a whiskey connoisseur, had complied by toting

along from the U.S. some good single malt. Macduff presented it to Jigme and suggested they imbibe.

"The last time I was in Kathmandu," Macduff began, swilling his brew, "was in 1968. The streets weren't paved, and there sure were a lot more cows roaming around."

"So you saw Kathmandu before I did," Jigme responded. It was an apt, compelling observation about the differentials of movement and senses of the world afforded by virtue of each of their births, and about the pace of change in the intervening years.

"Those were the early days of Freak Street, with all the hippies coming here," Macduff continued to reminisce. "Of course, I was one of them, more or less. I had been traveling around the world for a while at that point." MacDuff had spent much of his late teens and early twenties roaming, camera in hand.

"What seems most different to you now about Nepal?" Jigme asked.

"Well, the obvious things—pollution, noise, neon signs, traffic. But also the sense of the outside world—politics, Western popular culture, all of that. It seems like there is a lot of sophistication, and new types of creativity and possibility, but also tension about traditional Nepali cultures and values in relation to these modern changes," Macduff responded. His thoughtfulness came from three decades of intimate study of people in Mexico's Yucatán Peninsula, as they experienced the overarching forces and powerful undercurrents of cultural and socioeconomic transition. Macduff shared some of his stories from the years he had spent among Mayan communities.

"There is a lot of change in Mustang now, too," offered Jigme. "Some new ideas and influences are good, but others are difficult. You will see when you are in Monthang, especially at a time like Tiji. Sometimes I feel like my family, and others from Lo, are lucky to have so many foreigners wanting to visit our place. But other times, it makes things difficult, especially since the government has not kept its promise to the people of upper Mustang."

Macduff knew something about these conflicts. He responded, "Sienna told me about the permit situation and the money that should be going to Mustang. Is there anything that we can do? Can I write a letter of complaint?"

Jigme smiled, perhaps at what he saw as the futility of Macduff's good intentions. "You can write," he said, "But it would do no good. Besides, even if we get the money promised us, there will be endless issues among Loba about what to do with it. No matter what, there will be politics."

Shifting topics gently, Macduff enquired about traveling with his cameras and asked if there were any issues he should be aware of in terms of photographing. A look of worry passed across Jigme's face.

"Well, there are fees at some of the temples to photograph, and in other places it is not allowed. I will do what I can to make sure you can do your work, but this too has become difficult."

I knew what Jigme said to be true. Lobas had become particularly wary of photographers in recent years, in part due to a series of accidents, misconceptions, and unfortunate incidents. Specifically, an American photojournalist had been granted a year's free permit to live in Mustang in 1991—an offering made by the late king Birendra as a gesture of goodwill for the photographer's coverage of the 1990 People's Movement that transformed Nepal into a constitutional democracy. This photojournalist had lived and worked in Nepal since the early 1980s, spoke Nepali well, and was at home in the mountains. However, misunderstandings and cross-cultural snafus plagued his time in Lo. By the time he left, some Lobas were convinced he was a demon who had disturbed the balance of elements and angered local gods. Others had accused him of desecrating temples and stealing ancient art. I came to know this individual a bit over the next few years, and he always firmly disputed these claims and, perhaps rightly, felt like he was the scapegoat and the foil for a whole host of unresolved local tensions.

Whatever the truth behind these stories, this foreigner's presence inspired a sense among many Loba that photographers were not to be trusted, and that other sacred spots should be guarded against their presence. In many respects, ACAP encouraged this taboo; strict tariffs and rules had been imposed on the use of cameras inside Lo's temples and shrines. The irony was, of course, that many of Mustang's artistic treasures, particularly the frescoes in its temples, were being ravaged by the elements and time, and would be gone within my lifetime unless they were documented and restored.

I thought about this history a lot before my mom, Macduff, and I began our trek north. As photographers go, Macduff was culturally sensitive and anthropologically attuned. He felt instinctively the paradox that was the captured image: the blessings and the curses that could befall an image frozen in time. And yet, I wondered how he would behave when faced with the magnificence that was Monthang, the spectacle of Tiji, and the charged, crowded atmosphere in a place where he knew neither landscape nor language.

In some sense, the cast of characters that was about to descend upon Lo Monthang—myself and my parents included—represented a number of forces of transformation at work in upper Mustang. Some tourists saw this place through an exoticized lens. They hoped to find in this "hidden kingdom" something akin to an unchanged Tibet, a contemporary Shangri-la. For experts on Tibetan religion, history, and culture, Mustang was a fertile ground for study in its own right, and also part of a larger scholarly puzzle. Others, foreigners and Nepalis alike, saw in Mustang a place and a people that needed to be both "preserved" and "developed." These perspectives brought with it social and economic opportunities and deep paradoxes. As for Lobas themselves, their responses to these external bearers of change, as well as their own evolving sense of what Mustang meant to them, were quite varied. Locals seemed, by turns, baffled, affronted, and kindly curious about the foreign interests in their culture and landscape. Most were angered by the government's handling of the expensive restricted area fees. And many had varying, even competing, ideas about how Mustang should at once embrace change and honor tradition.

These thoughts swirled around in my head as my mom and I meandered through Kathmandu's markets, gathering up small gifts and supplies for our trip to Lo. They fed my dreams and filled my field notebooks. In that sense, they, too, became the baggage with which I journeyed through Mustang.

For all of the mixed agendas that were to surface during our days in Lo Monthang, the ride north was surprisingly quiet. Tshampa was off in India on his research, and Karma was more subdued in his absence. We stayed at the Dancing Yak for a night, before leaving Jomsom and heading to Kagbeni, where we spent a night in the jovial company of the sisters who ran the Red House Lodge, Pema Dolkar and Yödren. Macduff's penchant for puns was not lost on these women, and I translated dirty jokes late into the evening.

Macduff had once been a cowboy and a river guide in the Sierra Nevada. He took to the itinerant life implicit in a trek, and he knew the feel of backcountry. He was happy not to shave for weeks, and felt at home in a sleeping bag on the ground. And yet, his knees and back were not as strong as they once were. Decades of carrying forty pounds of camera equipment across countries and continents had slowed him. But he was capable of finding joy through the viewfinder, always. Mustang's vast horizons and wispy clouds suited his panoramic eye. Macduff had also brought a Polaroid camera and offered to take portraits of local families. Once word got out, women and children streamed toward our camp in each village in which we stopped, dressed in their finery, ready to be photographed.

Despite being raised by artists and photographers, I remain ambivalent about the extraction of photographs from a place or a people. The power of a photograph lies in its ability to preserve and document history-in-the-making, but in places like village Nepal, so little is usually offered as reciprocation for all those clicks of the shutter. In this particular instance, Macduff's Polaroid mitigated some of my concern, and I left him alone to negotiate these exchanges. He emerged from the trip with some beautiful portraits, while Loba villagers were left with mementos of their own. When Macduff wasn't shooting, he spent his spare time reading in his tent. Although he wouldn't have turned down a bath, he seemed content in Mustang.

My mother, on the other hand, had spent very little time in saddle or sleeping bag. Although the paths we'd traveled thus far had not been too rugged by Nepal's mountain standards, they had been difficult for her. In the context of Southern California, she was exceedingly fit. But she seemed to wither in this parched landscape, and confided in me that she often dreamt of oceans on those nights in the rain shadow of the Himalayas. As someone who came of age in North Hollywood in the 1950s and '60s, she teased that in her family, "camping" meant martinis and blood rare steaks on a barbecue in the backyard.

So, even though I know the people and landscape of Mustang moved her deeply, she was rarely at ease while she was there. As much as she came to understand how at home I felt in this environment, she could not fully acclimatize in or to Mustang herself. What I knew as the rhythms of a subsistence life, she experienced most clearly as poverty. What I understood as a Buddhist or a Bön ritual, she saw through an unfiltered lens as flashes of shapes and colors—archetypal spiritual incantations.

One morning, as we navigated through the villages of Tsug and Tsele, we all marveled at the network of irrigation canals that directed water through these villages. As I watched my mom examine the earthen pigments of this environment, I realized that while the customs were overwhelmingly foreign to her, she was familiar with Mustang's colors and textures, its medium. Although she could not speak the human languages of this place, the visceral languages of color and texture grounded her here. As she pointed out umber and cadmium, Venitian reds, Navajo whites, and the deep sienna for which I was named, I realized that she was experiencing Mustang deeply, but in a radically different way than me.

My mother and I have always enjoyed a deep emotional bond. She can put me at ease and comfort me in a way that is quintessentially maternal. Yet much of my childhood had been trying and chaotic, in part due to her choices. I had spent my high school years living with my father and his partner. By the time I left for college, my mom and I had traveled through a cycle of distance and rapprochement. In the years since, I had begun to forge a life for myself that was at once interdependent—entwined with those who raised and nurtured me—but also separate, and far away from California. In that sense, this trip to Mustang was not simply a superficial mother-daughter adventure. Rather, it was an attempt to meaningfully share my life, such as it was at this point, with the person who had given birth to me. Together we rode and camped and rode again, trying to find our way back to some common language with each other after the many months and worlds that had separated us.

On the day we approached Lo Monthang, my mom and I rode quickly and stuck together. From the saddle of a mountain pass, we stared down at the exhilarating sight of this ancient walled city. Together, we traced the adobe and stone perimeter of this maze of houses, alleys, temples, and chorten, looking to find the city gates. We studied the ways fields, not yet green in May, checkered the landscape outside the wall. We looked beyond the city to Ketchar Dzong, the ruins of the first king of Lo's fortress. We watched the river that runs below Monthang snake down toward the Kali Gandaki—now a day's ride southeast—and stared up at the black contours of a Himalayan griffin as it rode waves of wind in this cornflower sky.

Only then did we realize that it was Mother's Day.

After arriving in Monthang, we set up camp on the roof of Gyatso's family home. Soon, the Tiji festival began. During the three days of ceremony, monks dressed in sun-streaked silk danced inside an elaborate *mandala* traced on the ground in colored chalk. They moved to a symphony of Tibetan trumpets, cymbals, and drums, against the backdrop of a stunning two hundred-year-old brocade *thangka* of Guru Rinpoche that blanketed a building three stories high. Later in the ceremony, dough effigies that symbolized local demons were tied up in string. On the third day of Tiji, Monthang's lay and monastic priests cast these effigies outside the gates of the city and lit a fire at the entrance of Monthang. All the villagers (and some foreign bystanders) leapt over the flames. Local noble men shot at the effigies with ancient flintlock rifles. I could not help but wonder if these weapons once belonged to Khampa soldiers.

Throughout all of this fanfare, locals and tourists pushed against each other, vying for views of the destroyed demons and the elaborate costumes worn by twirling, masked monks. Macduff and the other professional photographers tried not to get in each others' way, and took turns shooting from different angles: the roof of the royal palace, the sanctified ground in which the masked dances took place. For the most part, they were respectful of the rituals, but I could not help but squirm when I saw photographers—professional and amateur—edging their way into the circle of the dance. "National Geographic" seemed as much an attitude as it was a glossy publication in a distant place called *Amreeka*.

Meanwhile, ACAP staff oversaw a local fashion show—"to promote Mustang culture"—as well as the tug-o-war tournament and, later, the horse races. The festival quickly took on a slightly macabre sensibility. The tug-of-war game lured most of Lo's young people away from the second day of masked dances. Youngsters had forsaken tradition for a new game, and Khempo Tashi Tenzin looked on with disdain.

One afternoon during the ceremonies, the Monthang Mother's Group surrounded me. They looked angry. I had no idea what I had done, but they knew that I spoke Nepali and some Tibetan, and that I was not exactly a tourist.

"Do you know how much money all these foreigners spend to come here?" One mother yelled at me, grabbing my sleeve. Before I had time to answer, another added. "People come to take our pictures without asking. They're rich but they don't spend any of their money here!"

"We need money just like everyone. Things are expensive now. We can't even afford grass." As one woman spoke, the group continued to close in on me, their *chubas* shuffling against each other.

"People come to say that they want to help or to learn about our culture, but what good is that? They're only interested in the king or our old customs. They don't care about how we really are!"

"And the government is stealing from us. We're supposed to be getting money from ACAP but they don't give any either. Long-nosed *rongba* swine! What do they know?"

"Only the ACAP doctor does any good, but they say he isn't even a real doctor. Nobody really cares about what happens here." The woman stomped her foot on the ground, another shook a fist.

"We want our money! We want our money!" One woman shook me as she spoke. I had no idea what to do except to try and explain that I understood why they were angry. But that did not appease the group. They were angered by circumstance, angered by the display of wealth that all these foreign faces, mine included, insinuated. I felt like they quite literally saw each of us as seventy dollars a day, sixty percent of which was rightfully theirs. Ironically, they'd targeted one of the few people here who was not paying the government of Nepal for the privilege of being in Lo.

I am still not sure how I would have extracted myself from that situation had Pushpa not happened along.

"What's going on?" he said to me in English.

"*Aama haru risaundaai chhan*," I answered, in Nepali. "The mothers are getting angry."

"About what?"

"*Paisa*," I said. "Money."

"Don't do this," he said, addressing the women in Nepali. Everyone in town respected Pushpa. He was a confidant to many, as much as he was an anomaly: definitely Nepali, but also American; not a monk, but monastic in his habits; a practicing Buddhist but someone who challenged local friends to do more than just "bonk their heads on statues" and then cheat on their neighbor. He knew how to bridge cultural worlds well, not only as an anthropologist, but also as someone who lived these divides personally.

"You know she is a student. Compared to these others, she is a 'small person,' for a foreigner. She can't do anything to help you get your money. You need to organize yourselves, go talk with ACAP, tell the nobility to push for your rights in Kathmandu. You know better than this." The group of mothers mumbled and began to disband. Pushpa turned to me.

"In a weird way, Sienna, you should be happy that just happened," he said. "It shows that at least they thought they could communicate with you. Don't let it bother you. This isn't an easy place to be. Look around us. This place is a three-ring circus right now." Although I took solace in Pushpa's words, I felt at once stunned, assaulted, and ashamed. I wished that I could make the situation in Monthang different. But I also realized that all I could do was spend my time here with integrity, making few promises, giving back what I could, and listening to the voices around me.

A PASSING

"MY FATHER is not well," Gyatso said to me one morning after our arrival in Monthang. Indeed, when I went to pay my respects to the elder *amchi* that day, I was shocked at his deterioration, even though it had only been a month or two since I had met him, while he was passing through Jomsom on his way back to Monthang. Cough and chills plagued him. To eat a handful of *tsampa* was "like swallowing a stone," he said.

Despite his worsening health, Tashi Chusang remained alert, and still seemed to take pleasure in telling stories. As his stamina allowed, I spent some hours with Tashi Chusang during the days surrounding Tiji, and learned something of his biography. The elderly *amchi* was born in 1927 into a Mustang radically different than today's. Tashi Chusang was considered a reincarnation of a local lama who once resided at Samdroling, a monastery just a short distance northwest of Lo Monthang's walled city gates—a place I would visit later that summer. His lineage had been associated with practitioners of medicine, astrology, and *nyingma* religious traditions for many centuries.

In more ways than one, Tashi Chusang hailed from a long line of royal servants. His mother had been a personal assistant to the previous king of Lo, and his grandfather had not only been a highly respected doctor but also a tantric practitioner of renown. It was from his grandfather that Tashi Chusang was afforded a classical education, including his introduction to the study of medicine. But this erudite grandfather died when Tashi Chusang was eleven, forcing his mother—who had also been widowed—to turn to others in Lo. Tashi Chusang eventually became the student of a Tibetan man who is remembered as a great physician, and who Tashi Chusang referred as *agu*, or "uncle," even though they were not blood relatives.

"My grandmother came to *agu*," Tashi Chusang explained, "and said, with tears running down her face, 'My fatherless child's lineage is that of an *amchi* and a *nakpa*. So he must be a physician.' *Agu* could not refuse." As the years unfolded, Tashi Chusang memorized the *Gyushi* and set to work on becoming a physician. The young *amchi*-in-training learned the disciplines of physiology, pathology, diagnosis, and treatment. He also became a skilled astrologer.

Although Gyatso was an accomplished physician at this point, he was always humble and deferential. "I was seven when I started picking herbs with my father, and eighteen when I completed my three-year retreat and began treating some patients," Gyatso had explained. "But by the time my father was my age, he had traveled all over Tibet and Nepal, studying with different famous *amchi*, from far away near China and from Lhasa. It is rare to find an *amchi* with as much experience as my father," said my friend.

Despite the relatively upbeat tone of these conversations with his father, Gyatso could do little to quell the sense that Tashi Chusang was dying. Even though Gyatso and I had only known each other a short while, he did not stifle his tears as we parted ways that afternoon.

As a result of his ill health, Tashi Chusang had been entirely missing from the Tiji festivities, though his position as a *nakpa* and royal astrologer and physician made him central to the ceremony. A slightly bewildered Gyatso took his father's place for the first time that year.

"I have never done this by myself before," Gyatso whispered to me, eyes brimming with nervous expectation on the morning before the Tiji rituals began. I spent those early hours preceding festivities in the musty sitting room of Tashi Chusang's home. By 7:30 AM, Gyatso and his father were already hard at work sculpting *torma*. The old doctor worked slowly, but this repetitive act, his contribution to the ritual, seemed to soothe him. He coughed less as he worked, and sipped tea slowly. Though Gyatso had made *torma* before, he had never formed the special offerings required at Tiji. This had always been his father's job. Now father and son sat beside each other. Their fingers worked steadily, almost in unison. Gyatso followed in step, one beat behind the old *amchi*. Every once in a while, Gyatso's mother offered me tea and tried to convince her husband to eat. Turning into the other room, she cried in her tea when she thought no one was looking.

As father and son made *torma* with diligence, I wandered into the family shrine room. On the walls hung half a dozen scroll paintings, *thangka* worn thin with age and blackened by the smoke released from Mustang's hearths. One painting depicted the Bodhisattva of Compassion, of whom the Dalai Lama is an incarnation. The face of this radiant image seemed askew, his eyes slightly off kilter, distinguishing this painting from the more uniform renderings on Mustang's monastery walls. Yet this *thangka* seemed to belong to Monthang like few images I'd seen. When I asked Gyatso about the work, he said that Tashi Chusang had painted this image several decades ago.

"He's also taught Tenzin to paint," said Gyatso. Tenzin was Gyatso's younger brother, a skilled *amchi* as well as a monk. "My brother is very talented. I don't have the hands for it."

My comment about the *thangka* seemed to spark a thought in Tashi Chusang. He mumbled directions to Gyatso, who jumped up and fetched another *thangka* from the shrine room. He unraveled it gently and hung it on the wall opposite where he and his father sat working. Prayers voiced by Tashi Chusang and Gyatso filled the near-dark room and the teaching of this morning grew deeper. *Thangka* are visualization tools used in meditation. Later, Gyatso explained that his father had sensed his son's nervousness. The painting had been meant to help Gyatso mentally and spiritually prepare for his new responsibilities during Tiji.

I sat quietly, privy to an intimate family ritual. Here, near the cluttered hearth of a home heavy with illness, the men's work breathed of lineage, and with it a sense of continuity and new life. I could imagine Tashi Chusang at Gyatso's age, directing his son to grind medicines, identify plants, and invest each powder or batch of pills with the correct *mantra* blessings so that his medicine would be as efficacious as possible.

Father and son shared the same face, the same thin lips. I watched Gyatso prepare, quietly and with diligence, for this rite of passage. He was aware of both his father's flagging lifeforce and the impending changes in his own life. Later that day, in the garish, golden sunshine and dust, among royalty and commoners and tourists, Gyatso wore his father's elaborate saffron hat and the maroon and white shawls of a householder priest with grace. And Tenzin twirled, incandescent.

I visited the old *amchi* again the next morning. Tashi Chusang hacked up phlegm as we spoke, and, as speaking required much effort of him, I did not stay long. Dr. David Shlim, an expatriate doctor who helped to run Kathmandu's most famous travel clinic, had arrived in Monthang on the American Himalayan Foundation–hired helicopter. He came to look in on Tashi Chusang. Without proper tests, Dr. Shlim said that he could not say specifically what was plaguing Tashi Chusang, but that the *amchi's* room "smelled like cancer."

What does cancer smell like? I wondered. The walls were caving in around this old doctor with an artist's soul.

As we prepared to leave Lo Monthang several days later, I realized that I might not see Tashi Chusang again. Although I had not spent much time with him, he had lodged in my *sem*, my heart-mind, as an exemplar.

Dr. Shlim offered to take Tashi Chusang with him in the helicopter, and attempt to diagnose and treat him in Kathmandu. The king and queen, as well as Jigme, thought this might be a good idea, but the *amchi* refused to leave Monthang. His sons were reticent to disregard his wishes.

Gyatso had insisted that he would continue to accompany me and my parents through the rest of our trek, but I knew that he was worried about his father and tried to insist that he stay in Monthang.

"We can make our way back to Jomsom," I said. "Tsewang or Tokme or Raju could travel with us. We'll be fine." But Gyatso would not budge. As we set off from Monthang, his usual lightness drained from his demeanor, Gyatso began to speak.

"I'm not sure I did the right thing by not putting my father on the helicopter. I know that he is sick, but I also know that he wants to be in his place, not in Kathmandu. Dr. Shlim's medicine is powerful. *Gyalchung* Jigme said he would pay for whatever expenses. But…I don't know…the decision. He's my responsibility." Gyatso's voice cracked, and for a time he walked on ahead of me, alone.

We arrived in the village of Dhi that evening. Prayer flags kissed the wind like tongues and eyelashes. Such soft images for a land of weather-beaten skin, lungs corroded by smoke, stomachs worn thin by *chang* and chilis, and flanks of earth delivered up by the relentless force of oceans and glaciers. Here, there is no choice but to realize that we live in deli-cate balance with our physical environment, and that the shifts of time that compose a life are nothing if not beautifully volatile.

That night, I pinched a nerve in my back. By morning, I could hardly move. Gyatso treated me with an herbal concoction that looked like the hot sauce served in Chinese restaurants. The recipe included cardamom, saffron soaked in oil, embers from the morning's fire—to drain heat and excess blood away from my ache—and "many other plants." He mas-saged the ointment into my back, commanding that I rest in Dhi while he took my parents to Luri, a chorten enclosed in a cave on the eastern edges of Lo, perched above the villages of Yara and Gara.

By reputation, Luri was a gem. The chorten was reputed to be eggshell smooth to the touch with images that looked more Persian or Kashmiri in style than Tibetan. The designs on the concave ceiling reminded one of the Taj Mahal, much more than they recalled any other Tibetan mon-ument. Propped up with sticks and brambles like an eagle's nest in the side of a cliff, Luri embodied both the harshness and the grace of Mus-tang's landscape. It was rumored that this chorten was one of six such edifices in Lo, but that the others had long since been rendered inacces-sible by the erosion of Mustang's sandy, fluted cliffs.

On that first trip, though, as I curled up in a corner of a darkened house in Dhi, I knew that my mother would be moved by the chorten at Luri and that she should go. She drew solace and inspiration from ancient places and had recently produced a series of paintings and an artist's book on the caves at Lascaux, France. The cave art was of a different period, and was the product of a different people, but I imagined it would inspire her greatly nonetheless.

"Don't worry. I will take care of your parents," said Gyatso. And with that, he, Macduff, and my mom headed off toward Luri. Although he had insisted, the fact that he was taking care of my parents, while his father suffered at home, disturbed and depressed me.

I spent the day sleeping and playing cards with our horseman from Tsarang. Late in the afternoon, a messenger arrived from Monthang with a letter for Gyatso. "Tashi Chusang is extremely sick," the note read. "Please tell Gyatso to return home immediately." When Gyatso and my parents returned to Dhi, I told him the news and handed him the letter. Gyatso's face fell as he read it. This always-smiling man was stone-faced now.

"You must leave at once," I said.

"But will you…"

"Don't worry about us. Your place is with your family. We've saddled your horse. I've packed you some buckwheat bread and eggs." For all the ways Gyatso has been my caretaker, I felt for a moment like his guardian, taking care of him in my insistence that he leave us.

As Gyatso prepared to leave, my parents pulled me aside.

"We want to give Gyatso something," my mom said. "It seems so horrible to say goodbye like this."

"I have a pocketknife," Macduff offered.

"I'll give him my sneakers," my mom added. "He liked them, right?" Gyatso had worn my mom's shoes earlier on during our trek, after he soaked his feet helping my mom cross a river.

"I'm sure he'll appreciate whatever you give him," I said, knowing that this was true but also that the gift of material possessions seemed a small gesture at a time of such inner mourning. Macduff picked up on this.

"I know it is silly, " he said, "but we want to give him something. We can't communicate with him to thank him. When you see someone torn with emotion, and your own eyes are tearing up, what do you do? If you do nothing, you have nothing."

And so it was that I wrapped up Macduff's pocketknife and my mother's shoes in a *kathag*, added some rupees for butter lamps and other offerings, and saw Gyatso off. The trail back to Monthang from Dhi led straight up a silty cliff, more dust than mountainside. I lost sight of Gyatso in minutes but stood listening to his horse's breath and the jingle of its bell until night closed in around me.

Tashi Chusang lived through that cycle of the moon.

✦ —— STONES AND LOST CHILDREN —— ✦

MY MOTHER and I have always found solace in shapes: the feel of a stone that fits perfectly in a palm, the full curves of a breast or cheek, the clean edges of a modernist painting, the saw-toothed horizon of mountains against sky. We share a love of the abstract, but also a love of the natural world and the rhythms of landscape as they map onto and shape human experience.

When I was about four years old, and my mother was still a graduate student in fine art, she won a scholarship to create a series of paintings and drawings on the American Southwest from the site plans and maps of Chaco Canyon and Canyon de Chelly. My father and I accompanied her on this trip. Under the dry heat of the desert sun, my mother sketched; my father, with his archaeologist eyes and vivid imagination, spent hours searching for shards and other remnants of an Indian past. I played among art supplies, field notebooks, and sleeping bags. At some point, I wandered over to where my mother was drawing from an on-site map. She traced for me the lines and shapes of this ancient place, intimating the world these maps had once depicted. Seeing this, I decided to "build" my own Indian *kiva*—a room for Native American rituals and spirit worship—out of pebbles. I set to the task of finding perfect rocks. "Earthwork," I called it. And so my mother and I began a relationship that involved creating beside each other, each in our own way.

Over the years, she and I have sent each other rocks and shells from our various journeys: she, bits of jade from Kyoto or seashells from Mexico; I, rocks found from among the reeds and dunes that border the northeastern shores of the Atlantic or green and ochre fragments from Mount Kailash in western Tibet. Together and alone, similar shapes have continued to catch our attention. Yet for all the ways I resemble my mother—our voices are nearly identical—we are actually quite different.

The trip to upper Mustang aged my mother. In her mid-forties at the time, she was in better physical shape than most people twenty years her junior. But the fierce wind, the butter tea, and the long, elemental days had made her feel weak and small. For someone who had spent most of her life at sea level, the rarefied air of the Himalayas drained her of energy. She struggled. And yet I also knew that she was seeing me as she had never seen me before, and that my ability to navigate this wholly other place impressed her. She also saw my Mustang friends for who they were: soulmates, teachers, and tough characters, by turns. As someone who lives for all that is visual and textual, I also knew that she was overwhelmed—in a good sense—by Mustang's raw beauty.

I wondered what my mother would make of this trip, after her return home. Would it, like so many of her other travels, transmute into painting? How would this place that meant so much to me come to live in her?

Faced as I was in Mustang with such vivid illustrations of family continuity—even at moments of death or heated dispute—I ached for my own sense of lineage. Coming from a culture, as I did, that valued youth over age and that so often involved an abject disavowal of our roots and the ways our families shape us, how would I carry my parents' teachings and yet grow into myself? Coming to Mustang was part of this experience, but only a part. Being in Mustang with my mom and Macduff had complicated and enriched my own sense of purpose and direction.

Some years before, my mother had written a short verse as part of an artist's statement accompanying a show of her paintings. Traversing Mustang's valleys, passes, and plains in her company, the verse came to me:

Suppose that everything that's happened
To me, or to you
Has left a mark, a smudge of color,
A scant trace of shadow or light.

Suppose, like the lizard or the snake,
That in order to grow
I am continuously sloughing off old skins
And that this re-forming occurs
Whether I know it or not.
Suppose that the bright joy a child feels
When she makes a pool of blue and a pool of
Yellow paint spill together and become green
Is no small matter.

Something about this poem seemed to capture the ways this landscape and these people were leaving their mark on me. My own passage through Mustang was an internal metamorphosis, even as
Mustang itself was adapting, changing, sloughing off old skins. Simul-
taneously, this particular time was opening up a new, shared space
between me and my mom. We were growing with each other through
this adventure.

In another respect, the poem also recalled for me those days of doing
my "earthwork." I thought about what it must have been like for my
mother to watch her child discover herself through simple acts of creation, and to have been something of a guide through this process.
Now, I saw my mother as that child, and it was I who was bearing witness, guiding her.

On our way back to Jomsom, after we had said goodbye to Gyatso in
Dhi, we had planned to head east from the village of Tetang, over the
Muya La pass, and down into the Muktinath Valley. But by the third day
of our return journey my mother was spent, both physically and emotionally. We shifted course, heading straight down the Kali Gandaki,
back to the relative luxury of Jomsom: beds and clean sheets, showers
and green vegetables. Afraid to disappoint me and deprive Macduff of
some valuable shots of Muktinath—one of the most dramatic and sacred
pilgrimage spots in all Nepal—my mom kept insisting that she would be
ready to travel after a day or two of rest. But Macduff and I agreed that
what energy my mother could cultivate would not take her far beyond

Jomsom. In the end, we compromised, and planned to spend a night in Lubra—just a two-hour walk from Jomsom, but a place I had wanted to share with them.

When we arrived in Lubra, the villages felt empty and still, aside from the rustling of the poplars and the gurgling creek that winds through these fourteen households. Dappled light shone through apricot trees. The old walnut tree at the foot of the village provided a few sleeping cows with shade. While Macduff disappeared to take photographs, my mom sat down near one of the village water taps. She looked peaceful.

"It's so quiet here," she said.

I just nodded and went off to find Palsang. She, like most of the other women in Lubra, was occupied with summer agricultural work. I found her among the buckwheat, high up above the village, and called out to her. She put down her hoe and waved. "The key to the house is in its usual place," she yelled back. "I'll come shortly. Tsewang Tenzin is in Jomsom, selling *arak*. Should be back tonight."

"I've brought my mother and little father," I called back. During our trip to Lo, I had taken to calling Macduff my "little father"—a term more easily understood in areas such as Mustang where polyandry had been, historically, more common than divorce.

"All this way?" Palsang responded. "You must be tired. There's tea in the thermos. I'm coming!"

I headed back down to the village and found Macduff and one of the village *nakpa*, Tashi Tenzin, engaged in sign-language banter. Tashi had a long face, huge hands, weathered skin, and coarse, unkempt whiskers. He was quiet and kind. Tashi was one of the old generation of householder priests who knew the myths and stories of the village by heart, and who could recount in incredible detail what Mustang was like as much as five or six decades ago. But he was shy and had little reason to consider tourism or other foreign encounters. Although there had been a time when he traveled and traded, he was village bound now.

I stood on the trail just above Tashi's house, watching him and Macduff. It was clear that Macduff wanted to take a picture of Tashi just as he had found him: dozing on his roof, amid piles of drying apricots in the magic light of late afternoon. But Tashi Tenzin had noticed Macduff and his cameras, and had begun tidying up his home to make it picture worthy. Macduff tried to get him to understand that he didn't have to do anything, but Tashi, in his slow, methodical way, would not have it. Macduff snapped anyway, as Tashi shunted half-dried apricots into a woven basket and picked up a broom to sweep the roof clean.

I called down in greeting and Tashi answered. "Tell your father to wait. I'm almost finished cleaning," he said. "How long will you stay?"

"Only one night. Going down to Kathmandu soon. Do you have anything for me to carry?" Tashi's son was a monk who had studied for many years at the Bön monastery in Dolanji, India, and he was now spending time at a sister institution near Swayambhunath, in Kathmandu. On a few occasions, I had carried letters, local *tsampa*, or dried apricots from Tashi to his son.

"No, nothing. My son is coming up soon."

I found my mom near Palsang's vegetable patch, under a tree. She was sketching in her journal and seemed, for the first time in three weeks, to have caught her breath and found her center.

"Palsang is coming," I said, "But I've opened up the house. You can go in and rest if you want. It's cool in there."

"No thanks. I'll stay out here for a while." My mother paused and then said, "I don't know how you do it, Sienna."

"Do what?" I asked.

"The quiet here, I need it. I can see why you like this village. But the lack of privacy, the dirt—I'm overwhelmed all the time. So much beauty, so much hospitality, so much that is made from so little. But don't you get tired of feeling like you're never alone, like you're constantly dirty and always misunderstood?"

I sat down next to her and looked at my boots. "Actually, mom, I feel like that's exactly what I am here—alone and yet never alone." But a great part of that was what I loved about Mustang. Despite—and, in some ways, as a consequence of—all the new cultural knowledge, the misunderstandings and the bare-bones, nomadic lifestyle I led, I felt that I was truly growing. There was nothing easy about life here, but I felt full and so deeply engaged. Here, I was "myself" but I was also someone new, emerging from this place and the languages I used to communicate. Although my Nepali or my comprehension of the local Tibetan dialect would never match the comfort I felt in English, I liked how I could not take the meanings of things for granted here. I was using every bit of my personality to communicate, to find a common thread, to form relationships, and I was becoming successful at that.

But there was a greater irony in my mom's reaction to Lubra. She had finally found the sense of emptiness and solitude she'd been craving in the one place in Mustang where I came explicitly for the company. In Lubra, I shared my deepest conversations with Palsang over steaming cups of tea. The most intimate of all my friendships in Mustang had grown out of time spent in Lubra, and I had repeatedly traveled to this village for the sole purpose of feeling comfortable in this land that was so distant from my own.

Of course, I understood on another level what my mother meant. Even though she could not understand the languages being spoken around her, she felt crowded in by Mustang's humanity. Here, most people slept and ate and were born and died within small, simple structures, shared by many. True solitude was rare. As we sat on the same ground, experiencing completely different emotions, I could not help but feel that, despite all we shared, there would remain so much of each of us that the other would not know.

That night, Palsang and I made vegetable *momo* and a soup of garlic greens and chard from her garden. Tsewang Tenzin came home from Jomsom eventually and tried out his English on my parents. We talked into the evening.

"So you really only have one child?" Palsang asked, nodding for me to translate to my mother.

"Yes, *ho*," my mother answered, using one of the few Nepali words she'd learned.

Palsang turned to me, "Is she well? She looks so healthy and not that old. I know about those medicines and things, but certainly she wanted more than one child. Why hasn't she had more children? Don't your mother and little father want to have children to take care of them when they're old? It will be too much just for you." I translated. In many ways, Palsang was right. Although my parents were still young, the thought of taking care of all four of them—my mother, Macduff, my father, and his partner Charles—seemed like an overwhelming task.

"Sometimes I wish I had other children," my mother said, asking me to translate. "But it is difficult to educate and take care of many kids in America."

Tsewang Tenzin understood. "*Yes. Schooling very expensive,*" he answered in English. "*In India also very expensive.*" I explained to my parents that Palsang and Tsewang Tenzin's boys were in boarding school in India.

"How many children do they have?" My mom asked.

"Three, but Palsang's given birth to seven," I responded. Palsang knew what I was talking about. She held up seven fingers and then pointed to her stomach. My mom stared at Palsang and then turned to me.

"Tell her that I've lost children, too," said my mother. Again, I translated, and then watched as the two women connected wordlessly. Without anticipating it, my mother had found a sense of intimacy and shared experience, creating a bond through their individual memories of loss.

The next morning, after a breakfast of omelets and thick wheat *chapati*, my mom and I walked upriver together. Macduff stayed back at Palsang's, supine and sleepy on the wooden cots I'd helped to finish and arrange in the extra room earlier that spring. Palsang had a full day of agricultural work ahead of her, but said she'd come back to feed us lunch before we returned to Jomsom.

The Panda Khola was subdued this time of year, before the rains came. My mom and I walked on the near side. We held hands, listened to the sweet rush of water, and gathered a few stones.

"Palsang is an amazing woman," said my mom, breaking the silence. "You've made good friends here." I nodded and squeezed her hand.

"You know, for years I really did want to have another child," she continued. "The first child I lost, after you—it was such a difficult decision. I was taking very strong antibiotics for a chronic infection, and when I missed my period I went immediately to the doctor. He said that the drug—tetracycline—could cause severe damage to the fetus. Your father and I decided it was better to end the pregnancy and try again. We both deeply wanted another child, and the thought of giving this one up was so hard. We were both pretty depressed." I imagined that such a decision, even if mutual, probably fueled distance and tensions between my parents at an already fragile time in their relationship. My mom and I did not look at each other as she talked, but held hands tightly and kept walking. I had known that there were losses, but she had never before shared these details with me.

"The second child was a disaster," my mom continued. "That was the ectopic pregnancy." I was about eight when my mother had started to hemorrhage in her studio. A family friend who made frames for my mom's paintings happened to stop by that afternoon, and was able to help rush my mom to the hospital. I remember visiting her in the emergency room and being scared by her weakness. I had seen my mother at the deep ends of sadness and anger in those years—the years when my parents' marriage really fell apart—but I had always imagined her as fundamentally healthy and strong. To see her there, among the antiseptic sheets and bedpans, and to touch the scar that ran across her belly, made me feel frightened and vulnerable. I imagine she felt the same, in her own way.

"The third loss turned out to be a 'false' pregnancy in my other tube," my mother continued. "A sort of bodily recoiling I guess. I never really understood. I dearly wanted another child, but it didn't work out. My body remembers it, though. I feel the loss sometimes. I know your dad does, too." My mother paused before continuing. "That is why you are such a gift," she said, reaching for a river rock. "I still have the smooth, round stone I held in my hand all through my labor with you." Touching her arm, I felt both the frailty of her tired frame and her innate strength. We stood there by the side of the Panda Khola, quiet in contemplation for a moment.

"Palsang and I have talked sometimes about her family, and the children she and Tsewang Tenzin have lost. But you and I have never really talked about this part of your life until now. That feels strange." I knew that things had been withheld from me when I was younger because I was simply that: too young to understand. But here, in Mustang, I had formed an intimate relationship with a mother who had lost children, and had come to grasp how precarious birth could be for both mother and child. Yet I remained somewhat ignorant as to what my own parents had suffered through.

"It's just different," my mother answered. "But also in some ways...I wonder. Her life seems so hard." I know that we were both considering the fact that an ectopic pregnancy to Palsang would have likely meant death.

"It isn't easy, but she is one of the most resilient people I've ever known."

"Seems like she has to be."

The sun was high. We turned and headed back toward the village.

The Story of the Ground

As spring bloomed and ushered in summer, I made several trips to Lo, spending much of the next two seasons in the kingdom. When possible, I traveled with Gyatso, who continued to serve as a local guide and a teacher. I was both learning much from Gyatso and forming a close friendship with him.

On one such trip from Jomsom to Lo, we arrived in the village of Ghami on a warm June evening and untacked our horses outside Raju's family home. After tea and niceties, Gyatso said he wanted to show me something. He and I ambled away from the village toward Maldang Ringmo. At nearly three hundred meters long and six feet high, this was the longest wall of engraved *mani* stones in Mustang, and quite possibly the longest such monument in all Nepal. I had seen the row of *mani* before, and had always found it impressive, but on previous trips I had not stopped to look at the actual stone carvings carefully. Now, I ran my hands along these carved rocks.

"We have many books in Mustang. You have seen the king's library. But these rocks are our history, too," said Gyatso. As my confidant and I stood in front of this snaking wall of stone, framed as it was by sky and wind, by the red cliffs of Drakmar village and the chalky gray hills, rich in iron, beyond, I felt overwhelmed by the power of this comment. I now realized that this wall was special in that it was not simply a collection of engraved prayers, but that it held stories, collective memories.

"Look at this inscription," he continued. "*Chip ta gi bön po—chipbön,*" the doctor muttered, running his hands over a slab of stone. "The *chipbön* is the master of the king's horses." I traced a row of Tibetan script carved into the rock, one line of text among thousands.

"My father remembered the last real *chipbön*. He was an old man who spent his days around the palace stables in Monthang. He took good care of the horses. Gave them rapeseed oil, eggs when he could get them, and more sweet peas than some families were lucky to harvest in a year. He could handle a horse, too. He used to ride through rivers that could drown a man and eat nothing but *tsampa* for days on end, all to bring the king superior horses from Tibet."

"Sounds just like Pema Ngotug," I said.

"Exactly," answered Gyatso. I had first met Pema Ngotug the same day in Jomsom when I had met Gyatso and the king. Pema Ngotug had been doctoring, trading, and breaking Mustang's horses for years. His body bore the scars of countless mounted misadventures. The ridge of his nose was crooked, his fingers formed a contorted yet solid fist, and his feet rested more naturally in stirrups than on the ground. All muscle and grit, his rough exterior gave way quickly when I told him that I was studying horses. He had since spent hours talking to me about what he knew.

"The last time I was in Monthang, Pema Ngotug told me that when he went to Tibet earlier in the spring, he came back with a new stallion for the king and a box of watches," I said. "He said that Tsangpo, the Brahmaputra River, almost swept him away, horse, watches, and all."

"I wish those watches did get washed away," Gyatso laughed. "He gave me one of them. It crows like a rooster and I can't get it to stop!" The *amchi* and I laughed, mouths open, heads thrown back.

"Pema Ngotug is similar to the *chipbön*," Gyatso continued, serious again. "They both know how to let blood, apply heat, and cauterize wounds with fire. The last *chipbön* also knew something about herbal medicines," continued Gyatso. "He learned some things from my father. At that time, some people did not like working for the king—our king's father. They were taken care of, but they weren't paid with *rupees*, and they were starting to understand what that meant. But the *chipbön*, he enjoyed his job, and so he stayed with the king taking care of the animals.

"The last *chipbön* died at the time of the king's father," Gyatso went on. "Nobody officially replaced the last *chipbön*. Horses still get treated, but Pema Ngotug, and others like him, are getting old. I guess things will have to change again."

Gyatso and I stared out over the landscape. He began to tell me how and why the row of *mani* stones was more than just a historical record. Encased in this string of stones lived the myths which gave life to this sacred geography. In the pale and fading light, Gyatso told me the tale of the *sinmo*, a demoness who once inhabited this land, and how she was subdued by Guru Rinpoche as he traveled through Mustang on his way to Tibet, spreading the teachings of the Buddha. The story involved shapeshifting, suffering, conquest, and all that the soil absorbs.

Such stories are common in the Tibetan culture. As it is recounted in myths and historical records, pre-Buddhist Tibet had a living, forceful geography that needed to be tamed. This "taming" was, in essence, the conversion of Tibetans to Buddhism, which lasted from the seventh century until the twelfth century. This was the height of the Tibetan Imperial Era—an age of *dharma* kings and religious as well as political expansion. Much of the literature of the time spoke about pre-Buddhist Tibet as a place of great inherent power, but a realm and a people who could benefit from Buddhism.

The ancient Tibetan landscape was guarded by various wrathful gods who ruled their sacred and earthly domains. While dedicated to the protection of the people and landscape, *sinmo* were particularly difficult to appease, and stories of their exploits and encounters with Buddhist figures such as Guru Rinpoche abound within Tibetan tradition. Here in Mustang, as in Central Tibet, these *sinmo* were literally and figuratively pinned down to this landscape by the power of the Buddha's teachings through the actions of Guru Rinpoche. Across the Tibetan-speaking world, these spiritual battles were inscribed in the landscape. They gave it both meaning and form. With the Buddhist conversion, these deities were not only subdued and transformed, but were then enlisted as wrathful protectors of the *dharma* and all those who practiced it.

Gyatso told me such a story, that waning afternoon in Lo, as we stood in front of Maldang Ringmo.

"Once, long ago in the kingdom of Lo, there lived a *sinmo*," Gyatso began. "She spent her days traveling the length and breadth of this country, a place of caves and canyons beyond the great Himalayas. Her hands—hundreds of them—smelled of sulfur and dusty earth. Her eyes shone the color of ocean by day and fire by night. Mysterious and powerful, she passed the centuries possessing animals with fear and crazy fright, drumming up hail that pelted barley crops and destroyed sheaves of unripened grain, and sneaking into the dreams of village children.

"The demoness wandered throughout the Tibetan world. She visited nomads in their tents on the cold northern plains and played tricks on their herds of yak and sheep, causing them to wander far from home. She sneaked into shrine rooms and rattled altars and offering bowls set out for protector deities in villages across the plains of U-Tsang. She rustled like wind across the prairies in the east, stirring up sickness and discontent among the warriors of Kham and Amdo.

"The demoness came to Mustang to make a home for herself. Restless and alone, her years of shaking up weather, disturbing dreams, and taunting the local gods with her magic had tired her. Even those beings that live by fire and mischief need to rest. Furthermore, in recent years she had begun to feel the rumblings of change coming up to Tibet from the south. She'd heard from other demons who ruled pockets of this great land that a mystic, a visionary wanderer, had discovered a great Truth somewhere in the lowlands of India and that he was determined to carry this *dharma* north to Tibet. This was Guru Rinpoche.

"But the demoness was not easily impressed. Like other demons and demonesses, she feasted on wild ass, antelope, and gazelle. She swallowed gulps of hail to quench her thirst.

"In those days, there was little thought given to compassion in this wild land. Instead, the *sinmo* kept people defensive and left them shortsighted, angry. They were preoccupied with small things: silly disputes, getting rich, petty village politics. Sort of like people are today," Gyatso mused. "For protection, they sacrificed animals and asked local gods.

"But the Buddha's teachings were spreading, and Guru Rinpoche was a very powerful master. He came in search of the demoness. He moved by flying more than by walking, and rode on a tigerskin, carrying a golden *dorje*, a thunderbolt scepter. When the demoness saw that *dorje* shine in the sun and snow, she felt fear like she never had before. But she was also stubborn and did not want to give up on this place. These hills and lakes and valleys had become her home. She decided to hide.

"Guru Rinpoche was not far behind her. He carried Tibetan salt with him—gifts from the local earth spirits he had encountered and subdued in other places—and he left bits of salt throughout Lo as he traveled, to mark his way. Salt can be a treasure, too. The *sinmo* tried to disguise herself as a village woman and trick Guru Rinpoche, but the *dharma* master could see right through this ruse. He continued to chase her.

"The demoness thought this place that she had ruled for so long would protect her from Guru Rinpoche, but he was more powerful. Where the demoness hid, Guru Rinpoche knew. He struck the spots with his golden *dorje* and hit her, ripped open her stomach. He removed her intestines and strung them along this plain, right where we are now. Maldang Ringmo is her intestine.

"Then, Guru Rinpoche emptied the demoness of her blood and splashed it on the cliffs of Drakmar. You know how red the dirt is there?"

"Yes," I said, recalling Drakmar's cliffs of deep umber and chalky scarlet earth.

"But Guru Rinpoche was not finished. Next, he took out her liver and flung it to the east of Ghami. Look, you can see it there," Gyatso pointed to a patch of slate-colored earth, above the now-abandoned settlement of old Ghami village.

"The last thing he did was to destroy the *sinmo's* heart—the most dangerous part of the demoness. In the end, he carried it up the mountainside to a lush valley, where he cut up the heart into a hundred and eight pieces, and buried each piece under a chorten, a cairn made of rocks and carved *mani* stones. Later, people built the monastery of Lo Gekhar on this spot. These chorten are still there, too. People say that Guru Rinpoche had to subdue this demoness before he conquered another *sinmo* in Central Tibet. There, Guru Rinpoche had to pin down the *sinmo* by building a chorten on each one of her joints, so that Samye, Tibet's first Buddhist monastery, could be built."

Although I had heard such stories before, Gyatso's tale of the demoness and her subjugation particularly spoke to me now. As much as I thought about the fact that the *sinmo* was a female force capable of both creation and destruction, her story also served as a metaphor for the current changes facing Mustang's landscape and its people. The *sinmo* embodied this animate landscape—a place bowing to the forces of change. At the same time, Gyatso's retelling of the *sinmo*'s tale spoke to Tibetan history and identity in a more general sense, and to Mustang's place within this. Although Mustang sat clearly within Nepal's border, the story I was hearing was one about the Tibetan assimilation of the *dharma* and the pervasiveness of Buddhist renderings of history. Finally, this story was a testament to the power of Tibetan places, to their beauty and their wildness, perhaps even to the human ambivalence that comes from making life in—and making meaning out of—a landscape at once near to the gods of earth and sky and yet on the edges of things, a place at once powerful and exposed.

To Heal a Horse

Evening in Lo is long shadows, turbulent winds, tired horses, and dry, dust-sore eyes. Hands buried in the pockets of my dirty jeans, heels dug into marble-sized bits of scree, I followed Gyatso away from the *mani* wall, down to the river's edge, and up again toward Ghami. Raju's house beckoned in the distance, but we still needed to feed, water, and let our horses out to graze before we could retire.

Once we reached the house, Gyatso and I stacked sweat-caked saddle carpets in the corner of the corral. I squinted against the wind and, even though it was summer, braced myself against night's chill. My *amchi* friend slipped feedbags over three groping noses. I reached for more bags, each laden with kilos of naked barley, and followed him. This was a ritual I had repeated countless times at barns back home, and it felt familiar here, too. The little gray gelding in the corner nuzzled my thigh as I passed him. As if I would forget this horse whose blood, let to cure an abscess, stained my jeans and remained encrusted under Gyatso's fingernails.

The day before, we had been on the road for the better part of the morning. Bena was three households propped up against each other like rain-worn standing stones, and we arrived just in time for tea. Bena is known throughout Mustang as the most filthy, smoky tea stop along the trail between Kagbeni and Monthang. The clientele, however, is never dull, as Bena is also known for its acrid barley home-brew and pretty, if also soot-smudged and tired, hostesses.

That morning we shared the hearth with an aging veterinarian named Norbu. Noticeably tipsy, Norbu explained that he had been traveling for days, letting blood. In late spring and midsummer, the nostrils of Mustang's horses are pricked and bled to combat the ill effects of blood turned noxious by months of physical exertion. Bloodletting has been shown to decrease the chance of edema and raise blood oxygen levels, particularly when horses are moved to high-altitude summer pastures, and the bloodletting I witnessed in Mustang left animals unharmed and, seemingly, invigorated. But it obviously left the practitioner drained. Norbu's withered body creaked and moaned in the morning sunlight. Well past sixty, his clients still expected the old man to ride or walk for up to eight hours to treat their horses during the auspicious window in early summer.

"I've got five horses to bleed in Chuksang tomorrow," said the doctor, begrudgingly, physically spent. "Haven't stopped working for the last week. Worked on three horses yesterday. A few more are waiting in Tangbe," he mumbled. Smearing a dab of yak butter on his palm, he began massaging the grease into his hand and examining his fingers against a stream of sunlight. Perhaps heat and light would mend his fossilized joints.

Gyatso noticed my stare and whispered, "He lives alone with nobody to take care of him. His wife died years ago." Norbu's fingers cracked. Human tinder, those brittle bones.

In a few minutes, Gyatso went outside to check on the horses. He returned, hands on his hips, wrinkles creasing his forehead. The gray gelding had been acting sluggish all morning. Cowering when asked to move forward, its usual quick pace slowed to a languishing trot, not at all the organ-rattling four-beat gait that is preferred by high-mountain horsemen from Mongolia to Mustang. By the time we approached Bena, the horse was merely creeping along, moving its bit across its teeth, alerting Gyatso that something was wrong.

"*Meme*," he said, addressing Norbu as "grandfather." "My gelding doesn't move well or eat. Will you look at him?"

Norbu grunted. "You've been working them hard. The grass is not very good these days," he said. Though far from congenial, the doctor took notice of Gyatso's fallen face and straightened up.

"I saw two horses suffering from *hre* last week and another who had an old case of *gen* that didn't eat for several days," I offered. "I wouldn't be surprised if it is *hre*." The fact that I knew the local names for several types of gastrointestinal disorders caught Norbu by surprise. I'd seen Tshampa Ngawang and others diagnose this problem many times before, and by voicing my thoughts I hoped to challenge Norbu into examining the horse. The old doctor rose and mumbled "maybe" as he headed out the door. I hurried behind him and out the door to watch him work.

Norbu propped the gelding's mouth open with one end of Gyatso's whip. The doctor then pulled out the horn of a ghoral, a wild ungulate found in the Himalayas and Tibet. He then pinned down the horse's tongue and swiftly punctured with the tip of the horn a small abscess that had formed on the roof of the horse's mouth.

"*Gen*," said Norbu. He motioned for me to come closer. "See how the roof of the mouth looks more black than usual? See how his tongue is fine, no discoloring? That is a sure way to tell the difference between *gen* and *hre*. With *hre*, the collection of bad blood forms in the tongue. *Gen* is the gathering of blood in the mouth cavity. Makes this small sore." Norbu pulled me aside and grabbed a twig. He sketched the inside of the horse's mouth in the dirt and explained what he had done.

"You must prick between the third and fourth ridges of skin that run horizontally across the roof of the mouth. Too far forward, you don't get rid of the disease. Too far back, you risk the horse not being able to eat. The roof of the mouth is very sensitive, and ghoral horns are less harsh on horses and better for curing *gen* than cold metal. If I used a metal instrument to bleed this horse, he could run a fever." I marveled at the old doctor's sketch in the dirt, with its accurately traced contours of a horse's jaw and mouth.

"How did you learn about horse care?" I asked.

"I learned by watching. Nobody in my village knew how to do this work, and somebody had to do it. I started traveling around with a doctor from another village, and once he got too old, I took over."

"Have you studied horse texts?"

"Those books are useless," continued Norbu. "Pretty pictures and lots of wasted time. You learn through experience. But who wants to learn anymore? Not my son! When I was young we were fed and given grain for our work. Twenty, thirty years ago that was fine, but where does that get me now? Old and tired and poor. All these young people off to Korea, Hong Kong, India. They don't know the first thing about horses. They only want to buy the most expensive animal they can." I heard echoes of Mayala's consternation, his stubbornness, in this Loba horse healer's refrain. Wiping his brow and huffing, Norbu walked back inside for his payment: a glass of *chang*, refilled for about an hour, courtesy of Gyatso.

Gyatso had walked off while Norbu was explaining the procedure, but now he returned clutching a handful of shrubs and a bowl of boiled water that he'd requested from the Bena hostesses.

"This plant guards against infection and fever in horse and human blood," the *amchi* explained. "The old man knows a lot about some things, but he doesn't know much about medicinal plants." As he spoke, Gyatso mixed water and plant, kneading the handful of herbs like dough.

"Norbu said the horse texts are not very useful," I commented.

"That's just because he is illiterate. How can you believe in something that you can't understand? The texts are the source of his knowledge. He knows that. Norbu just doesn't want to admit the books might have as much to offer as his practical skill." As Gyatso spoke, he propped open his horse's mouth again and swabbed the punctured abscess with the herbal mixture he had made.

"When we get to Monthang, I'll put one of the protective charms my father made on the horse," Gyatso continued. "The power of our medicine depends on good plants, but it also depends on good intentions. Simply curing the horse's physical pain is not enough."

As the morning slowly crawled into afternoon, Gyatso and I saddled our horses and headed on toward Ghami. The little gray gelding had seemed to improve as we made our way north, and that evening ate his well-earned meal with vigor.

Early the next morning, after cups of tepid tea and *tsampa*, Gyatso and I had headed north in the direction of Drakmar, and from there, on toward the village of Tsarang.

If it had not been for the vultures, perhaps Gyatso and I wouldn't have noticed the animal's corpse and would have instead ridden on. But

Gyatso spotted the body and we rode up to investigate. Its frame lay unmoved. A lumpen shape on the horizon, the dead horse did not draw attention to itself, but instead receded into Mustang's landscape: ruins, desert wildflowers, and suede-colored hills. Only tufts of dried grass remained where once there had been tongue and nostrils and tail flesh. The horse's skeleton was mostly intact, yet the skull, once a web of delicate lines, had been smashed to invite vultures to feast on the body.

Gyatso guessed the horse was about thirteen. Its teeth and lips hinted at scars from a bit, while its hooves bore no shoeing marks. This horse, like countless others of its kind, had probably spent its life walking this river valley, carrying loads. A sunken ribcage suggested a death brought on by slow starvation, internal parasites, and perhaps the dreaded "hot" disease that I had learned about during my winter excursions to Kaji Pokhara with Wangdi—afflictions locals attribute to the winter migration south.

We stared at the dead animal. I wondered if anyone had read the *Bumchung* as this horse was laid to rest. Literally "concise vessel," the *Bumchung* is the *Heart Sutra*, a brief text of the Buddha's teachings on highest wisdom. This text helps guide the dead toward auspicious gateways of rebirth. I had learned from Tshampa that it could be read for the benefit of humans and animals, alike. "If the *Bumchung* is not read, beings, dead to this world, can wander toward realms of hell and hungry ghosts," Tshampa had once explained to me.

Sometimes, an animal's owner will even place the head of the dead horse on the roof of his house to ensure that his wealth and property, embodied by horses, does not die with the animal. If the dead horse had been a prized mount, this exposed burial ground might have been scattered with remnants of a ritual: charred incense, grains, dabs of butter, spilled *chang*. As it was, there was only wind, thin mountain air, and a trail littered with hoof prints leading north.

We arrived in Lo Monthang the next day. Monthang's fields blazed. Rapeseed glowed: a plush yellow carpet across the high, dry earth. Barley swayed, high as rushes and electrifyingly green. Many Loba were busy directing irrigation canals, passages without which this oasis could not exist.

Approaching the enormous compound, I immediately felt over-whelmed. Though I knew where I was, it was still difficult to distinguish where one house ended and another began. This walled city was an elab-orate labyrinth, with a four-story, whitewashed palace looming over all other dwellings. The city's north-facing gate was lined with chorten, and old Loba men huddled around it, spinning wool, prayer wheels, and gos-sip. This passageway divided royalty from common folk: nobody except the king, queen, and *gyalchung* was allowed to pass through this gate on horseback.

Gyatso and I parted ways at the gate, and I went to settle in to my room at Pema Rinzen's home, where Pushpa welcomed me back. Our friendship had blossomed during my first trip to Lo, with my parents. Knowing that I would need a place to base myself over the coming months, Pushpa offered to share his room in the home of the widow Pema Rinzen Bista when I returned to Monthang and I accepted his offer with enthusiasm.

Later that day, I stopped by Gyatso's house to pay my respects to Gyatso's family and see how his little gray gelding was faring. Tashi Chu-sang's passing still lingered in the dark house. The look of abandon on Gyatso's mother's face was a poetry of loss, and she sat draped in yak-wool blankets in the corner of the main sitting room. Gyatso's brother Tenzin plied me with Chinese orange soda and handfuls of dried cheese while Gyatso shuffled around in the family prayer room, and finally returned carrying a woven charm in the palm of his hand.

"This is one of the protection charms my father made before he died." Less than two inches square, it smelled of juniper and was bound by crosshatched yarn in the color of the five elements: red for fire, yellow for wind, blue for water, green for earth, and white for space.

"He folded up prayers to Tamdin inside," whispered Gyatso. "This will help keep the horse well. Go, take some incense, and string the charm around the horse's neck." The deity Tamdin was the Tibetan name for Hayagriva, a wrathful deity with the body of a man and the head of a horse. Tibetans invoked him as a protector of horses, as it was said that his powerful neighing would ward off demons.

I went out to the corral. Gyatso's gelding stood munching hay. He did not flinch as I fastened the charm around his neck where a bridle's throatlatch would normally hang. I emptied my pockets of the loosely ground juniper Gyatso had handed me on the way out the door, placed the incense in a small pile, and lit it. The bittersweet smell filled the air, tickled my nose, and caught the horse's attention. Gyatso's gelding seemed almost fully recovered. I have seen dozens of horses suffer from colic and other digestive problems at home in California: sick animals who spent hours, sometimes days, rolling in pain, staring at their bloated stomachs and twisted intestines—that is, if they survived that long. Others suffered quick, painful deaths from ingesting poisonous plants or moldy hay, or convalesced for months with pneumonia and severe lameness, all with the benefits of high-tech veterinary care. And in these arduous environs, where grass was sparse, skilled veterinary care scarce, and weather always threatening, Gyatso's rugged Himalayan mount healed quickly. I was astounded, really.

I crouched in the stall next to the gelding and deeply inhaled his sweet smell. Like the horse's fragile health, I felt that so much of Mustang's equine tradition was faced with inevitable change. Quite literally, horses were the vehicles on whose backs this culture has been carried for centuries. Given the pace at which life was changing in Mustang, and the number of young people who were vested with different educations, different expectations, and different dreams, what would they know of Mustang's "horse culture"? I wondered what would become of knowledge that lived in the minds and hands of people like Mayala and Norbu? Would they go the way of the *chipbön*, set in stone?

The horse muzzled me with a soft caress, bringing me back to the present. In the dark stall, I sat cross-legged, alone in the world with only a horse who, by skill and sacrament, had been made whole again.

During my summer of research in Lo, Chandra Thakali was appointed as my "liaison officer" since he was not only personal secretary to the king of Mustang but also someone well connected in district-level government in Jomsom. Although we did not spend much time together, Chandra and I shared some time on the trail, chatting as we rode. One day we headed to Tsarang, where Chandra had business and I hoped to conduct some interviews. Gyatso came along, as he had a few patients to see as well.

We had been riding since early morning, but had been moving slowly, and had stopped at several other villages along the way. Chandra's mare was pregnant. She had been struggling to keep up all day. Though well fed and muscle toned, she struggled up the morning's passes and was panting by noon, sweat trickling between her ears. Chandra rode quietly and tried not to push his horse. His position as an official intermediary between the royal family of Lo and the government in Jomsom, a post he had held since his twenty-first birthday, bespoke his savvy, diplomatic nature. A consummate political advisor, he always looked clean, even in dust storms.

In the case of his horse, Chandra was also no fool. He realized that, if born healthy and trained well, the developing foal would fetch upward of 50,000 rupees (about $800 at the time) on the local market; a miscarriage, however, would only harm his mare. The day had begun to wane and we still had a way to go before reaching the village of Tsarang, but Chandra would not let us hurry. Instead, he let loose the reins, lowered his head, and dozed, lulled to sleep by the easy rhythms of his mare's walk.

We dismounted and began the descent to the river at the edge of Tsarang. Chandra's mare lumbered with the added weight of the life inside her. She shied away from a piece of rock that broke off from the cliff and came tumbling down. Alert and protective, she seemed to be guarding the vessel of her body as she stepped gingerly toward the river, swollen in late afternoon. Gyatso's horse and mine balked at the force of this muddied current, but we convinced them to step in, brace themselves, and cross. Chandra's mare refused to budge, and, oddly enough, strained to drink the river water. The mare's exertions had brought on a thirst that was indifferent to rapids.

"See the way the baby flips in the mother's stomach while she drinks?" said Gyatso. "Maybe the foal is a lake horse," he continued as the mare drank. Tibetan legends speak of horses fathered by deities incarnated as horses who live at the center of lakes, emerging only to mate with mares grazing at the shore. Developing foals are said to "swim" inside their mother's wombs. Mares birthed from such unions are thought to travel with exceptional strength and ease, as if moving through water when on land. Colts, however, don't like to approach water for fear of being paralyzed by their father's reflection, the fear of not knowing to which world they belong.

Lake horse or not, I hoped that the unborn foal would survive Mustang's bleak winter and imagined it grown—as tenacious and fluid as the currents we now crossed.

By late July, Lo Monthang's fields blazed with cadmium mustard flowers and pale pink buckwheat. According to Tibetan astrology and local lore, these glacial streams ran with "water medicine" during this brief moment in the lunar cycle. Each year at this same time in the Tibetan calendar, Mustang's horses were bled from their noses and bathed in streams running high with new glacial melt. This shedding of "old" blood was a ritual of renewal that prepared horses to move to the high summer grasslands. Spilled blood was mixed with grains and fed back to the horses. Life force was reborn as sustenance.

I left Monthang at daybreak and headed for the king's yak pastures. All thirty of the royal horses had been brought there the day before, as the bloodletting and baths would begin at first light. The king, Pema Ngotug, and a handful of helpers were soaked, their pants stained by grass and blood by the time I arrived. All but the king's favorite horses had been bathed, bled, and let out to pasture. I sat watching as one musclebound beauty followed the other into the water, through this ritual. It was the finest showing of horses I had seen in Mustang.

Until the final horse. It seemed a bit unusual that the king would save a dingy-looking two-year-old for last; but it didn't take long for me to realize that this animal was more than just a horse. For months now I had been hearing about a god-horse said to be one emanation of Dung Mar, the king's protector deity. As Dung Mar's mount, this horse is never ridden. Immediately after the horse dies, a new incarnation must be recognized by the king. Tradition stipulates that any gap in the Dung Mar succession could disrupt the balance of this living landscape.

Such god-horses surface as protector deities and village guardians throughout the Tibetan-speaking world. Perhaps the most famous of such god-horses is Kyang Gö Karkar, the mount of Gesar of Ling, the heralded warrior-king whose life is recounted in epic song across Central Asia. As the story goes, a reincarnate lama was sent from the realm of the gods to become Gesar's trusty horse. Endowed with the wisdom and compassion required of *dharma* warriors, this pair fought many battles against evil, illusion, and ignorance, emerging victorious. Gesar's heroic, triumphant depiction is commonplace in everything from children's stories to mural paintings.

I stared down at the valley below, thinking of Gesar and his mount, sitting next to a contemporary Tibetan king and the current incarnation of his "god horse." The king of Lo glanced toward where the young Dung Mar was grazing. Although this half-grown stud bore the markings and color demanded of these horses—a red body with white socks and blaze—he seemed no match for his previous incarnation. Most Loba I had asked about the last Dung Mar remember the horse as grand and fearless, deep chestnut in color. He had led the procession at a yearly harvest festival saddled in gilded silver and turquoise, coral and gold. Though riderless, the horse pranced and sweated, moving with the conviction and grace of a god.

This young Dung Mar skittered across marshy tundra and refused to be caught that summer morning. The king, not one for sloshing through bogs, handed Pema Ngotug a rope and sent him off to fetch the colt.

"The last one," said the king, gesturing toward the young horse, "was surely Dung Mar. This one, well..." His eyes drifted into the distance, watching as the horse deftly avoided Pema Ngotug's snare again and again, in an awkward, comical dance. "I'm actually still looking for the next real Dung Mar," the king continued. "But this horse will do for now. He has to." The king looked east. I followed his gaze toward Samdzong, a village at the outer reaches of his kingdom.

"Samdzong used to be a very rich village," the king explained. "People there had water, fields, plenty of pastures. Dung Mar horses had been born there for five generations. The horse that died two years ago was the last to come from Samdzong. Now, those pastures have turned to desert. The river is drying up. There are rats in the fields and the water in the river is running green. Now Samdzong is the poorest village in Lo, and this two-year-old is nothing compared to his forefathers," the king mused, his round, wrinkled face hung slightly, in deep contemplation.

Pema Ngotug returned with the special colt in tow, coaxed the animal into the river, and bathed him. Although he was faith manifest in horse-flesh, the young animal was not enough of this world to be bled. Half wild, Dung Mar leapt out of the river and galloped off, pausing only to shake water from his mane and nicker at the king. Here was the pulse of Mustang's landscape, of change and continuity, of lost ancestors and the ghosts of greatness.

After spending these months in Mustang, I realized that I found dips and peaks along the trail and the distances between villages no longer a surprise. By early August, I needed to return to Kathmandu to renew my permit for Lo, and I felt confident enough to travel solo. For the ride south, Raju lent me his crow-colored gelding, a powerful horse that once belonged to a Tibetan nomad. Although Raju and I were still just coming to know each other, we had continued to spend time together in the saddle, and I felt like his initial skepticism of me, and my interest in things equestrian, had given way to a sense of mutual affection—for horses, and for each other. I knew that he would only give me a horse to ride if he truly trusted I could handle the animal.

Before I left Monthang, I looked this horse over. Judging from marks on the gelding's teeth, I guessed the age of the animal to be eleven—well beyond middle age for most of Mustang's horses. The tips of his ears had been split soon after birth, earning him the name "four ears." Raju had explained to me that horses born to mares that have previously lost foals have their ears cut down the middle, an act that renders them "imperfect" enough to mature in this world, filled as it was with suffering. Now grown, this gelding was one of Raju's strongest. We left Monthang early.

There is a saying in Tibetan that likens the Buddhist concept of "mind" to a horse: a powerful tool rendered useless without training and discipline. The ubiquitous Tibetan prayer flags—rainbows of flapping color strung up on mountain passes and offered to the sky—are called, literally, "windhorse" because they carry the image of a horse on whose back is balanced the jewels of the Buddha's teachings. This "windhorse" is also a Tibetan Buddhist practice. The *ta chog* or "excellent horse" is a spiritual metaphor for traveling with wisdom, transmuting obstacles, illusion, and misfortune with the greatest speed. Yet, the sort of insight found within these teachings never comes instantly. One needs to plod along before one can ride on the wind. During these days of summer in Lo, this metaphor of the windhorse resonated with me. I still had much to learn about horses and about life in Mustang. This movement of horse and rider—like the movement of cultures and people toward each other—is a subtle act of discipline, skillful means, and trust.

Thoughts of the windhorse came to me as I rode Raju's gelding south. The stretch of trail after Samar invited speed. If the horse had been young, or if I had been less familiar with the trail, I might have been anxious. As it was, any sense of nervousness was dispelled by the joyful harmony of eyes and arms and solid seat, hooves and mane and half-pinned ears. My left hand was raised and gripping reins, heels urging the horse forward, right hand flicking whip at my mount's right eye, but never actually touching horseflesh. I could feel the gelding's power well up from behind as he taught me patience, lent me his speed. The strain of muscles, his and mine, became as effortless as exertion can be. Moments of balance, found, lost, found again.

Although Mustang is in the rainshadow of the Himalayas, it is not immune to monsoon. Clouds had been gathering all day, and the sky darkened behind me, an inky indigo. Lightning split the sky and heat and light charged the earth in an electric, ionic resonance. Miraculous light. The earth seemed to crack with thunder—called the "sound of the dragon" in Tibetan. Raju's horse had been undaunted by steep hills, high waters, porters carrying boxes and planks along the trail; but now, as the storm broke, he stopped short, whinnied at the northern sky, and pawed the ground.

The horse and I arrived in Jomsom drenched. Small rivers ran between houses, over slate cobblestones, down to the swollen Kali Gandaki. Willow trees keeled to downpour. I headed toward Chandra Thakali's house. I knew Chandra would take good care of Raju's horse until someone from Lo could ride it north again. When we arrived, both the horse and I were shaking, steam rising from our bodies like smoke from the kitchen fire. I unsaddled and stabled the black gelding, Chandra fetched the horse some grain, and the animal and I began to dry. Chandra's wife prepared tea.

The next morning my pretty black gelding was feverish. His nose ran and his eyes were dull. My hosts had gone out and the horse needed immediate care, so I decided to call on Mayala. I had succeeded in having a few stilted conversations with him in past months, but for the most part, he remained aloof and difficult.

The door to Mayala's house swung open, though nobody answered my greetings. I could see the old man upstairs. He sat repairing a bridle on the cool wood platform of his unlit hearth.

"Mayala," I called, "Raju's horse is sick with fever. We rode in the rain all yesterday afternoon. Please come look at him." The old man made no move to answer me. "Mayala, please. The horse is not mine." Again, no reply. I left. Later that day when I told Chandra about my unsuccessful visit to Mayala's, my friend burst out laughing.

"Mayala is difficult. If I had asked him, he couldn't have refused. But you're just an outsider to him," said Chandra, sheepishly. He had seen enough foreigners, tourists and researchers alike, pour in and out of Mustang. His reluctance to speak to me, or help my horse, had been an initiation as well as a teaching for me.

"That old man has taken care of horses for nearly forty years," continued Chandra, shedding his smile. "Don't worry. I'm sure the horse will be fine."

By the time I checked on the horse that evening, Mayala had visited and prescribed twelve black hay beetles, ground live and mixed with grain to quell the fever. A tender pile of juniper incense burned in the corner of the stable, and the horse wore a new protection amulet around its neck. The animal looked peaceful, and perfectly at home.

PART V

AN INTIMATE DISTANCE

COMING TO KNOW Mustang was also a process of entering into and participating in family life. The contours of my own family back home in California were complicated, fractured in places, if also imbued with much beauty and love. As a result, part of me had learned to retreat from family at an early age, and to manage both my expectations of, and my responses to, the people who raised me. The barn often felt like a less volatile and more emotionally secure place than home. I could let my guard down at the barn. Although being with horses never felt lonely to me—quite the opposite—it represented at once a deep engagement with the world and a certain detachment from it. In this sense, part of what I intuited when I first went to Mustang and met Tshampa and his family was my own desire for different kinds of domestic experiences, distinct frames through which to understand, and feel, the profound connections of kinship.

Of course, no family is perfect. Each functions within the contours of its own shadows and light. But seeking out a certain kind of familial belonging, however tenuous, was part of what I logistically needed and emotionally craved during my time in Mustang. Tshampa, Karma, and their children had provided one such experience, as had coming to know Palsang and Tsewang Tenzin. Once I moved north to spend the summer and autumn in Lo Monthang, I began to know another family, that of Pema Rinzen Bista.

The widower Pema Rinzen had been married to one of King Jigme Palbar's sisters. She had died nearly two decades before I came to Lo, but Pema Rinzen and his children had remained within the inner circle of palace life. Pema Rinzen's eldest child, Mahendra, was married to a beautiful woman named Dawa who had come to Lo Monthang from Shigatse, Tibet, as a teenager. Dawa was the niece of the queen of Lo, who also hailed from Shigatse. Pema Rinzen's second child, a daughter named Chimi Dolkar, no longer lived in Lo Monthang. She was married to a *nakpa* whose lineage was that of the presiding lama of Muktinath. They lived in Kathmandu and were, at that time, building a guesthouse near Boudha.

Like most families in Mustang, home economics and the harsh winters in Lo meant that Pema Rinzen and his family moved with the seasons. Mahendra often wintered in India, selling sweaters with others from Mustang, while Dawa and Pema Rinzen alternated between spending winters in Lo and taking refuge at Chimi Dolkar's more comfortable Kathmandu home. Dawa and Mahendra had two children at the time I lived with them: a young girl named Rinchen Wangmo who was in boarding school in Kathmandu, and a little girl named Sonam Chödren who was still young enough that she lived at home and attended the local government primary school. I imagined, though, that she would join her sister in Kathmandu as soon as she was older.

Like most of Lo Monthang's two hundred-odd households, Pema Rinzen's home was nestled close to its neighbors and abutted the city's wall on one side. The family's animals lived below us, penned in beneath an open courtyard on the ground floor. The main living quarters were formed as a horseshoe of small rooms, framed by a wrap-around balcony that looked down on the animals below. Thankfully, a small but serviceable latrine occupied one corner of the house, kept clean with hearth ash and incense. Other spaces were divided up to make room for the work of subsistence, the need for food stores and for warmth, and the requirements of worship. The kitchen abutted a pantry, sleeping quarters, and the family shrine room.

Yet one of the rooms in Pema Rinzen's house was quite unique. This was the old storage room that Pushpa had turned into his quarters, and that he now offered to share with me for the duration of my stay in Monthang.

Pushpa's room was the cleanest place in Mustang—even cleaner and more comfortable, some joked, than the palace. When he had arrived in Monthang to begin his fieldwork, Pushpa had transformed a once-cluttered space in Pema Rinzen's home into a virtually dust-free haven—not a small feat in Lo—in great part to protect his video equipment. He had whitewashed the walls and painted the beams Christmas red and green. He'd spread plastic tarps on the floor and had even gone to the trouble of bringing industrial carpeting up from Pokhara by mule. As a vegetarian in a land of meat eaters, Pushpa kept a trunk filled with various soy products, as well as tins of Scottish shortbread and dried fruits, which he reserved for guests. He also had a solar-powered boom box, solar panels to charge his video battery, and a small library filled with novels and anthropology texts. As such, his room became the *de facto* hangout spot and, at times, counseling center, for many a young Loba. Pushpa was quite universally liked and trusted. He lived without much privacy, but in style.

In one corner of Pushpa's room was his shrine. A devout Tibetan Buddhist practitioner, Pushpa woke up every morning at five to recite a Tibetan text and meditate. I usually woke to the chanting of this handsome, almost ageless man, his long braid down his back, his profile delicate against the morning light. After Pushpa broke his meditation, he emptied each of his seven water offering bowls and filled them up again with fresh libations. As this was summer and wildflowers were abundant, he often sprinkled blossoms atop these bowls. His room was an utterly cultivated, pristine place in a rough land. Although much different than Palsang's house in Lubra, this little room became for me another kind of sanctuary.

The room was good for fieldwork, too. From the window near Pushpa's bed, I was afforded an ideal location to conduct a specific type of livestock census. His room overlooked the corral that we dubbed the "animal jail." Whenever an animal—many a horse among them—was caught venturing into a field that did not belong to its owner, the animal was rounded up and placed in this dusty penitentiary for four-legged creatures. Owners of said livestock were obliged by local custom to pay fines to those fellow villagers whose fields were impinged upon. Such reparations were sometimes tallied in hoofprints: ten rupees per step for a horse, a few less for the cloven-hooved beasts. In the afternoons, I often sat on Pushpa's bed, staring out the window, and counting animals, trying to gain a sense of how much was locally lost and gained through these transactions on a given day.

Pushpa had been born in Tukche, a village in lower Mustang, but he left his mountain home at the age of seven and spent his youth in Kathmandu. Educated at St. Xavier's, a Jesuit school for boys, Pushpa became interested in documentary film and eventually ended up a graduate student in Visual Anthropology at the University of Southern California. At the time of our co-residence, he had been living in Monthang for the better part of the previous two years working on his dissertation research. It became obvious to me early on that Pushpa's passion, and his gift, was film.

Pushpa kept his small archive of Mustang video footage in a metal chest, near his shrine. Sometimes, when the ACAP generator was working and the night air was not too cool, Pushpa would show clips of his videos to an audience of Loba and interested ACAP staff. Although several documentaries already had been made about the kingdom of Lo, few locals had actually seen their lives depicted on film as raw footage, without the veils of edits and translation. These evening video screenings were something like a Mustang Drive-In—except that people walked. Villagers sat on blankets laid across the cool and dusty ground and watched their lives projected on the side of Chimi's Coffee House, with its large swath of whitewashed stone and mud brick.

Pushpa's presence in the household of Pema Rinzen had already changed the family dynamics quite a bit, before my arrival. Although Pushpa was not really a foreigner, neither was he truly a local. Everyone in the family had gotten quite used to his participation in family life, his assistance as well as his idiosyncrasies. My presence certainly added a layer of complexity to the household that summer, but it was not without precedent.

Pushpa became like an uncle to me during these months in Monthang, and even a teacher. I learned to read and write the *devanagari* Nepali script alongside Sonam Chödren, whom Pushpa also tutored. Although Pema Rinzen could be surly at times and had a tendency to indulge his love of *chang*, he also had a gentle side and was an excellent storyteller. Pushpa and I would sit together with the old man of the house in the evenings, listening as Pema Rinzen told stories of Khampas and yetis and festivals past. Pushpa's sense of humor often got the better of him, and he had embraced the local penchant for tall tales and ribald jokes. Pushpa also insisted on helping with the mundane tasks of the household: fetching water, harvesting crops, and helping with meals. Any resistance to my helping out in a similar manner was resolved by Pushpa's example. And so, we laughed with each other and worked together and, as such, were some sort of family.

Pushpa and I became quite close during that summer in Lo, but it was with Dawa that I garnered the strongest emotional connection. We were close in age if not life experience. I found in her someone who, like myself, could be by turns shy and outspoken. As much as one can know this for certain when working through the layerings of second and third languages, I felt that Dawa and I had a similar sense of humor, and that we bore kindred sensitivities. I could tell, for instance, when Dawa felt wounded by her father-in-law's coarseness, and identified with her capacity to take to heart—for better or for worse—things that were not her doing or beyond her control. In that sense, as much as we could laugh about similar things, we also shared a certain embodied sense of responsibility. Our shoulders were broad and tended to carry a lot, in both a literal and metaphoric sense.

Also, I identified with the fact that Dawa carried something of another place with her, even though Mustang had been her home for well over a decade at the time we met. The circumstances of each of our early leave-takings from our natal homes were quite different—at sixteen she was sent across a firm geographic and political, if not cultural, border from Shigatse to Monthang to be a maidservant for the queen and a future wife for a Loba of aristocratic blood. I had the luxury of leaving home at seventeen for an Ivy League education. Yet we talked a lot about what it had meant, for each of us, to feel at once unmoored and yet obliged to embrace the challenges and opportunities that had been presented to each of us.

Dawa was one of the few people in Mustang with whom I could easily practice my Tibetan, as she spoke the Central Tibetan dialect. Nothing marked Dawa's outward appearance as a Mustang emigreé. Yet she seemed to cherish our detours, through language, back to memories of her own youth in Tibet. When I was not chasing down shepherds or local veterinarians, I could usually be found with Dawa: making *momos*, tending the hearth, washing clothes, picking lice out of her daughter's hair.

After several weeks of living together, Dawa invited me to become her *rogmo*, a term that literally means "female friend" but that also implies fictive kinship. The invitation meant that I was to be ceremonially accepted into Dawa's life, and she into mine.

I accepted Dawa's offer to become her *rogmo*. We invited the king and queen, along with the Bista Boys—*gyalchung* Jigme, Tsewang, and Raju— and a few other friends to join us in celebration. On the evening of this ceremony, Tsewang and Raju came bearing *kathag* from the palace and small gifts from the king and queen. Pema Rinzen recited some prayers and gave us his blessing.

As I stood beside Dawa, each of our bright, silky blouses peaking out of the fitted bodices of our clean summer *chubas*, I felt at once happy and apprehensive—and even a little self-conscious, particularly in front of Raju and Tsewang. I knew that for some people, such a "special friend" was as dear, or more, than blood relations. For others, the bond was more casual. People could have several such relationships in different locations. As much as I liked Dawa and had begun to care deeply for her, I did not know how our friendship would evolve. However, I still felt willing to mark this connection, to take that risk.

After Pema Rinzen said some prayers, Dawa and I exchanged gifts in the halflight of the family shrine room. She gave me a beautiful Bhutanese jacket, and I gave her a new *chuba* and a silver and turquoise necklace. Pushpa filmed the ritual. As the videotape whirred, he joked that now Mahendra could enjoy the pleasures of two wives, which promptly sent shy Mahendra, his face a deep crimson, off to feed the cows.

In proper local fashion, we plied our guests with alcohol and treats. One of the younger ACAP staff with whom I had also struck up a friendship brought out Pushpa's radio, and to the sounds of Nepali folk songs and a smattering of rock and roll, we danced arm-in-arm late into the evening. As *rogmo*, Dawa and I were obliged to each other in new ways, even though the contours of this relationship were still nascent.

When Dawa had first suggested that we become *rogmo*, this offer of such a friendship surprised me, caught me off guard. The suggestion was made simply enough, while we were slicing zucchini one afternoon, in preparation for the evening meal. Yet even before Dawa raised this possibility, I had begun to wonder how we would share our lives over the years to come. Now that we were so joined, I asked myself even more questions. How would we maintain an interest in each others' lives after I left Mustang? Would our children come to know each other? How would we continue to honor this friendship? These were concerns I could not answer at the time. And for all of these ways that my friendships in Lo were deepening, I was also becoming increasingly aware that I would not—could not—remain here much longer. The validity of my *gratis* permit was stamped into my passport and etched into my mind, and this had begun to weigh on me.

When I close my eyes, I can still see Raju's black hair and wide shoulders framed by Mustang wind and light. In these memories, he is always riding, his body swaying side to side ever so slightly, his legs and feet solid and still against his mount's flanks. Like his horses, Raju was completely at ease in the Mustang landscape. Raju exuded confidence, belonging. He seemed to at once honor and command this place he called home.

By Mustang standards, Raju was not a small man: five foot ten and strapping, with a slight bulge in his belly after a summer of local barley beer and his mother's cooking. As a nephew of the king and the eldest son of the noble family of Ghami, Raju could have spent his youth in educational exile, at boarding schools in Kathmandu or India, like some of his cousins. Instead, he stayed at home, venturing south to Jomsom only for high school, after which he joined his uncle in business.

Throughout the summer, I watched Raju ride. My eyes followed him across the chalky plains north of Monthang, past the ancient fortress of Ketchar Dzong, and on to meet an old horseman named Darchen. I took note as Raju asked his horse to gallop and slow, watching for river stones and uneven ground. On the flat stretches, he demonstrated his skill, racing off ahead of me. I lounged by riverbanks in the company of local shepherds, sipping a warm, weak brew made from riverwater, tea stems, and Tibetan salt. Raju helped interpret and translate the gritty, often toothless banter of these animal experts into a Nepali I could understand.

On one such outing, Raju had been pushing his white gelding forward at a quick, rhythmic pace for the better part of an hour. Sweat ran the length of his horse's gaskins and stippled its rump with moisture. White foam dripped from his gelding's mouth as it worked a thin snaffle bit across its tongue, neck arched and nostrils wide. Yet, for all the exertion, the horse moved with equanimity and resolve: equally the marks of a good horse and a skilled equestrian. It seemed Raju had always been riding.

Weeks passed quickly during that summer in Lo. At one point, I had to make a midsummer trip to Jomsom to renegotiate my next round of liaison officers since Chandra Thakali had been called to Kathmandu for some pressing work. Fortunately, I was able to arrange a return trip to Lo in the company of *gyalchung* Jigme and a group of tourists who had hired Royal Mustang Excursions to arrange their tour. Raju, who had accompanied me down to Jomsom the previous week, was now also returning home.

Our party had set out from Kagbeni that morning, and we had been riding steadily. The stone irrigation canals and gnarled willows of Tetang were behind us and we rode on toward the Mustang Gate, a dramatic narrowing in the Kali Gandaki just before the ascent to Tsele, where we would spend the night.

"What's the matter? Can't keep up?" Raju turned around in his saddle to face me. I answered with a flick of my whip in the direction of my horse's face, careful not to touch the animal. The sight of the whip was enough to make the horse surge forward obediently. I moved up beside Raju. Before us stretched clusters of thorny shrubs, sandy soil, and cliffs that held up the sky.

"Good. So maybe you can ride!"

"Maybe." I met his smile. "But be careful what you say. You're the one who gave me your whip." I dangled the end of Raju's braided leather crop in front of his face, joking with him. But instead of grabbing the whip, he grabbed my wrist, then my hand. This startled me, but I did not pull away. The simple gesture felt momentous. Raju and I rode on like this for a time, palms touching, until we were no longer alone.

The others with whom we were traveling—Jigme, the group of French trekkers, and their Nepali liaison officer—had been lagging behind since the moment we set off from Kagbeni. The liaison officer had never ridden a horse before, and even though Jigme had given him one of the king's strong and docile mounts, the Brahmin's progress along the trail was painfully slow. The half dozen Parisians didn't seem to mind. It was August and they were on vacation. They rode ahead, until the liaison officer became a speck in the distance. The French travelers dismounted on occasion and leaned back in the Mustang dust for a cigarette, hoping this would give the liaison officer a chance to catch up. They'd already been through this routine three or four times by the time Jigme finally excused himself and rode quickly toward me and Raju.

"Are you planning on riding all the way to Monthang today?" Jigme's voice called out, as he urged his horse to catch us.

"Good thing the *rongba* can ride, eh?" Raju smiled, letting go of my hand. I stared straight ahead and squinted. A shiver ran through me, despite the warmth of the day. I could feel Raju watching me, and I suddenly became aware of my body in a way that I had not considered it in months. I ran my tongue across my lips, moistening them. I straightened my shoulders and looked down at the rest of my body, noticing that my jeans were filthy. I hadn't bathed in several days, but only now became self-conscious about it.

"All he has to do is sit there," Jigme sighed, still fixated on his bumbling Brahmin. "That horse is like a Land Cruiser: smooth ride, comfortable seats, even Mustang air conditioning! I just hope he doesn't start to feel the altitude and decide to turn around. The last thing I need to do is spend time at the police check post, explaining why our liaison officer didn't show up. 'Altitude sickness again?' they'll say. I should just start budgeting in a few thousand rupees to pay for the work the liaison officers don't do, or at least for their return trip to Jomsom once they realize they don't want to spend ten days in the mountains." Jigme was bringing up a common excuse used by these government officials who, after tiring easily, would return to Jomsom and skirt their duties in favor of satellite television and decent food.

"I suppose there is no way to stop this sort of thing," I said.

"What would I tell them? *You can't get altitude sickness*! It's a perfect excuse."

"Well, he'll need the four-wheel drive to get across the river if we don't start moving. It's already noon. Water's rising," Raju added.

"Even if we get to Tsele late, at least the mules will beat us. The others should have the members' tents set up and tea will be ready," Jigme grumbled. As the *gyalchung* scanned the landscape he had seen so many times, he set his jaw and looked disaffected.

"I know why foreigners come to Mustang. It's exotic and remote. Like Tibet, but smaller. There's a walled city, even a king," said Jigme, in a rare moment of irony and grit. "But sometimes I can't understand why foreigners would choose to spend their vacation and so much money to eat tinned meat and powdered soup, to sleep in tents and not have a shower for two weeks."

"People will always want what they can't have," I responded. "Some people come looking for something, others just come to look."

"And you?" Raju interjected.

"You know what I've come for...your horses!"

"But you can never take one home," said Raju. "All you've really got are your notebooks in the end. And your friends, and what you remember."

His words were honest and plain, but they filled me with a new sadness. I struggled before I was able to respond. "True," I said finally, "but what does anybody really have but that? A few things, some memories. Nothing more than your mind can carry." The idea fermented in me, making me become nostalgic for something I was still very much in the midst of. Where, in the truth of the present, does forgetting hide?

Jigme reached into his saddlebag and tossed an apple to each of us. We ate, savoring the sweetness.

"From Pema Dolkar's orchard," said Jigme, motioning toward the apple. "She wouldn't let me leave Kagbeni this morning without stuffing my bags full of them." We reached the descent to the Kali Gandaki River, and dismounted.

"Another reason to come to Mustang," I joked as I fed my apple core to my horse.

"Do you still need a reason to come here?" Raju responded, more serious than I'd seen him all day. The comment held me for a moment.

"No, I suppose I don't."

"Then it's becoming a bit like your own place—like home."

"Yes, in some ways."

"But won't you have to pay to come here once your scholarship runs out?" Jigme added, his eyes trailing back toward the sauntering liaison officer and the tourists.

"And who has to pay to come home?" said Raju.

"Those aren't my rules and they're not yours either," I answered, feeling a flush of defensiveness. "At least I don't have to pay now."

"Of course, you're always welcome," said Jigme, ever the hospitable *gyalchung*.

"Thank you," I answered. "Just because I can't be here all the time doesn't mean I love a place any less."

"No, but it changes how well you can know it," said Raju. "And what it means to you."

Our conversation came to an abrupt halt as we reached the water's edge. Raju, Jigme, the trekkers and I spent the afternoon fording the river. The Mustang Gate's narrow archway was carved into red rock by the force of the Kali Gandaki—a point where the watercourse was forced to narrow and then, as if in rebellion, burst out the other side. A river enraged. Water, muddied by silt, churned as if the wrathful goddess Kali herself were being squeezed through this thin passage on her southward journey. Just the week before, several horses and a mule had been washed clean away by the force of the river's current at precisely this spot. We crossed carefully, water welling up past stirrups and shins. Making it safely across, we climbed the vertical trail up from the river's banks to the village of Tsele, our horses still dripping water from their bellies. I was more anxious and expectant than I had been at any point in the journey so far. And also the saddest.

That night, after the French tourists had retired to their tents and Jigme had gone off to bed, Raju and I sat up talking in the kitchen.

"What is it like in New York?" Raju said between drags on a Surya cigarette.

"Big buildings. Bright lights. Lots of different kinds of people," I fumbled for explanations. "It is hard to describe, but amazing. Why do you ask?"

"My younger brother, Dorje, is going to New York." Raju said, at once guarded and proud. I had heard stories about a cousin here and a brother-in-law there who had spent time working in Korea, Taiwan, or Japan. But to that point, America was dream than destination for people from Mustang.

"Why is he going?" I asked.

"There is nothing here for people like my brother," said Raju. "And people keep saying that New York is the place to make money. Better than Japan, since their rules about foreigners are too strict. And America is better than Europe because people speak English.

"Besides, Dorje is the baby of the family. It would be different if I wanted to leave." Raju stared up at the stars. "Who knows, maybe I will go to America someday, too. But Dorje left Mustang when he was young to go to boarding school. Since then, he's only come home for holidays." The implications were clear. A few weeks at home each year did not leave enough time for children like Dorje to foster a sense of possibility in such a place.

"What is there in Mustang for someone like Dorje? Dust and fields to manage? Boring village politics? That's for old men. I'm only involved in these things because I'm the eldest son in my family and my father expects it of me." Raju paused. At that moment, a flash of resentment passed across his face.

"Village life can be fun, of course," continued Raju, his tone changed, "and it's nice to be at home, but we can't make a living here like our parents did." Raju snubbed out his cigarette and reached for a glass of local liquor that had been set out for him by the woman of the house. He dipped the ring finger of his right hand into the glass three times—an offering to the gods—before he continued.

"Even if we wanted to stay and build hotels and make pizza for tourists, we still would not benefit much, because they come up here on organized treks, live in tents, and eat noodles that some Sherpa has carried from Kathmandu or Pokhara. What kind of an opportunity is that?"

"If Dorje wanted to live in Mustang," Raju continued, "maybe he could be hired by ACAP, but then he would have to report to a bunch of *rongba* who think they know Mustang even though they don't. Why should he bother with all of this if he can go to America?"

"Life isn't that easy in America, Raju," I said, sipping my tea as the moon rose outside the window, casting a pale light on the floor. "New York especially. People work very hard. What kind of life will Dorje have in New York? Where will he live? Where will he work? Is anybody else from Mustang going?" I felt obliged to question what lay in store for Dorje once he arrived.

"We have some connections, our own people, there already," Raju answered. His tone had suddenly changed. It had grown more guarded, if not defensive. "*Gyalchung* Jigme's wife's family—from Tibet. They run a restaurant in New York. He will probably start there. Maybe you can see him when you go back to America," Raju smiled, flooding what had become a tense moment with affection. "Then, you could bring him memories from Mustang. And *churpi* and chilies."

"You'll have to get me out of here first!" I teased, thankful for his change in demeanor. "Of course I will meet him. I plan on seeing friends in New York next winter, when I go home for a visit," I said. The thought of returning to the U.S. suddenly jarred me.

"But how is Dorje getting to New York?" I asked. "How did he get a visa? Isn't it really difficult?" I asked.

"Yes, difficult, but not impossible," Raju answered obliquely. I had heard from friends in Mustang and in Kathmandu about various ways that coveted U.S. tourist and business visas could be procured, and I decided not to push the issue.

Raju then explained that his family had paid for young Dorje's plane ticket, and some pocket money to get him started in the City. This nephew of the king would live in Queens with a few other Nepalis, one of them a Loba, and try to find work. "He is leaving in a few weeks. He has a tourist visa for now, three months. But everybody says that when he gets to America they will give him six months and that he can renew it for another six months after that, no problem. A few other Loba have done the same thing," Raju continued. "My brother is smart and he speaks good English. He will be fine. He will make it in America."

"I hope you're right," I answered. It was difficult for me to imagine at that time the extent to which our conversation foreshadowed the Mustang diaspora that was to come over the next decade.

The house was quiet. The French trekkers were snoozing. Our Tsele hostess had made up beds for Jigme, Raju, and me. Jigme had already retired. Raju and I stopped talking. Our eyes were fixed on each other, acknowledging the charge between us. Raju reached out for my hands and pulled me into his embrace. He smelled faintly of tobacco and sweet summer hay, his palms warm against my own. Within the simple gesture of our kiss, I felt intimacy and distance, by turns. It was as if this one small act of affection spoke to the deepest truth of my experiences here— a commitment to living the sentient rhythm, between changing and being changed.

A horse neighed in the corral nearby and a mastiff answered with a low, rumbling growl. Then all grew silent around us.

Mustang Tour Guide

I ROSE EARLY, stirred by the sounds of Pushpa's morning rituals. His low chanting and the cool tinkle of offering bowls were familiar now, and generally did not disturb my sleep. But today was different. I got up, threw on jeans and jacket over my long underwear, grabbed my notebook and camera, and headed out of the warm room.

Dawa and I joined each other in the kitchen. Her one gold-plated tooth glimmered in the pale, pre-dawn light as she smiled in greeting. I sat watching my *rogmo* make tea while I wrote in my journal. A few minutes later, Gyatso arrived at house. A group of British tourists had asked to see the yak pastures north of Monthang, and Gyatso had been asked by the king to travel with them. Worried about his lack of English, Gyatso had asked me to help and act as a translator. "Besides," he had said, "It will be a chance to ride one of the king's horses!" I needed little more to convince me that the outing would be a worthwhile way to spend a day.

"Are you ready?" said my friend as he ascended the hollowed tree trunk whose deep foothole scoops served as a ladder, connecting the ground floor stable to our second-story dwelling.

"Yes, but come have tea," I responded. Gyatso sat down beside me and Dawa poured us two scalding, frothy cups of butter tea. Gyatso looked sleepy, his hair disheveled.

"Too early!" he moaned. "The chickens aren't even awake."

Mahendra, who would also come along on this day trip to help with the horses, sorted through saddle blankets and prodded Kancha, their household helper, awake. The tourists were to ride our family's two horses, as well as some from the palace livery. Mahendra was in charge of readying the animals and he needed Kancha's help saddling the ten mounts before the tourists finished their breakfast.

"Go fetch the horses," grumbled Mahendra. "We have to get going or the tourists won't see the yak!" Mahendra glanced down at his Chinese-made watch. We had planned to leave Monthang before dawn so that we might reach the nomad settlements up near the Tibetan border in time to see the female yak being milked, and before the grown bulls meandered up to high pastures to graze for the day.

The horses were ready by five thirty. We met the group of British tourists near the city's northern gate. After a brief orientation to Mustang horsemanship and a final round of backpack adjustments and water bottle fill ups, we headed out. The group rode northwest in sleepy silence, mist clouding our vision. Gyatso and I led the way toward the nomad's encampment. Since his father's passing, the bond between me and Gyatso had grown stronger. I trusted him implicitly. We rode slowly, so as not to worry Mahendra. He had a tender, almost motherly streak, always concerned about foreigners getting hurt or losing their way in Lo. It had taken several weeks for me to convince Mahendra that I was capable of saddling and unsaddling a horse, that I could fetch water and help make food.

Gyatso had recently returned from Kathmandu where he, like his father before him, had bought various "hot" medicinal ingredients to augment those he and Tenzin would collect throughout the summer from the hills and high pastures of Lo. Since his return, he had been working late into the night alongside Tenzin, grinding many ingredients into powders and rolling them into pills. Piles of medicinal herbs remained to be processed. For an *amchi*, the summertime was the busiest moment of the year. Plants, as well as patients, required diligent attention during this brief window of abundance.

As we rode on, I noticed Gyatso nod off in the saddle. His hand went limp in the reins, and his torso swayed gently with the rhythm of his horse's gait. We had a river to cross soon, but Gyatso woke as if on cue when we reached the water's edge.

"You look really tired, Gyatso," I said, once we had crossed.

"I was up late again last night, making medicines," he answered. "But it is also my mind. It is not at ease. My mother still cries all the time, remembering my father. She is not in good health. She can't walk well. Tenzin and I are talking about the Amchi Association, and the school we hope to build. All this new work is flooding in. We need more than just the two of us to make medicines and care for people—to keep our *amchi* tradition alive. At least my father had us to help with the work. But with him gone—" Gyatso went quiet. The forty-nine day mourning period, in which a departed soul passes through the *bardo*, the liminal space between death and rebirth, had come and gone, but Tashi Chusang's widow and sons still felt the loss daily.

Our horses lumbered up the gentle incline that led us from the twelve-thousand-foot basin that cradles Monthang, toward the community of nomads who lived in the pastures at fourteen thousand feet. It began to rain softly. Gyatso said a *mantra* under his breath as we rode north in the misty morning.

I watched my friend closely. I wondered how he would come to wear the cloak of his lineage, how he would carry himself through the future and the many opportunities and challenges he would face in living up to his father's vision. As with my *rogmo* Dawa, I wondered how, and in what capacity, our friendship would continue after I was no longer living in Mustang. How and when would we see each other, grow with each other, in the years to come?

Our mounted group continued on past Thinker, the village where the king's summer palace was located. Gyatso and I spent a few minutes explaining Lo's history to the British travelers at this juncture. Sometimes he would speak and I would translate. Other times, I would speak from what I knew.

"We will visit the cave monasteries, Nyiphug and Garphug, after a snack of fresh yogurt with the nomads," I translated for the group. They nodded. Some of them looked sleepy, too, perhaps woozy with altitude, perhaps still lost in their dreams. Our horses carried us up the loping hills ahead, fog still lingering even though Monthang's fields were speckled with sunshine below. We rode over wet, woody shrubs and low-lying sedges.

It was just past seven by the time we reached the nomads' tents. These moveable dwellings are ingeniously designed to keep in heat, exhale smoke, and shelter nomads against the harsh elements in which they live. Whittled saplings—poplars and willows from a lower land, where there are trees—supported the tent flanks, which were made of spun yak wool. A circle of stones covered with sod formed the tent's base, and makeshift corrals were built beside these encampments.

The trekkers, Gyatso, and I climbed into one of the larger nomad tents and sat down by a yak dung fire. Outside one of the tents, a hollow statue of drying dung, reminiscent of a termite mound or an oversized bee hive, marked camp and provided shelter for a female mastiff and her two pups.

"We see yak!" said Mahendra in gleeful, self-conscious English as he poked his head into the tent. The males had already left for high pastures, but just around the corner we would spy a group of female yak—dri—and their fuzzy offspring.

"Could you tell us a bit about these animals?" one of the tourists asked. "I have heard they can withstand outrageously cold temperatures, and then can carry hundreds of pounds."

"You're right," I answered. "In a sense, yak epitomize the Tibetan frontier. Nomads couldn't really live without them." Yak provide wool, meat, and dairy products. These animals can porter up to two hundred pounds at altitudes nearing twenty thousand feet. For people who both farm and keep animals, yak-cow crossbreeds are also essential agricultural beasts of burden.

"But it doesn't seem like there are all that many yak in Lo these days. We had to travel quite far to reach them," said one Brit.

"True. Compared with other parts of northern Nepal, the yak herds here are smaller. This is in part because of all that has happened since the Chinese annexation of Tibet," I continued. "Now people here have less access to pasture land than ever before. This is especially a problem for keeping large herds of yak. Sheep and goat are easier to maintain. But yak are revered; they are a marker of identity as well as important in economic terms. These nomads up on the border still keep yak, and the king still has a herd in the care of these families."

Just then, Mahendra peeked in the tent again. "They haven't finished milking the females," Mahendra said to me. "We can still catch them." Noticeably excited by the animals, Mahendra seemed proud of these powerful beasts, and he nearly skipped up the mountain toward the herd. The Brits breathed heavily in this light air and struggled to catch him, trudging up a gentle incline to where about twenty female yak and half as many yearlings stood grazing. Since the fog had still not lifted, on several occasions a startled tourist found him or herself face to muzzle with one of these creatures.

"The word for 'yak' in Latin is actually 'grunting cow.' They can be incredibly quiet when they choose," I said, quietly. I had not spent much time around these creatures, but I was immediately attracted to their wild beauty and bovine grace. I liked their deep brown eyes. Their curved horns reminded me of manzanita boughs. "I have never felt so small," one of the tourists whispered to me. Baby yak scampered and fell, fell and scampered at their mothers' sides, pining for milk.

I looked over and found Gyatso leaned back against a shelf of dew-soaked earth. He was watching the foreigners as they marveled at his world, taking pictures and commenting on the animals. I sat down next to him and could feel his melancholy, palpable as fog in the morning air.

"The nomads work so hard up here," he said. "I don't work at all compared to them." A foreigner posed with one of the more timid yaks while another took his picture. Their laughter was shrill in the peaceful morning, and two nomads turned suddenly as if shocked by the timbre. "I wonder what they would think of the tall buildings in places like England and America," Gyatso mused. They would probably be scared of all the cars—even in Kathmandu." He patted my arm gently and stood up, motioning that we should gather our tourists and lead them back down to the tent for tea.

Finished with her milking, the lady of the tent came in behind us and brought out the tea for us. Counting our steaming heads, she quickly began searching the tent for enough cups. As it was, she could only find six, and so we drank gritty, ashen butter tea by turns. I tried not to laugh as I watched our guests' faces pucker. Their expressions changed from thanks to disgust. Expecting tea more suitable to the British Isles, they had accepted hastily and then recoiled at the cups when handed to them. To say Tibetan salt-butter tea is an acquired taste is a vast understatement.

"*You like?*" said Gyatso in simple English, pointing to the one mug of tea in the tent that had been drained by a middle-aged man from Bristol.

"Quite good, quite good," he answered, sincere. "Tastes a bit like Roquefort cheese soup." His wife nudged him. "Remember your arteries, Harry, your cholesterol. This is bloody *wretched*."

"What is the English word for *sho*?" Gyatso asked me.

"Yogurt," I answered. Then, in his best English, Gyatso announced to the group, "*We eat youu-gyurrt now! Very health. Fresh.*"

Several snotty-nosed children huddled near the door and inspected us as the daughter of this family appeared. She fumbled behind several of the tourists and then pulled out a large pot covered with a stainless steel lid, bent in places. The vessel had been wrapped in blankets to help the fermentation process. She removed these layers and lifted the lid to reveal a vat of yogurt the color of warm white silk.

Her presentation of the yogurt pot prompted squirming and shuffling in the tent, causing two of the tourists to nearly sit on a baby goat that had been wrapped in blankets and stuffed in the corner like a mottled piece of laundry. The goat's muffled squeals were soon replaced by a high-pitched scream. "Oh my! There's a kid under my tush!" a tourist exclaimed. Everyone laughed, even the shy daughter with her gritty hands and downcast eyes. Her younger sister simply smiled as she stirred a cauldron of fresh milk on the stove, waiting for the fat of the creamy liquid to rise.

Gyatso was resting near the fire and to the right of the shrine, in a place of honor. A carpet cushioned him against damp ground. "This house is my *netsang*," he explained to me. *Netsang* are adoptive family, homes away from home. These relationships, which also serve as trading partnerships, are bound not only by common economic purpose or familial bond, but are also *dharma* connections—not unlike the bond I now shared with Dawa, my *rogmo*. Maintenance of these relationships are often viewed as religious and social duty.

"My father was the older man's *netsang*. They used to go to Tibet together. Sometimes, in the days when we kept more animals, this family used to look after some of our yak." The nomad family, like many others straddling the border between Mustang and western Tibet, were part of a vast network of patients and patrons once served by the hands of Tashi Chusang, now under Gyatso and Tenzin's care. Overhearing our conversation, I turned and explained this relationship to the tour group.

"Before the Chinese took over Tibet," I continued, "Gyatso's father used to spend most of his summers traveling, seeing friends, treating people, and gathering up medicinal plants. This family is close by, for a *netsang*, since their camps are only a couple of hours from Monthang. But many of Gyatso's other *netsang* live much farther away. Some of the families that his father used to visit are now across the border in Tibet. Others are in exile in India."

"Others disappeared, or we lost track of them, after the Chinese came," said Gyatso as I continued to translate. "But now the Chinese army is loosening up their hold on the border, at least for trade. Maybe we will find them someday. I go to Tibet now to help sick people."

Just then, the father of the house interrupted Gyatso. Kneeling now, he approached the doctor for treatment. In this darkened tent, one of his daughters poured us tea while another shooed chickens out the door. Gyatso reached his fingers around the old man's wrist to read his pulse. The group of Brits grew quiet and watched, squinting against thick smoke. "What is he doing?" one of them finally asked me.

"Gyatso is reading the man's pulse to figure out what is wrong with him," I explained. "Tibetan medicine determines a lot from pulse analysis. Some people say it's as exact as a dialysis machine or an x-ray. See how Gyatso moves his fingers? He's applying different levels of pressure to the veins and arteries running through the old man's wrist. After he does that, he will feel the pulse on the other hand."

As our female host ladled out scoops of yogurt into available vessels, Gyatso pulled out his medicine kit: small round herbal pills in labeled plastic bags and stuffed into a worn knapsack. The doctor fidgeted with satchels, finally placing three different kinds of pills in makeshift envelopes of Nepali newsprint. With some patients, Gyatso would write the dosage on the outside of these prescriptions. In this case, he simply explained—in slow words for the nearly deaf ears of this old man—the course of treatment. The nomad couldn't read.

The group slurped fresh yogurt as the aging patriarch retreated. He seemed shy, perhaps wary of us, perhaps bothered by his sickness, or both.

"This is fantastic!" said one tourist as he finished his helping of yogurt. "Is there any more?" Though I could see a bucket in the corner still half-filled with the stuff, I hesitated to have him pass his cup.

"I know that it is really good," I said, "but I don't want to take it all. If I ask, they will give it to us. Gyatso and I will pay them for our tea and yogurt. But if we eat more, then most of them won't have much yogurt for a day or two. Most likely, none of the girls will get much until more is made. People are served according to age, and sometimes according to sex. Women tend to get fed after the men, especially when there is not enough to go around. It isn't a huge problem now, but in the winter, people often eat mostly *tsampa*, and whatever they've been able to cure and dry from the summer—cheese and meat, mostly." I translated what I had said to Gyatso.

"That's true," Gyatso responded. "But they would just as soon have the money now. Everyone needs cash these days. It isn't like old times when people didn't buy as many things like thermoses and clothes. Now, people would rather have rupees or Chinese money. All the nomads have to sell is what they make. Most of them don't go to sell sweaters in India, or go off to foreign countries. They're lucky if they can buy things in China and sell them down here. Tell the tourists that they can have more yogurt if they want." I relayed this to the group, and was humbled by Gyatso's commentary. It was an apt reminder of all that I still did not understand about Mustang, and the changes this culture was experiencing.

The man who had asked about the extra yogurt looked confused. His appetite seemed to wane and he grew pensive. I could see that he was facing a decision that he felt incapable of making. Muddled by the choices, he put down his mug and opted to cuddle the scrawny baby goat. At least he knew where he stood with this little being.

A few minutes later, we said good-bye to the nomad family. Cameras clicked. The younger nomad children scampered about, saying the only English word they knew: "Hello, hello, hello."

The father of this nomad tent took Gyatso's hands and they touched foreheads, briefly, in leavetaking. I imagined that the old nomad saw Tashi Chusang in the eyes and face of Gyatso. "Go slowly," he said, as we mounted our horses. Fog lost the battle against high altitude sun. Our steaming ponies dried and then began to sweat as we rode down the mountain.

THE BROTHERS

SUMMER had ushered in a new season of rites in Mustang. These were bucolic, long-lived days, filled with feasts and celebrations. Several weeks after my outing with the British tourists, Pushpa and I accompanied the king and his entourage to the village of Chung Jung to witness the annual shearing of the king's sheep.

Chung Jung consisted of no more than a dozen humble dwellings. Their whitewashed exteriors were worn in places, revealing rain and wind-inflicted wounds. Like most houses in Mustang, these roofs were lined with brambles, although dung burned more often than wood in village hearths. We headed toward a house at the edge of Chung Jung that bordered on some of the king's pastureland.

By the time we arrived, a number of local herders had already corralled the sheep. Crouched against the walls, they sharpened knives and slurped butter tea, chatting. As was Tibetan custom, when the king arrived, they took off their caps and stuck out their tongues in deference—and to prove that their tongues weren't black. The rosy color of their palates proved they meant the king no ill will, and that they were not demons capable of black magic.

The king nodded to his subjects and surveyed his flock. His large, beautiful head cocked to one side, and beneath the rim of his fedora, his mouth puckered in disapproval.

"Winter was a pack of wolves this year," he muttered. It was true. Snowstorms across the Tibetan Plateau had plundered herds of yak and sheep. Sleet-soaked winds had howled, leaving animals frozen in their tracks—a bloodless slaughter.

"How many lambs?"

"Only seventeen," answered one of the laborers.

The king nodded. "Well, let's get to work," he said. The king removed his arms from the sleeves of his *chuba* and knotted them around his waist. He set down his hat and pushed back his hair—two thinning, gray-black plaits tied with red yarn—and fastened it atop his head. Without his fedora, the king looked vulnerable, older.

In the hours that followed, I watched these men work with startling efficiency. Sheep were hobbled and shorn in minutes. Naked, dazed, and sometimes nicked by the knife, they wandered around the pen, trying to recognize each other. The king bagged and sorted wool, his gold tooth flashing in the sun each time he called to another shepherd for assistance.

The woman of the house spent her morning making rounds with a teakettle, and later, a pitcher of barley beer. Gulp to gulp, the beer brought on jokes.

"Looks like this one isn't going to stay warm this winter," said one of the laborers, poking at a ram's genitals with the blunt end of his knife. "I've seen bigger balls on a marmot!"

"I wouldn't talk," said another. "Not from what your wife says."

"At least I *have* a wife," the first man retorted. Tough humor, told in good fun. "I've seen you handling those sheep. You're moving pretty slowly over there." And so it went. Pushpa filmed while the men sheared. Every once in a while he stopped and played back a clip of video for the workers.

"Look, you're a movie star!" the hired hands kidded each other. Even the king chuckled as he stared through the camera's screen and watched the frames of instant history: sheep scurrying about and the men who lunged after them, swallowing dust. When viewed through a camera lens, this mundane event suddenly became imbued with a new kind of novelty, and humor.

After the shearing was done, our hostess stepped out from the kitchen with a pot of glowing embers. The king submerged a thin iron rod into the hot cauldron, and then branded each of the yearling sheep. After he finished, all of the wool was gathered and stuffed into woolen sacks. Then, the king swung open the courtyard door just enough for one sheep to pass at a time. Ewes butted up against their offspring and their mates as the king counted.

"One hundred thirty-eight," he announced when the pen was empty.

"How many did he have last year?" I asked one of the workmen.

He put his hands on his hips and considered the question. "I was in Tibet last year trading, so I'm not sure. But not long ago he used to have more than a thousand."

The day stretched on into late afternoon, made darker with the lack of windows inside the small home. Tokme Bista had come along to help the king, and he now busied himself making *thukpa*, a noodle stew, for all. I helped him chop garlic. A local woman mixed coarse Tibetan salt and dried chili peppers with water, pounding the spices into a paste. The king closed his eyes.

We were all surprised when the door swung open. In a flood of light, in walked an enormous man. His saddlebags were slung over one shoulder, making his silhouette appear even more imposing than his broad frame alone. Smoke and sun obscured his features, but I intuited who he was, who he must be. This was the king's elder brother, the man referred to as Shabtrung Rinpoche. This powerful local lama was reputed to be a *drupthop*, a mad yogin with clairvoyant powers and a deep gnosis of the *dharma*. He was also known to be fond of drink.

Shabtrung Rinpoche moved through the small home, and settled beside his brother. I studied his features. He looked bloated and scarred. I caught a whiff of juniper and alcoholic sweat as he pushed past me. A brocade shirt poked out of his cloak like a golden poppy in a field of scorched grass. For an old, sick man, he was wild-eyed. Although I was encountering this lama for the first time, I sensed immediately the truth in what others had said about him. He embodied so many paradoxes: uncannily wise yet deeply troubled, bound by the physical shackles of age and ill health and yet transcendent of them.

King Jigme Palbar turned to face his elder brother. "Have you eaten?" asked the king, in greeting. I couldn't tell if Shabtrung mumbled yes or no. It really didn't matter, as he would be brought the first bowl of *thukpa* when it was ready.

"The rivers are high in Tibet now," said Shabtrung to his brother. They spoke in low tones, as if they were the only two people in the room.

"We got word that you returned yesterday. Did you have problems on the road?"

"The day before yesterday, at night. We could have camped just near the border, but I wanted to get home."

"And our *netsang*? How are they?" The king asked, referring to several nomad families across the border in Tibet. "Are they recovering from the winter?"

"It was bad. They lost many animals. I performed some rituals." Shabtrung was in great demand as a ritual specialist.

"The soldiers? Did they give you any trouble at the border?"

"We didn't see a one," Shabtrung answered. "They were probably all at the trade fairs."

After dining on tea and *thukpa*, Shabtrung reached into his saddlebag and produced a Tibetan text wrapped in silk and a brass ritual bell. The king followed suit, and for a moment the brothers were mirror images of each other, slouched in concentration as they prepared for an afternoon of prayer. Shabtrung poured barley grains into a cup and motioned for someone to fetch him some water.

"We're making an offering," the king said to me and Pushpa. "To protect the sheep."

I had heard many stories about Shabtrung Rinpoche. The lama and his wife, a younger woman who was originally from Dolpo, lived in Thinker. They occupied one corner of the king's summer palace. Shabtrung was the second son of the previous king of Lo, Angun Tenzin. From a young age, he was revered for his spiritual acumen.

When he was still a young man, Shabtrung took up his ancestral role as the abbot of the monastery in the village of Tsarang. Later, against the will of his family, Shabtrung decided to marry, and marry for love. His wife soon became pregnant, and bore a son. However, the woman died when their son was still an infant. Stricken with grief after the loss of his wife, Shabtrung apparently went mad. It is said that he carried his boy from door to door, begging for food.

Eventually, Shabtrung left Lo for Dolpo, where he lived for many years in retreat. Eventually he remarried a woman from Dolpo, and had, in recent years, returned with his second wife to Mustang.

In the years leading up to Shabtrung's madness, his elder brother died and his younger brother, the current king, became heir to the kingdom. Jigme Palbar had by this time married the woman who would become his queen, and she had given birth to a son. But the child was weak and died young. Meanwhile, Shabtrung's son lacked a proper guardian. Now childless, the noble couple decided to adopt their nephew. So it was that Shabtrung's biological son, my friend Jigme, became the *gyalchung* of Lo.

After we had known each other for some time, and well after I had heard this story from other Loba, *gyalchung* Jigme told me of this history himself, as we sat in his Boudha home far from Monthang and what I imagined was the sting of his childhood.

"You know I was adopted, don't you?" he said at the time.

"Yes," I answered. "How old were you?"

"Very young, about eight. Shabtrung is my father, but the king and queen are my parents, the ones who raised me."

"*How* were you adopted?" I asked, "I mean, was there a ceremony? Did you have to file papers with the Nepali government?"

"Khenpo Tashi Tenzin read some prayers." Jigme had reached for a bottle of Johnny Walker Black Label and poured himself a splash. "It was a long time ago. My birth mother died when I was very small," the *gyalchung* continued.

I noticed a picture of the king and queen of Lo that hung in Jigme's living room as he retreated into his memories. The black-and-white photograph had been taken in 1973, the year I was born, when the king and queen had come to Kathmandu to celebrate the coronation of Nepal's late king, Birendra Shah. In the photograph, the King of Lo's face is perfectly round and he wears a neatly trimmed mustache that comes to a point at either side of his full mouth. I already knew that Jigme and the king had similar voices, both resonant and deep. But that day, I had studied Jigme's face alongside that picture of the king, and had seen the resemblance one could expect from an uncle, but not quite a father. The thought was unsettling. Now, sitting in Chung Jung near these two men, I kept thinking of Jigme. Transfixed, I watched as his two fathers chanted in unison. The lyrical rhythm of their prayers brought William Blake's *Songs of Innocence and Experience* to mind.

> *Father, Father, where are you going*
> *O do not walk so fast.*
> *Speak, Father, speak to your little boy*
> *Or else I shall be lost.*

In the half-light of that smoky Mustang home, I imagined what it might have been like for Jigme to have witnessed his biological father descend into madness—at least for a time. My thoughts then turned to the passages through darkness that my own father had traveled after his marriage to my mother ended. I closed my eyes and could see so clearly my dad's lanky form approaching me at the stable where I kept my horse. I was just ten at the time. I could smell his grief: white sage, scotch, and sweat.

During those months and years of my father's mourning and anger, I felt as if I had lost someone I loved, and that I was now confronted with someone I did not know. This revelation, mixed with the innocent hope that my father would resurface and be made whole again, led me to rush into his arms. My dad withered against me and sobbed. And in that instant something of the child in me was replaced by an elder self, not unburdened but also, somehow, stronger.

Akin to my identification with Dawa, I felt my connection to Jigme grow deeper after this encounter with the father who gave him life, as well as the father who had raised him. Tears welled up in me. I was thankful for the half-light of this Mustang home and the shadow it cast across my private sadness. The sorrow sprung from a primal place, a place that I imagined Jigme and I shared—for all the ways that our upbringings diverged. Intermingled with this personal recollection of loss—of being a child unmoored—I felt a wellspring of compassion for Jigme, for Shabtrung, and for my own father.

Pushpa poked me in the ribs. Startled, I turned my gaze away from Shabtrung and King Jigme Palbar. The brothers had begun to pack up their thumbed and smoke-stained texts, their prayer beads and silver-plated teacups. They spoke softly. A cup of tea sat on a wooden table in front of me.

"Where have you been, daydreamer?" Pushpa whispered. "Come on, drink your tea. We're leaving soon."

"Sorry," I said. Words tumbled loose and quiet. I resurfaced.

"It is remarkable to see them together," said Pushpa. "But he looks so much older than the king." He has a pockmarked face like the moon, I thought. And just as remote.

"Had you met the lama before?" I asked Pushpa.

"Once, at a village ceremony. But I didn't get to talk with him."

We walked out of the house after both of the older men. The king led his elder bother by the arm and hoisted him onto his horse. Shabtrung coughed. His face flushed red as he found stirrups, groped for reigns. The lama's chestnut gelding grunted under the weight of Shabtrung's corpulent frame and then broke into a trot down the trail.

"Ride with Shabtrung back to Thinker," the king instructed Tokme. With a nod, the young man mounted his horse and sped off after the lama. As I watched Shabtrung's imposing frame recede, I found myself thinking about the arc of his life. How had he reconciled, in his own heart-mind, the ties of love and lineage with the crazy wisdom that was both his gift and his curse? The lama and his horse disappeared over the hills toward Thinker. The movement of these figures across the horizon seemed like a certain foreshadowing of Shabtrung's passing, and of the transcendence that seemed to dwell in him.

RUINS

THE MONASTERY at Samdroling, or what is left of it, rests on a small bluff northeast of Monthang—two crumbling rooms on the edge of time. Over the years, this structure has been reduced by the elements to a sad outcropping. The place is quiet and the landscape around Samdroling is dotted with animal dung and small shrubs. Chortens that surround the old temple have been ripped open at the seams, revealing remnants of the relics once safely housed inside these small shrines. Even though Samdroling is a regular picnic spot for travelers and shepherds, it feels like it has not been visited in centuries. It is difficult to imagine that these ruins once held valuable statues, *thangka* paintings framed in brocade, and a library of religious texts.

And yet Samdroling was a functioning temple just over twenty years ago. Both *Amchi* Tashi Chusang and Pema Rinzen Bista spent months in retreat at Samdroling when they were young, while Gyatso and his brother Tenzin are the great grandsons of the lama who once presided over this site. In Mustang's dry environment, things do not decay easily. Even sheep dung holds its shape for years. Something about Samdroling's decomposition looked deliberate.

I had spoken with several Loba about Samdroling and its current neglected state. One morning I even approached the king to ask him about the temple. He had just finished circumambulating Monthang, his practice each dawn. As far as I could tell, it was the one moment he was truly alone during his day. He seemed to cherish the ritual. Sometimes a villager or two would join him, but they would walk in silence by his side.

Here, as he moved slowly and with a definite rhythm, the king seemed most in his element.

When I told the king of my intent to visit the ruins, his lips turned down like a river shifting course. "Samdroling, hmm." He seemed to frown unconsciously. "There is little left of it."

"I know, but I'd like to see it anyway. It is the only Kagyu monastery in Lo, right?" I asked. Most people in Lo identified with either the Nyingma, or "old" school of Tibetan Buddhism, or the Sakya School. The Kagyu, or "oral lineage" school, was associated with Milarepa, the Tibetan yogi and saint who was known for his songs and his thin frame, tinged green from the years he had subsisted on nothing but nettles. Milarepa was most famous for the fact that he had achieved enlightenment in just one lifetime through his diligent practice.

"Yes, it is the only Kagyu temple. But for some time there has been no caretaker, nobody living there. But it is a peaceful place, so good for practice." The king was a devout Buddhist practitioner and had a sense of cultivated wisdom that seemed, at times, to belie the political position into which he was born.

"I tried to convince Shabtrung to live at Samdroling with his wife when he returned from Dapo, but he didn't want to live there," the king continued. "It would have been very beneficial if someone with his knowledge lived at Samdroling. It would have made much merit. He is so powerful that nobody would have dared loot Samdroling, had he been there. But what can you do? He didn't want to go."

The king did not hide his sense of disappointment, but our exchange about Shabtrung ended there. After all, everyone knew Shabtrung could hear what people said about him from miles away.

On this first visit to the ruins, I traveled with Pushpa. As we hiked toward Samdroling, we talked about why this monastery had fallen into disrepair so completely, while other temples in Lo remained much more functional, even though they showed their age and were in need of renovation. I thought of Tubchen Lhakhang, the largest and oldest temple in Monthang. Pillars made from whole tree trunks hold up its grand roof, housing larger-than-life statues and intricate wall paintings. And in Monthang's Jhampa Lhakang a seven hundred year-old statue of the Buddha to Come loomed two stories high and golden. Even though the Buddha's dark encasing was thick with dust, even though the roof of this temple had caved in under the weight of the elements and time, the space still felt sacred. Intricate mandalas covered the walls. These painted geometric designs are also blueprints for transcendental palaces and Buddha realms, and those in Jhampa Lhakang were among the most beautiful I had ever seen. Many villagers were ashamed of the monastery's dust and neglect, and yet proud that such a temple existed at all in Monthang. For, etched into its walls and displayed in the statue's smooth, gilded features, was the resonance of Monthang's greatness, its history.

A group of foreign experts would eventually restore these monasteries and their frescoes. Artisans from Italy and America would work alongside a local team of laborers, cleaning the frescoes and renewing the temples' architectural integrity. But at this point, such plans for restoration were more dream than reality. Many locals were distrustful of what this restoration would entail. Some were worried that more of Lo's treasures would be taken out of Mustang and sold on the foreign antiquities market, which was not an unfounded concern. Others had heard rumors that the Italian experts were going to remove the frescoes from the walls in order to clean them, and they saw this effort to restore as a violation of the temple, an act that would upset local gods. The royal family was cautiously enthusiastic about the restoration projects, but the king and *gyalchung* knew the process of negotiating between local villagers and international interests would not be easy. They also wondered if this project would simply turn into one more way that outsiders were encroaching on Mustang, placing their visions of what Lo should be before the ideas and feelings of those who actually belonged to this land. Pushpa and I talked about this as we walked up toward the ruins one morning.

"They are beautiful paintings," he began, "but I can't help think that all the money and energy that is likely to be spent on restoration might be better put to use by helping Loba care for their living culture, the things they use need. Schools. Health care." My friend sighed.

"Maybe if it's restored, it will reignite a deeper interest in Lo's young people—an inspiration to know their history," I responded. "But I have my questions about the restoration projects, too. The art is stunning—"

"But the politics will be intense," Pushpa interjected. "In some ways it feels like another effort to keep up the image of Mustang as a timeless place, rather than a place that has a rich heritage, but that should be allowed to change on its own terms." Pushpa paused, and we walked along in silence for a moment, our strides lengthening across a stretch of grassy plain.

"Sometimes I think it is really ironic," Pushpa mused. "The restoration projects will bring a lot of foreign money and energy here, to protect and preserve these temples. They see them as 'world heritage' and there is truth in this perspective. The artwork is special. But meanwhile any young Loba with the means to do so is leaving Mustang to forge a life elsewhere, and all the local people with money invest in business abroad or property in Kathmandu. Nobody invests much in Mustang these days. They expect foreigners to do it. If it weren't so sad, it would be funny."

"And this is called 'cultural preservation,'" I muttered.

We continued to walk in silence, both lost in our own thoughts. "I could spend months out here," said my friend, finally. "This would be a perfect place to do a retreat. No teacher, of course, but I would do okay just sitting here by myself, as long as somebody brought me tsampa, tea, and a few good books!"

Pushpa's thoughts struck me. In some sense, just being in Mustang was a retreat for both of us. Reflection and a slower pace to life were born of Lo's sheer remoteness. And yet the same remoteness we enjoyed often made our Loba friends feel trapped, made their lives more difficult and the place of their birth feel like a burden.

As we approached the piles of stones, beams, and half walls that was Samdroling, Pushpa sighed.

"It looks worse than it was last year," he said, walking toward a cairn to inspect the damage. "Last fall this one was still intact. It was the only one that hadn't been broken. Now look at it." We moved closer to the decimated shrine and peered into its midsection like two surgeons inspecting a wound. Inside dirt mixed with shards of tsa tsa, clay relics made as offerings after a person's death.

"I don't understand why people would even want to break into these chorten," I whispered to Pushpa.

"They've stolen all parts that were made of gold and left those made of clay." Pushpa moved away from the cairn and headed toward what was left of the main shrine room. As he looked around the remains of the building, I could sense that my friend was searching himself for a way to reconcile Mustang's past and present, to make peace with change and yet not avoid the disquieting aspects of what it means to be a culture in transition.

In the near distance, a Himalayan griffin swooped down onto a piece of carrion. Pushpa and I headed away from the ruins, leaning into the afternoon winds as we headed back toward Monthang.

The next time I visited Samdroling, I was in Gyatso's company. We approached Samdroling on horseback, from the east. The temple looked much as it had on my last visit: abandoned and leaking broken offerings. Gyatso grabbed my hand and pulled me toward the main temple, up its cracked stairs, and in through what remained of the doorway. Not one for anger, Gyatso's face turned tense.

"Look at this. How can we say that we care about this place? Look at these bricks, destroyed. This place is ruined because nobody has watched out for it. My father spent time in retreat here, you know?"

I knew.

"This is disgraceful. How could we have let this happen? How can we say that we are any better than the Chinese, when they came and ate up Tibet, if we do this to our own places, our own religion? We did not even need an army to do the damage," said Gyatso.

As Gyatso recounted all the different texts that used to be housed at Samdroling, and all the things his father told him of his time in retreat here, I thought back to something I had read in the *Popol Vuh*, a sacred text of the Maya: *Don't wait for strangers to remind you of your duty; you have a conscience and a spirit for that. All the good you do must come from your own initiative.*

Gyatso and I sat down on the steps outside Samdroling, the heat of the day upon us.

"I have an idea about this place," said my friend. "It would be wonderful if Syangpa Rinpoche could come up here and make Samdroling
new again. He's powerful enough to make it work." In his previous incarnation, Syangpa Rinpoche had wielded great influence in Mustang and
Dolpo. Tshampa's father had been a disciple of the previous Syangpa Rinpoche, and both Gyatso and Tshampa knew the present incarnation.
This current Syangpa Rinpoche had spent some early years in Dolpo
with his mother, after they escaped from Tibet. Eventually, he was taken
to the Tibetan refugee camp in Pokhara, where he spent most of his
youth. Now Syangpa Rinpoche ran a *dharma* center in Singapore and
most of his devotees were from urban Southeast Asia. He traveled exten-
sively, giving teachings to students in many countries. Given this trajectory, I asked Gyatso what made him think that Syangpa would be a
suitable caretaker for Samdroling.

"The times I have met him, Rinpoche always said that he wanted to
come back to Mustang. It would be perfect if he came to Samdroling. A
few monks, some new buildings, a library for texts, a new altar. He could
keep spreading the *dharma*, like the last Syangpa Rinpoche did, in remote
places!" I didn't have the heart to voice my skepticism at that moment,
but Syangpa Rinpoche struck me as an urban lama, with no dirt under
his fingernails, no scuffs on his shoes. Soon enough, Gyatso's thoughts
began to echo my own.

"He definitely has the money to do it," Gyatso reasoned. "But I don't
know if he would really want to live in Mustang. He probably thinks
he should spend time up here, but that doesn't mean that he will.
Monks are supposed to practice in quiet, peaceful places. But people
don't want to live where it is empty anymore. Besides, he's used to
clean cities and fancy cars." Tracing the arc of his own idea, Gyatso now
looked as disheartened as he had been excited a few minutes before.
He stood up and led me out of the ruined building.

"You know," said Gyatso, as we headed back to Monthang, "this isn't
the first place to be damaged like this. There have been many *gompa* robberies recently. Ghami's monastery was broken into last year and they
lost some of their old *thangka*. This year, one of the first volumes of
Tsarang's *kangyur*, the complete teachings of Buddha, was stolen. It was

the one that was written in gold. And you heard about the horrible theft in Gelung several years back, right?"

"Yes. That one had to have been an insider's job."

"They all were," said Gyatso. "None of those robberies could have happened without local connections."

A friend in Gelung had told me about this robbery. The event had already become legendary. As the story went, a group of four men—two lowland Nepalis and two Lobas—caught and tortured the caretaker until he gave them the key to the monastery. After they robbed the place, the bandits tied up the monk and cut off the tip of his tongue. Sadly, many stolen items from the village monastery ended up in the homes of wealthy art collectors in the West. Even if they were not melted down for scrap, as they might have been had the loss occurred several decades earlier on the other side of the border, these objects remained far out of Mustang's reach.

As Gyatso and I walked around Samdroling that afternoon, I recalled a story Jigme had once told me, about an attempted robbery that occurred when the Khampa were in Lo. A guerrilla approached the king and asked if he could take one of the gold statues that belonged to the king's private prayer hall. The soldier explained that the statue was not for him, but that he was going to take it to Dharamsala and present it as a gift to His Holiness the Dalai Lama. The Khampa wept. He said that he was only trying to help re-establish Tibetan religion in exile and that this statue would be greatly appreciated by the Dalai Lama himself.

The king was not convinced. He sensed the Khampa would sell the statue for the value of its gold and precious inlaid stones. But since the Khampa invoked the Dalai Lama's name, the king could not refuse. He let the Khampa remove the statue from his altar and carry it out of the palace.

Pleased with his trickery, the Khampa headed south in the direction of Tsarang, carrying the statue. As he headed down the path, the statue grew heavier and heavier. Soon, the Khampa could no longer lift the statue. Confused, for he had hauled the statue out of Monthang without any initial difficulty, the Khampa sat down and contemplated his dilemma. "If I return," thought the soldier, "the king will surely judge me a fool, if not a thief. If I try to keep going, I might be crushed by the weight of this thing. And what use would that be?"

Disheartened and a bit baffled, the soldier turned back to Monthang. To his surprise, when he picked up the statue and headed north toward Monthang, the object weighed nearly nothing. But when the Khampa turned around and tried to head south again, the statue crippled him with its mass. And so, the soldier returned the statue to the palace, where it remains to this day.

I wondered where this divine force that once guarded the king's statue had gone in the atmosphere of modern Mustang. Where is the sentiment, expressed in this local story, that objects retain a rightful place as much as sentient beings, and that both yearn for a sense of belonging?

But then, myths are only as strong as those who honor them.

WINDHORSE

MOST OF THE PEOPLE I spoke with in Mustang had at one point or another traveled north of the Nepali border, into Tibet. Some had attended trade fairs in Ngari or Tsang, the western and central provinces of the Tibet Autonomous Region. Others had gone on pilgrimage to sacred sites. Yet few had seen Lhasa. Many of the massive changes that had accompanied the Chinese annexation of Tibet in the 1950s had remained something of an abstraction. But as Chinese goods continued to make their way down into Monthang, and as Loba tuned in to Tibetan broadcasts from Lhasa on their shortwaves, they began to gather that Tibet, as a part of China, seemed more prosperous and powerful than the country to which they belonged. The history of political oppression in Tibet was not lost on most from Mustang, but neither did this suffering feel entirely personal—beyond what they had experienced during the Khampa years and had learned from exile Tibetan friends, or how the closing of the border impacted their access to grazing lands. Few Loba, save the royal family, had extended family members in Tibet. Yet more and more Loba were coming to rely on Chinese-made goods and the Tibetan traders who brought them to Mustang's doorstep. Many of the Loba I spoke with about the changes in Tibet remarked first on the quality of roads across the border, the ease and relative comfort afforded by travel and trade in trucks instead of by yak caravan or horseback, and the strength of the Chinese government to deliver "development" to remote areas and, for better or for worse, to implement social change.

"Tibet is so much more developed than Mustang," one man said. "And Lhasa is richer than Kathmandu. Even though the Chinese have sinned—they have treated Tibetans badly—at least they've also brought roads and hospitals and greenhouses. That's more than the Nepali government has done for us!"

Other Lobas told stories, often experienced second or third hand, about life in Lhasa: *There are discos near the Potala. Young women wear mini skirts and smoke cigarettes. There are many Chinese. People cannot even wear Buddhist protection cords, but they have money coming out of their stuffed pockets. People cannot study Tibetan in school, only Chinese.*

This latter comment interested me, though, in that people in Lo often felt disadvantaged by their relative lack of schooling in Nepali or English. One afternoon I asked Tokme and his cousin, Rajendra, about this, as we sat around eating lunch at Chimi's Coffee Shop.

"The only way we can learn anything that will help us is to leave, to go somewhere where we can really learn English, or at least learn to speak and write Nepali well. You cannot receive an adequate education here. At least those people in Lhasa are learning a language that will get them somewhere," said Rajendra. "They may be speaking Chinese, but a lot of Tibetans are better educated than we are."

"But if you lose your language, then you lose your culture," Tokme added. "I've heard that the only reason Tibetans are learning Chinese is because they can't learn Tibetan in schools. It's illegal." Although this was not true, it was accurate in that sending children to Tibetan medium schools in Tibet basically ensured that they would have fewer social and economic opportunities compared with those who mastered Chinese.

"It is similar here, though, with Nepali," added Indra, Chimi's husband, as he stoked the fire. "Our children even get Nepali names at the government school. Look at us! Indra and Rajendra and Mahendra? These aren't our real names. The schoolmasters just give them to us because they think it will make us more like other Nepalis. Like giving our *gyalpo*, our king, and all the Lo nobles the name *Bista*. This isn't our culture, but it is what we've grown up with."

"But it matters more in China. Nepal is just a small country with no power," said Rajendra. "Not like China or America."

The time passed quickly that afternoon. This was my last research trip to Lo Monthang. My Fulbright was coming to an end, and my *gratis* permit would expire at the end of September. On this final trip to Lo, I had brought with me a videocassette copy of *Windhorse*, an independent feature film about Tibet that had been filmed in Boudha, Lhasa, and in lower Mustang. *Windhorse* was written by a young American woman named Julia Elliot and her Tibetan partner, Thubten Tsering, and was produced by Julia's uncle, Academy Award-winning documentary filmmaker Paul Wagner. The previous winter, I had participated in the making of the film and even appeared as a bit character. Eventually, the film would receive accolades in the United States and Europe. It would even win Best Film at the annual Santa Barbara Film Festival, in my hometown.

Several Tibet-related films had already come out of Hollywood, Beijing, and Europe in recent years. Scratchy copies of both Martin Scorcese's *Kundun* and *Seven Years in Tibet* starring Brad Pitt had already made their way in backpacks and saddlebags from Kathmandu to Jomsom. But *Windhorse* posed something different than these features. Instead of being shot in Morocco, Argentina, or the American Rockies, it was filmed in Nepal and Tibet. Instead of being shot in English, it was filmed almost entirely in Tibetan, with smatterings of Chinese and English. Unlike these major motion pictures, *Windhorse* tells a story about Tibetan history and the Tibetan present that people in Lo could directly relate to. The film showed angry, frustrated Tibetan youth, underground networks of information and resistance that exist between Lhasa, Dharamsala, and the West, and vestiges of the last generation to know Tibet as it was before 1959. The story also highlighted human rights abuses and provided viewers with footage of modern Lhasa that were still relatively difficult to obtain at the time *Windhorse* was shot. Made in collaboration with Tibetan exile communities in Nepal and India, *Windhorse* had a cast and crew who were mostly Tibetan, with virtually no previous film experience.

I knew that Loba who viewed the film would notice these differences between Hollywood's vision of Tibet and this more "independent" production, but I was not sure what their ultimate reaction to the film would be. So, after the evening meal at Pema Rinzen's house, after the sun had gone down and the cows had come home, I headed off, cassette in hand, to the Monthang "movie hall": the bottom floor of a house with a dusty television in one corner, saddle blankets and carpets thrown on the floor, and a bench leaning against the back wall. The room smelled slightly of barley and mice droppings, wool and Chinese laundry detergent. Before it was a movie hall, it had been a storeroom.

I met Indra at the entrance to this screening room, where he was fiddling with the generator. As the generator roared, we found places on the floor of the hall. Soon, the space was packed with locals, including Mahendra and Dawa. There were no lights to dim, no curtains to raise. Indra simply pressed play and turned up the volume to drown out the generator. The audience became entranced by the image of paper prayer flags, from which *Windhorse* takes its name, fluttering through a cloudless sky near a mountain pass.

The *Windhorse* script begins in the dry hills and valleys of western Tibet in the mid-seventies and follows one family's story until the present. The death of the family's grandfather at the hands of Chinese Red Guards during the violent and chaotic years of Mao's Cultural Revolution poignantly transitions into mid-'90s Lhasa, where the family—grandmother, mother and father, two children—migrated after the grandfather was murdered.

No sooner had the peaceful, pastoral opening scene of prayer flags on the wind melded into a shot of a village, with the subtitle "Western Tibet 1976" floating below it, did murmurs clutter the Monthang movie hall. Loba recognized the sweeping Kali Gandaki running winter low and shimmering in the sun. Most of the men in the room immediately recognized the village that came into view.

"*Ah mo*! That is Lubra," said one person.

"Look! That's where I go to buy *arak*," said another. Most of the local women in the room had never been to Lubra, and stared at the cluster of adobe dwellings with a vague notion of something shared.

"See how many trees they have down south," one woman whispered to another.

Someone asked me to translate the subtitle, which was written in English. When I told them what it said, some folks erupted in peals of laughter.

"Ha! We're in Tibet? Then where are the Chinese?"

Others found this meshing of a fictional story and the reality of place confusing, especially as the story progressed. During one scene shot in Lhasa, a woman leaned into me and said, "How can they be in Lhasa if they were born in Lubra?"

The entire room giggled during the scenes that took place in Lhasa's discos and brothels. One of the local women chided her husband, "What are you laughing at? You just drink *chang* and go to sleep!"

An image of me darted across the screen. My friend Abraham and I played the traveling companions of the Western female lead character, a young woman who gets entangled in a Tibetan family's tragedy. Mahendra pointed and teasingly called me "heroine." I was far from this, but I blushed anyway.

I was sitting next to Dawa. As the movie rolled on, Dawa found herself in the strange position of translating between Central Tibetan, Mandarin—which she had learned during her childhood in Tibet—and the local Loba dialect. She was the only person in the movie hall who knew all three languages. As the film progressed, this added responsibility to communicate the content of the film seemed to weigh on her. Translations grew truncated. By the moment in the film when one of the main characters, a nun, was recounting her arrest and torture at the hands of Chinese security officers, Dawa had fallen silent.

During this most disturbing episode, everyone gasped as they watched flashback images of the nun being dragged from an armored vehicle and then interrogated by the prison warden, a fellow Tibetan. In the half-light of a dingy prison office, the man struck her on the head. The video hall instantly filled with the sound of clicking tongues—a motion, not unlike the call of crickets, which condemned this abuse. Calls of *"ninje"* echoed through the small room, followed by whispers about bad karma and the pollution inherent in such acts of violence.

Everyone in the room could follow the basic story, but as we watched the film, I kept a close eye on Dawa. I knew that she had not been back to Tibet since she had left as a young teenager, but that she was hoping to return for a visit soon. Though she and her parents continued to correspond, Dawa often wondered what her family's life was like. Her parents' letters revealed the details of their routine: chronic coughs, the purchase of a new cow, the profits garnered from the small store they keep in Shigatse's central marketplace. But they could say nothing of politics or their inner lives. Dawa had always been close to her family, and she missed them terribly. The film had clearly upset her.

The credits rolled and then a blue stillness filled the screen. Indra reached up and flipped off the television and VCR, but the questions and commentary continued. To them, the story of torture and exile is one they have lived, albeit vicariously, through the Khampa and through their diasporic Tibetan friends. It was impossible for them to imagine the family's story as fiction. It was much too real, too close to home.

"What happened to Dorje?" one Loba asked. "Did he go to Dharamsala and work for the government?"

"Did Dolkar keep singing?" asked another.

"What about the mother and father? What about grandmother?" said someone else. "Were they caught by the police?"

"How terrible!" said another. "I have a cousin-brother whose mother's sister was a nun, and she ended up in prison like that. She eventually made it to Dharamsala, but by then she was *nyomba*, mad."

Later that evening, I sat in my room in Pema Rinzen's house, unable to sleep. Although I had seen the film before, I was particularly moved by it after this viewing. A few minutes later Dawa walked in. My friend's cheeks were tear-streaked, her eyes red from crying. I took Dawa's hands in mine. Unlike her smooth, pale skin and streams of ink-black hair, her hands were marked by Lo. Although fictional, *Windhorse* had afforded her a vivid, painful glimpse at what she had left and, in many ways, the world in which her family still lived.

Without question, there was difficulty in Dawa's life in Monthang. Even as the queen's niece and as the wife of a noble, she still toiled in her fields in spring and fall, sat close to the hearth and waited out winter. By material standards, Dawa was probably worse off than her relatives in Shigatse. But in terms of freedom and security, she knew that she was afforded great luxuries compared to her family members still in Tibet. After a few moments of feigned composure, my friend buried her head in her hands and began to cry again. I stroked her hair while she wept.

"There is so much suffering," Dawa said plainly, her tear-streaked face swept raw and clean.

During my final week in Monthang, I spent more time walking than I had in months. After all the hours I had passed on horseback, I felt the need for a slowed pace, a sense of internal rhythm unbound from my research, or any other "official" agenda. I needed to feel this place, to breath it, in order that I might leave. And, perhaps in anticipation of this leave-taking, I felt myself retreating from social scenes and becoming more solitary.

Some mornings, I walked around the city's ancient walls and down to the river's edge. Other days, I walked toward the stretch of chalky earth to the north and east of Monthang, and back through the salt flats where Loba took their horses and cattle to graze. These walks were filled with questions: When would I return to Lo? What would I do with all the stories I had gathered? How might they find a coherent form outside my journals, and myself? What would happen to the friendships I'd begun to forge?

As I contemplated leaving Monthang, I reflected on how different things felt now than they had when I left lower Mustang for several seasons in Lo. This was, in part, because I still had so much to look forward to. But this was also because returning to lower Mustang required none of the permissions or resources that being in Lo demanded. A return was less certain. I tried to remind myself of Rilke's gentle admonishments to his young poet. *Resolve to be a beginner, to love the questions themselves, and to live along some distant day into the answer.*

On one of these last nights in Monthang I dreamt that I had dyed my hair black, dressed in my oldest *chuba* and tried to sneak in past the checkpoints at Kagbeni, to visit again. I made it as far as Monthang before the local police discovered me. They returned me to Jomsom with admonishment, but a certain kindness. "You will find your way back," said a lanky lowland policeman, this figment of my sleepy imagination.

Aching for perspective, the next morning I hiked up to the remains of Ketchar Dzong, the fortress founded by Amepal, the fourteenth century western Tibetan noble who made Lo his kingdom. From that vantage, amid the crumbled adobe bricks and the blonde, parched soil, I stared out across Monthang's fields and the city walls, past the homes of Pema Rinzen and Gyatso, beyond the looming palace roof, and south toward the stretch of earth for which the city was named. The age of this place moved me. Shadows of long-abandoned fields and the remains of chortens filled out a view that was otherwise framed by burnished barley, near to harvest, and the delicate remains of summer sweet peas.

The next day, I walked out to this "plain of aspiration" filled with my own sense of longing and fulfillment, by turns. Some months had passed since I last traversed this dusty stretch of earth. This had been the site of the ACAP-sponsored horse races during Tiji—an afternoon of stirred up dust, much excitement, and plenty of Mustang machismo. Raju's three-year-old bay gelding had won the race, spirited forward by a young man from Ghami. In celebration of the victory, Raju had led a group of us on a galloping circumambulation of the city's walls. The day was jubilant, brisk. I went to sleep that night smelling of horses, happy, with grit under my nails. Now the same stretch of land was quiet, contemplative. An open space, dwarfing my frame against the sky.

Back in Pushpa's room later that evening, I took out Pablo Neruda's *Memoirs*—one of the few books I had contributed to Pushpa's little library. And as I tried to make sense of my own leave-taking, I turned to the poet's prose. "We stopped inside this magic circle, like guests in a holy place...There with my inscrutable companions I came to understand then, in some only vaguely defined way, that communication existed between people who did not know one another, that there was solicitude, pleasant answers to those pleas, even in the most far-flung and out-of-the-way places in the world." As I read about Neruda's experiences with the cowboys of Patagonia, in his native Chile, my own experiences in Mustang—in this landscape, among its horses and its men, its women and its children—resonated. I felt full and yet empty, deeply changed and yet peaceful, grounded. I seemed to be finding my way.

The morning Ken left for Dolpo dawned cold. Kathmandu was shrouded in fog. We huddled together under layers of cotton duvets and down sleeping bags, waiting for the sun to break through. Ken cupped my hands in his. We let ourselves swell with tears and some laughter.

In Ken, I had found a soulmate. Throughout the year I had spent in Mustang, we had written letters and flirted with the possibilities of our affection, though my heart-mind had been diligently trained on Mustang. But I had found myself thinking more and more about this beautiful young man.

Serendipity nurtured our blooming relationship. By the winter after my return to Kathmandu from Mustang, we had fallen deeply in love. With Ken, I began to make a new kind of sense out of my connection to Mustang. I started to understand that what I valued—and what I longed for—was not only a sense of allegiance to a place and a group of people, but to a way of being in the world. As formative as all of my experiences over the past year had been, I now began to discover that the place I had grown into was not only a specific locale, but also a path, a life's trajectory. The longing I felt for Mustang, and the hardest parts of leaving, had come along with the fear that once I left Mustang I would lose the momentum that I'd just begun to build. I had a desire to keep learning, to follow this path—to have confidence in it—even though the direction remained unclear, the horizons obscured. Ken shared this sensibility, and I admired the ways he moved through his own evolving relationship to Nepal, and to himself.

Yet falling in love with Ken was at once a homecoming and another process of departure, of taking leave. Ken was now setting off on his own passage, this time to Dolpo. He had been awarded a Fulbright grant the year after me, and was now preparing to spend much of the long, cold winter immersed in the sartorial rhythms of Dolpo's pastoralists, studying the ways they stewarded their landscape, and how the region was changing.

When it came time for him to leave, I lifted Ken's backpack onto his smooth shoulders, kissed him, and slipped a poem I had written into his hand. Such began our own cycles of presence and absence, of singly and jointly moving through this world.

Reap this harvest well my dear
You will not feel this blanket—
Snow draping wool
'Neath bursts of paleolithic sky—
For lifetimes to come

Learn this language well my dear
To taste woodsmoke and radishes
In single mouthfuls
Of the simplest exchanges
For all that is dramatic in this place

Walk these miles well my dear
These treeless lands
Balance ladders of wood—
Petrified sculptures held up in homage
To feet that take you there,
And back again

I taste it still
This burnt and bitter hospitality
Blessedly dirty, even on the
Cleanest of tongues

EPILOGUE

FROM WHERE I SIT in this Kathmandu coffee house, I can feel the Himalayan sun on my back. The din of traffic on the streets below is deeply familiar, as is the tangle of telephone wires just beyond this balcony, the acrid scent of petrol, a cacophony of horns and hawkers. It is easy to place myself here, to feel at home.

It is more difficult to unravel the years between my departure from Mustang and the present. In short, the relationships that began more than a decade ago have continued to evolve. Mustang and Nepal have changed, as have I, but my commitment to this place and the people I've met there endure, and have unfolded with a serendipity for which I am grateful.

My year in Mustang bled into two more years of living in Nepal. During this time I traveled with Ken through other regions of far western Nepal: Humla, Mugu, Jumla, and Dolpa. Although I did not fully realize it at the time, we were walking through unstable terrain, on the topographic and ideological fringes of the burgeoning Maoist insurgency. Over the next decade, conflict between this guerrilla People's Liberation Army and the Nepali armed forces would leave fifteen thousand Nepalis dead, thousands more Nepali citizens orphaned, traumatized, and displaced, the Nepali monarchy in shambles, and the state of the nation transformed.

At the time of our travels through these regions, I could not have anticipated all of Nepal's impending political dramas—from the bloody civil war to the royal massacre whose plot twists rival the best Greek tragedies. But I did carry with me a sense of foreboding during those long hikes through some of the country's most desperately poor territory. I also emerged with a sense of how relatively fortunate my friends in Mustang were, compared to many of their fellow citizens.

During the years following my Fulbright fellowship in Mustang, I continued working with both Tshampa and Gyatso. Tshampa used the experiences granted through his World Wildlife Fund fellowship to help found the Himalayan Amchi Association, a Kathmandu-based organization that draws together Nepal's *amchi* in an effort to defend and transform their traditional medical practice in the face of huge changes—social, economic, and political. After the death of Tashi Chusang, Gyatso and his brother Tenzin founded a school for Tibetan medicine in Lo Monthang, and have also been active members of the national *amchi* association, of which Gyatso is the current chairman. I have felt privileged to both participate in and observe Tshampa and Gyatso's transformations—as healer-physicians and simply as human beings. My own engagement with *amchi* and, more broadly, with Tibetan medicine, has continued to the present and remains a core focus of my scholarship and activism in Nepal and Tibetan areas of China.

After my year in Mustang, the intimate friendship that Ken and I had kindled continued to grow, fueled in part by bittersweet cycles of shared domesticity and distance. We encouraged each other. Ken saw the poet in me. He pushed me to write, and to move with grace and humility from one stage of life to the next. I watched with pleasure and awe as Ken immersed himself in Dolpo, and helped inspire in him the discipline and confidence to keep up his study of high Asia's human and natural environments.

Ken left Nepal in 1997 to start graduate school at Berkeley, and I followed soon thereafter. Our relationship weathered the transition from Nepal to the U.S. and we were married in 1999. That same year we founded a small non-profit, DROKPA, a word which means "nomad" in Tibetan. Our wedding was our first fundraiser. Over the past decade we have channeled energy and resources into grassroots projects in the areas of health, education, alternative energy, and social entrepreneurship.

Later that year I began my graduate study in anthropology at Cornell University. We moved our household across the country, to Ithaca, New York, and found there a remarkable community that made the distances between Nepal and North America feel smaller. Both the founding of DROKPA and the commencement of my formal training as an anthropologist further instantiated my commitment to Nepal, and, in a more personal sense, to the life course that Ken and I were mapping, independently and together.

After Ken completed his master's degree in rangeland ecology from Berkeley, he wrote a book about Dolpo and then went on earn a doctorate in development studies from Oxford. Ken now teaches at the University of Vermont. I completed my Ph.D. in 2006, and have since been teaching anthropology at Dartmouth College. I have also taken joy in other writing projects: a book for children produced with a painter friend from Dolpo, and a collaboration with my mom on an artist's book about Tibetan and Himalayan sacred landscape. Ken and I were blessed by the birth of our daughter, Aida Claire, in November 2004.

But what of Mustang? The year I left Nepal for Berkeley commenced a steady stream of Mustangi migration to the U.S.—primarily to New York City. Many of the friends about whom I have written in these pages have now found their way to the Big Apple. Some have made quite permanent lives for themselves, while others continue to survive, five or six to a room, in the netherworld of our underground economy, navigating the Five Boroughs with limited English and a sense of indentured servitude to those who funded their visas. Others still have been able to negotiate a life between the worlds of New York and Nepal. Remittances from the New York Mustang Association filter back to Mustang's villages and families, just as videotapes of marriages and annual rituals are sent to kindred in Brooklyn and Queens. Through this process of exchange, people from Mustang are remaking their geographies of home, these maps of belonging.

Back in Mustang there have also been many changes. Villages that had no electricity and only dreamed of telephones during my tenure now benefit from these basic resources. Perhaps most significantly, a new set of motorable road projects—one coming north into Mustang from the Pokhara roadhead and one snaking south from the Tibetan border—are reshaping Mustang's landscape. In this process, tractors and motorcycles have come to take the place of horses in many families—a change akin to what one finds throughout nomad communities on the Tibetan plateau. As one friend from Kagbeni put it, "We don't have to feed and shepherd a motorcycle every day, the way we do with horses. We can just feed it petrol!" Yet horses retain a symbolic and worldly importance in this corner of the high Himalayas. Midsummer horse festivals continue and god horses wander Mustang's ranges.

All of these changes have brought to bear a certain nostalgia about what one might call "pre-industrial" Mustang, both from outsiders with a love of the area and, at times, from people from Mustang themselves. In short, Mustang feels closer to Kathmandu and even to the U.S. than it ever has. And yet the sense of distance remains.

Earlier today I was sitting with a friend from the village of Jharkot, in the Muktinath Valley, looking at pictures of his daughter, a former nun who is now in boarding school in Florida, and other Mustang youth now living in New York City. In one picture, my friend's daughter, radiant in an emerald green *chuba*, stands with her hand draped over the shoulders of another Mustang beauty—Tshampa's eldest daughter. They are dressed to celebrate the Tibetan New Year, in the basement of a Russian Orthodox church on the Lower East Side.

Seeing the picture reminded me of one of the last times Tshampa and I spoke, just after the birth of his daughter's first child, and only days before the birth of my girl, Aida. On a snowbound winter evening in 2004, I was resting in bed when the phone rang. Ken answered. His usual "hello" was followed by a pause, and then the lilt of Nepali. "How are you Tshampa-la? Yes, I will get Sienna for you." Ken handed me the receiver. I was greeted by a voice at once distant and familiar—that of my first teacher.

"Have you had your baby yet?" Tshampa asked me, by way of greeting.

"No, not yet, but I think I will soon. Are you a grandfather yet? Are you in New York?" I asked. Tshampa had spent some time a few years prior lecturing at Virginia Tech, and, as such, had luck procuring a visa for a return trip to the U.S. for the birth of his first grandchild. He was now camped out in his daughter's apartment in Astoria, tending to the new mother and child with herbs and incense that had made the long journey from Jomsom.

"Yes, I am in New York and I am a grandfather now," he continued, his voice infused with his usual confidence and a new kind of joy. "The child is a girl. She was born a few days ago. I have named her Yangchen Lhamo. She is beautiful, Sienna, and she is one of the first Mustang-Americans." We both laughed.

A few weeks later, I received a package from Nepal. I remember unwrapping it as Aida nursed. A *kathag*, infused with the smells of Mustang, spilled out over my newborn, blanketing her. Wrapped in this offering scarf was a letter from Gyatso. In it he told me that he had done a ritual for my birth, and that he had thought of a name for my child. *Yangchen Lhamo*, the note read. The words brought tears to my eyes. Tshampa had given his granddaughter the very same name. What were the chances? A flood of emotion washed over me, of loving and being loved, of knowing and being known, by two such remarkable teachers.

Just yesterday, Gyatso and I emerged from the United Nations Development Programme office, where we had been meeting with program officers to discuss this year's progress on a medicinal plant conservation project underway in Lo Monthang. The midday sun had taken the chill off the city's winter briskness, the meeting had gone well, and Gyatso and I headed toward a tea shop to relax for a bit.

"My book about the year I spent in Mustang, studying horses, will be coming out in a few months," I said.

"*Ah mo*, that was so long ago."

"Yes, more than ten years," I responded.

"We're getting old," Gyatso laughed. "We were so young and carefree then, in the days before we had so much work and responsibility." Gyatso paused before continuing. "Those will be good stories to remember," he said.

I agreed.

Kathmandu, Nepal
December 2007

◆ ———— ACKNOWLEDGMENTS ———— ◆

M Y GRATITUDE to many people runs deep. As in any story of becoming, this book distills years of experiences, formed into a narrative and refracted through memory. An inaccuracies are my own to bear. Most importantly I thank my friends and interlocutors in Mustang. First, I would like to thank Tshampa Ngawang and his family. This story could not have been written—would not have come to be— without Tshampa's friendship and teachings. Likewise with Gyatso and Tenzin Bista as well as their late father, Tashi Chusang. I owe many thanks to the royal family of Lo Monthang, particularly Gyalpo Jigme Palbar Bista and *gyalchung* Jigme S.P. Bista, as well as to Tsewang, Raju, Mahendra, Chime Dolkar, and Pema Rinzen Bista, and my sweet sister, Dawa-la. I also owe heartfelt thanks to Nyima Dandrul, Wangdi Lama, Nirmal and Laxmi Gauchan, Angya and Pasang Gurung from Jharkot, Karma Jigme, Chandra Thakali, Pema Dolkar and Yöden at the Red House in Kagbeni, as well as Yonten Lama, Lubra Karchung, and Palsang and Tsewang Tenzin. Kunzom Thakuri and Pushpa Tulachan, I treasure our shared time in Mustang.

The Mustang field research that forms the basis for this narrative was conducted intensively from October 1995 through December 1996, with support from the United States Educational Foundation / Nepal (USEF/N) through a research grant from Fulbright / Institute for International Education. I am grateful for this support, and I owe particular thanks to Penny Walker, Director of USEF/N during my tenure as a Fulbrighter.

Many other people in Nepal deserve recognition for the ways the have taught me, and inspired me to know their country. Among them, I would particularly like to remember Mingma Norbu Sherpa and Yeshi Chodron Lama, both of whom passed away tragically in September 2006. I would also like to thank Vincanne Adams, Judith Brown, Carroll Dunham, Ethan Goldings, Hiroya Iida, Sarah LeVine, Charles Ramble, Harold Roth, Nicolas Sihlé, and Mark Unno. Each of you has been friend and exemplar, both.

Edmund and Sylvia Morris, I am grateful for the ways you've shaped my words and my desire to write. Leila Hadley Luce, Pico Iyer, Gretel Ehrlich, and Helen Tworkov have also encouraged me to tell these stories and have inspired me as a writer. At Wisdom, I would like to thank David Kittelstrom for his belief in this project and his guidance early on, as well as my editor, MacDuff Stewart, who has shaped this book with so much grace.

Although this book predates my tenure in graduate school at Cornell, the experience of being a Ph.D. student in anthropology, as well as the incredible Nepali and Tibetan communities in Ithaca, have contributed to this project. At Cornell, I would like to thank my advisors, both formal and informal: David Holmberg, Kathryn March, Davydd Greenwood, Viranjini Munasinghe, and Lamar Herrin. Elana Chipman, Alexandra Denes, Erik Harms, Farhana Ibrahim, and Brenda Maiale, thank you for your friendship and insight over the years. Steve Curtis, Susan Hangan and Tika Gurung, Heather Harrick and Kunga, Anjali, and Amber Delotsang, Sondra Hausner, Anne Rademacher, Sara Shneiderman, Mark Turin, and Abraham Zablocki thank you for all the ways you make my life more complete, and the distances between the US and Nepal smaller.

Daniella Mayer, Kiki Thorpe, Lucy Raimes, and Pia Singer, best friends from Brown days, thank you for your curiosity, love, and support through the years of our friendship – for the couches to sleep on during forays back to the US and the ways you've listened and understood, lessening the boundaries of time and space between us. Sam Masson, you have kept me in music, and in your heart, wherever I've been. Thank you for providing the refrain: "You'd better be home soon."

This book owes a lot to the 'barn sisters' and riding instructors of my childhood and adolescence. These people not only taught me how to ride, but also how to be more fully human by coming to know the horse. Anne Blecker and her daughters, Tricia, Marcia, and Leslie as well as Kip Goldreyer grounded and toughened me, inspired hard work and compassion, by turns. I learned composure in the saddle and camaraderie in competition from Courtney Cochran, Danielle Holzer, Laura Fairbanks, and Chantell Taylor – and we had so much fun. Betsy Woods encouraged in me self-confidence and an appreciation for clear instruction, be it given inside or outside the ring.

To my parents, grandparents, and others who raised me, particularly Steve Craig, Mary Heebner, Charles Rowley, and Macduff Everton, thank you for always encouraging me and for the numerous ways my upbringing has led to the creation of this book. Ken, my partner in all things, I invoke the mountains where we found each other, and the distances we've traveled. And to Aida, my little monkey, joy of joys, I wish for you a life of love, equanimity, and adventure on your own terms.

✦ — Sources and Suggested Reading — ✦

THE WORK of many scholars and writers has been instrumental in the development of this book. I list some of the most pertinent and illuminating texts below.

MUSTANG

Dhungel, Ramesh. *The Kingdom of Lo (Mustang): A Historical Study*. Kathmandu: Lo Gyalpo Jigme Foundation, 2001.

Fisher, William F. *Fluid Boundaries: Forming and Transforming Identity in Nepal*. New York: Columbia University Press, 2001.

Peisel, Michel. *Mustang, the Forbidden Kingdom*. New York: Dutton, 1967.

Matthiessen, Peter. *East of Lo Monthang: In the Land of Mustang*. Photography by Thomas Laird. Boston: Shambhala, 1996.

Ramble, Charles. *The Navel of the Demoness: Tibetan Buddhism and Civil Religion in Highland Nepal*. Oxford: Oxford University Press, 2007.

Tucci, Guisseppi. *Journey to Mustang*. 2nd ed. Bangkok: Orchid Press, 2006.

TIBET: HISTORY, POLITICS, AND CULTURE

Avedon, John F. *In Exile from the Land of Snows: The First Full Account of the Dalai Lama and Tibet since the Chinese Conquest*. New York: Vintage Books, 1986.

Dunham, Carroll, and Ian Baker. *Tibet: Reflections from the Wheel of Life*. Photography by Thomas L. Kelly. Foreword by the Dalai Lama. New York: Abbeville Press, 2001.

Goldstein, Melvyn C. *A History of Modern Tibet, 1913–1951: The Demise of the Lamaist State*. Berkeley: University of California Press, 1991.

————. *The Snow Lion and the Dragon: China, Tibet, and the Dalai Lama.* Berkeley: University of California Press, 1999.

Knaus, John Kenneth. *Orphans of the Cold War: Cold War America and the Tibetan Struggle for Survival.* Washington, DC: Public Affairs, 2000.

Laird, Thomas. *The Story of Tibet: Conversations with the Dalai Lama.* New York: Grove Press, 2006.

Lopez, Donald, Jr. 1998. *Prisoners of Shangri La: Tibetan Buddhism and the West.* Chicago, IL: University of Chicago Press.

Norbu, Jamyang, 1987. *Warriors of Tibet: The Story of Aten and the Khampas' Fight for the Freedom of Their Country.* Boston: Wisdom Publications.

Shakya, Tsering, 2000. *The Dragon in the Land of Snows: A History of Modern Tibet since 1947.* New York: Penguin Classics.

TIBETAN BUDDHISM

Goldstein, Melvyn and Matthew Kapstein, eds. 1999. *Buddhism in Contemporary Tibet: Religous Revival and Cultural Identity.* Berkeley: University of California Press.

Lopez, Donald, Jr., ed. 2007. *Religions of Tibet In Practice, Abridged Edition.* Princeton, NJ: Princeton University Press.

Kapstein, Matthiew, 2001. *The Tibetan Assimilation of Buddhism: Conversion, Contestatin, and Memory.* Oxford: Oxford University Press.

Samuel, Geoffrey, 1995. *Civilized Shamans: Buddhism in Tibetan Societies.* Washington, DC: Smithsonian.

NEPAL: HISTORY, POLITICS, AND CULTURE

Bauer, Kenneth, 2004. *High Frontiers: Dolpo and the Changing World of Himalayan Pastoralists.* New York: Columbia University Press.

Bista, Dor Bahadur, 2000 [1976]. *People of Nepal.* Kathmandu: Ratna Pustak Bhandar.

Cameron, Mary, 1998. *On the Edge of the Auspicious: Gender and Caste in Nepal.* Chicago, IL: University of Illinois Press.

Childs, Geoff, 2004. *Tibetan Diary: From Birth to Death and Beyond in a Himalayan Valley.* Berkeley: University of California Press.

Gellner, David, John Whelpton and Joanna Pfaff-Czarnecka, eds. 1997. *Nationalism and Ethnicity in a Hindu Kingdom: The Politics and Culture of Contemporary Nepal.*

Hutt, Michael, 2004. *Himalayan People's War: Nepal's Maoist Rebellion.* Bloomington, IN: University of Indiana Press.

Snellgrove, David, 1988. *Himalayan Pilgrimage.* Boston: Shambhala.

Thapa, Manjushree, 2007. *Forget Kathmandu: An Elegy for Democracy, Nepal.* New Delhi: Penguin India.

Whelpton, John, 2005. *A History of Nepal.* Cambridge: Cambridge University Press.

MEMOIRS, TRAVELOGUES, AND (AUTO)BIOGRAPHIES
Adhe, Ama and Joy Blakeslee, 1999. *The Voice That Remembers: A Tibetan Woman's Inspiring Story of Survival.* Boston: Wisdom Publications.

Barnett, Robert, 2006. *Lhasa: Streets with Memories.* New York: Columbia University Press.

Crow, David, 2001. *In Search of the Medicine Buddha: A Himalayan Journey.* New York: Tarcher.

Goldstein, Melvyn, William Siebenschuh and Tashi Tsering, 2000. *The Struggle for Modern Tibet: The Autobiography of Tashi Tsering.* New York: ME Sharpe Publishers.

Guneratne, Katharine Bjork, 1999. *In the Circle of the Dance: Notes of an Outsider in Nepal.* Ithaca, NY: Cornell University Press.

Gyatso, Tenzin, 1997. *My Land and My People: The Original Autobiography of His Holiness the Dalai Lama of Tibet.* Boston: Warner Books.

Matthissen, Peter, 1998 [1973]. *The Snow Leopard.* New York: Vintage.

McHugh, Ernestine, 2001. *Love and Honor in the Himalayas: Coming to Know Another Culture.* Philadelphia, PA: University of Pennsylvania Press.

Scot, Barbara J. 2005. *The Violet Shyness of their Eyes: Notes from Nepal, Revised Edition.* Corvallis, OR: CALYX Books.

Zeppa, Jamie, 2000. BEYOND THE SKY AND EARTH: A JOURNEY INTO BHUTAN. San Francisco: Riverhead Trade.

◆ —— About Wisdom Publications —— ◆

Wisdom Publications, a nonprofit publisher, is dedicated to making available authentic works relating to Buddhism for the benefit of all. We publish books by ancient and modern masters in all traditions of Buddhism, translations of important texts, and original scholarship. Additionally, we offer books that explore East-West themes unfolding as traditional Buddhism encounters our modern culture in all its aspects. Our titles are published with the appreciation of Buddhism as a living philosophy, and with the special commitment to preserve and transmit important works from Buddhism's many traditions.

To learn more about Wisdom, or to browse books online, visit our website at www.wisdompubs.org.

You may request a copy of our catalog online or by writing to this address:

Wisdom Publications
199 Elm Street
Somerville, Massachusetts 02144 USA
Telephone: 617-776-7416
Fax: 617-776-7841
Email: info@wisdompubs.org
www.wisdompubs.org

The Wisdom Trust

As a nonprofit publisher, Wisdom is dedicated to the publication of Dharma books for the benefit of all sentient beings and dependent upon the kindness and generosity of sponsors in order to do so. If you would like to make a donation to Wisdom, you may do so through our website or our Somerville office. If you would like to help sponsor the publication of a book, please write or email us at the address above.

Thank you.

Wisdom is a nonprofit, charitable 501(c)(3) organization affiliated with the Foundation for the Preservation of the Mahayana Tradition (FPMT).